DEPARTMENT OF ECONOMIC AND SOCIAL INFORMATION
AND POLICY ANALYSIS

D0313486

# WORLD
# SOCIAL SITUATION

# IN THE 1990s

UNITED NATIONS
NEW YORK, 1994

UNITED NATIONS PUBLICATIONS
*United Nations, Room DC2-853, New York, New York 10017 USA*

UNITED NATIONS PUBLICATIONS
*Palais des Nations, 1211 Geneva 10, Switzerland*

U.N. Sales No. E.94.IV.4
ISBN 92-1-130161-0
Copyright © United Nations 1994
All rights reserved
Manufactured in the United States of America

# CONTENTS

## 4. POVERTY

**Part II: Human development, basic needs and social services**

## 5. POPULATION GROWTH, URBANIZATION, MIGRATION AND REFUGEES

## 6. HUNGER, MALNUTRITION AND FOOD SUPPLIES

## 7. HEALTH

## 8. EDUCATION AND LITERACY

## 14. SOCIAL CONSEQUENCES OF ADVANCES IN TECHNOLOGY

# PREFACE

The *World Social Situation in the 1990s* is derived from the *Report on the World Social Situation 1993*, the thirteenth in a series of reports on the subject dating back to 1952. The *1993 Report* is an in-depth synthesis and interpretation. This concise edition provides ready access to most of the subjects covered in the *1993 Report*.

The *World Social Situation in the 1990s* describes major improvements in social conditions in the difficult economic circumstances of the 1980s and early 1990s. It points out emerging situations and discusses a variety of policies responding to these situations. Income distribution and inequality, employment — including especially low productivity employment — and poverty are presented in Part One. Part Two takes in human development, basic needs including hunger, health, education and housing, and social services such as social security and quality of life. In Part Three the emphasis shifts to emerging social issues and dilemmas, with an analysis of ethnic conflicts and national disintegration. The concluding chapter discusses the profound importance of the new technological advances in electronics, biotechnology and material sciences.

*World Social Situation in the 1990s* was prepared by the Department of Economic Information and Social Policy Analysis with the cooperation of other agencies and offices of the United Nations system.

# 1

# Introduction

As fears of global confrontation between opposing ideological and military camps receded during the past few years, international attention is increasingly drawn to the objectives of higher standards of living and economic and social development. The present report analyses, in varying degrees of detail, the extent to which these objectives had been achieved at the beginning of the 1990s. It highlights major improvements in social conditions in the difficult economic circumstances of the 1980s and early 1990s, decribes emerging situations and discusses a variety of policies adopted by Governments and international organizations in responses to those situations. These findings gain significance in the light of the World Summit for Social Development to be convened early in 1995.

The issues that confront each group of countries and their significance to policy makers vary significantly. Poverty, unemployment and low productivity employment are of the highest concern to many developing countries. In the economies in transition, poverty and unemployment have emerged as significant problems as they change from one set of institutional arrangements to another. High levels of unemployment have persisted over a decade or more in most developed countries.

Chronic hunger and malnutrition are concomitants of poverty. These deprivations have been made more severe by natural disasters such as drought and flood and civil wars and other conflicts. In the absence of adequate infrastructure, natural disasters have taken a heavier toll in the least-developed countries, especially in Africa. The limited resources available to Governments have reduced their ability to respond adequately to the needs of those affected.

Human resources development has received much attention in all groups of countries, but for different reasons. Nutrition, sanitation, primary health care and primary education remained significant for all developing countries, especially the least developed. In the developed countries, the significance of education and training increased due to the persistence of high unemployment rates. Likewise, rising costs of medical care and equitable means of paying for such services received much attention. The economies in transition need to change their systems of education radically to meet the challenges of new institutions. Attention has also been focused on the wider concern of human development, including the enjoyment of certain civil rights.

Demographic changes and growing restraints on public sector resources on the one hand, and persisting weaknesses in the delivery of social services on the other, posed new challenges to social security policies in developed countries. In economies in transition, new institutions and organizations have yet to emerge to replace those dismantled in the process of transition. In developing countries the major problem remained those of wider coverage and greater equity in the availability and sharing the costs of social security.

Major changes in economic and social institutions are in process in the formerly centrally planned economies. These institutions range from the ownership of the means of production, forms of government, factor and product markets to social security arrangements. In developing countries there has been a change over from military or one party governments to elected governments. Almost universally, attempts have been made to limit the reach of Governments in the economy. In developed countries, markets have been made freer of government regulation.

As international conflicts abated and societies became more liberal, ethnic and religious conflicts and civil wars among groups seeking to capture political power erupted, most recently in Africa and Europe. New nation states were formed and ethnic groups within nation states strove for self-determination.

This volume highlights the nature of these social development issues and discusses the variety of policy responses.

## A. THE ECONOMIC CONTEXT

One reason for the deep concern with social development issues is the slow-down in the pace of economic growth. The slow-down in the world economy which began in the 1970s continued all through the 1980s and worsened in the early 1990s. Total world output dipped in 1991 and grew by less than 1 per cent in 1992. Since some three quarters of total world output originated in developed market economy countries, the total was heavily governed by changes in output in those economies where economic growth was anaemic during 1991-1992. Output in economies in transition fell drastically in 1990, 1991 and 1992. In developing countries economic growth was higher than in the rest of the world. Economies in Asia, generally, grew rapidly during the 1980s; those in Africa and Latin America grew much more slowly and more slowly than in the developed economies. Total output in West Asia fell during the last decade. Except for sub-Saharan Africa, there was some recovery in most developing economies during 1991 and 1992 and growth in Asia has continued to be robust. Growth has been especially impressive in China and East and South-East Asia, which have seen their GDP per capita double in the last six or seven years.

Since the rate of growth of population was well above rates of growth in GDP in Africa, Latin America and West Asia, per capita income fell in these three regions. Economic conditions were worse in 1992 than in 1971 in much of Africa. In Latin America, gross domestic per capita was lower in 1992 than in 1981.

Negative per capita growth in Africa and Latin America can be attributed to a combination of external and domestic factors. Some developing countries were affected by adverse weather and other natural disasters, while others had their opportunities and potential for growth destroyed by civil wars and political unrest.

Recession in developed countries in the early 1980s caused a slow-down in growth in international trade, declining prices for a large number of commodities exported by developing countries, deteriorating terms of trade and an increase in protection. International interest rates became positive and high in real terms, after having been negative in the mid-seventies. There was a massive net transfer of resources from capital importing Latin American countries from 1983 to 1989. They have turned positive since 1990.[1]

Constraints on import capacities reduced both current production and the potential for future growth.[2] A shortage of imported inputs reduced capacity utilization and current output. They also reduced investment by denying machinery and equipment for the construction of capital assets. Finally, net transfers abroad reduced total resources available for deployment in the domestic economy and, because investment is often postponable, investment was disproportionately cut back. The drop in investment, in turn, compromised future growth.

Many developing countries undertook domestic policy changes, partly in response to the international challenges and partly to correct past mistaken policies. In most of these instances, policy packages were arrived at in negotiations with the International Monetary Fund and the World Bank.

The new policies were expected to bring about shifts from production of non-tradeables to tradeables, and resources were to be allocated in a way that would ensure a pattern of production that would be viable at international prices. Price distortions existing in the economy were to be eliminated. The latter usually required the abolition of price controls, cuts in most subsidies, the rationalization of the tax and tariff structures and the (gradual) elimination of protectionism. Adjustment policies mostly implied that disequilibrium in the balance of payments was to be removed by a reduction in domestic absorption. Reductions in aggregate domestic demand were to be obtained through a mix of policy instruments of which wage repression, limits to credit supply and cuts in government expenditure played important roles. Some economies have emerged from these processes robust and vigorous. Others, however, have taken longer than earlier envisaged to achieve these objectives.

The experience of a large number of developing countries in the 1980s ran counter to their principal need for rapid sustained growth with equity in a manner which is environmentally sound. They need to grow rapidly as conditions of living at present levels of output are unsatisfactory and in many instances below any reasonable standards. Rapid growth is a necessary condition for their improvement. Growth must be sustained over three or four decades, especially in the least developed and low income countries, if significant improvements are to be achieved. Growth in the economy needs to be well distributed for more than political reasons. Inequitable growth may flounder after some time because rising inequalities can reach politically unacceptable levels. Besides, growth in all parts of an economy will itself generate internal dynamism to sustain growth in the long term. The equitable distribution of the benefits from growth among persons and households implies fairness to women, to backward regions, and to distinct ethnic groups within each society. Sustained rapid growth over a considerable stretch of time is essential to reducing environmental degradation due to poor living conditions. At the same time, patterns of development and the technologies adopted need to receive constant attention to avoid damage to the environment from the very process of growth.

## B. INEQUALITY, UNEMPLOYMENT AND POVERTY

One consequence of the variegated patterns of growth during the last decade has been changes in the distribution of world output among countries (see chapter 2). Rapid economic growth in China and East Asia, and more recently in India, Indonesia, Malaysia and Thailand, helped raise the share of world output accruing to the bottom 40 per cent of income recipients in the distribution of world output in the late 1980s.

Although output grew faster in developing countries than in

the developed countries, population growth was three times faster in the latter than in the former. The rate of growth of output per capita 1982-1991 in developing countries was about half that in developed countries.

The distribution of income among households in many countries underwent significant change. In the former centrally planned economies where there was a high degree of evenness in the distribution of income, that distribution became more skewed. Rapid price inflation, rising unemployment and new opportunities to accumulate wealth all contributed to this process. In fact, larger inequalities in income and wealth are to be expected within the framework of new institutions and incentive structures, as they transform themselves into market economies (see chapter 12).

In developing countries, inequality in the distribution of household incomes declined in some of the rapidly growing economies, including Indonesia and Malaysia. In Africa, disparities in income probably fell as higher paying employment, wages and earnings were reduced. In Latin America the drop in real wages reduced incomes accruing to the bottom deciles, while high income receivers were able to profit from a number of sources, including the purchase and sale of foreign currency.

Low productivity employment and unemployment have been chronic in developing countries (see chapter 3). Stabilization programmes — during the initial stages of implementation — imposed additional employment losses. To stabilize prices and exchange rates it was necessary to restrain government expenditure and credit to the private sector. Trade liberalization drove out uncompetitive domestic enterprises, throwing out both workers and capital equipment from employment. Although exports of developing countries became more competitive abroad, there were delays in establishing additional capacity and undertaking investment. The severity of the unemployment problem has been eliminated only in those economies, including Mauritius, the Republic of Korea, Singapore and Taiwan (province of China) marked by sustained high levels of investment, both in physical and human capital.

In the longer term, the major problem in developing countries is that of low productivity employment rather than unemployment. High productivity employment for the growing labour force requires investment both in physical and human capital and an environment conducive to entrepreneurial activity. Internationally, it requires growing international trade and inflows of capital and technology.

In developed market economies the pre-occupation of Governments with the stability of monetary values as an objective has gone hand in hand with persistently high levels of unemployment. Although a wide range of policy instruments have been used to reduce unemployment in these economies, the problem persists and deteriorated even further with the economic recession of the early 1990s.

One consequence of slow growth and low productivity employment and unemployment has been that poverty remains a major economic and social problem (see chapter 4). Poverty affects more than 1,000 million people living in sub-Saharan Africa, South Asia, China and parts of Latin America and the Caribbean. The speed with which economies deteriorated in sub-Saharan Africa and parts of Latin America to aggravate conditions of poverty has demonstrated how long-term deficiencies in economic policy and unfavourable international conditions can push large masses of people over the edge into poverty. The success of some east Asian developing economies in raising employment and alleviating poverty, as noted earlier, demonstrate the feasibility of successfully grappling with these problems in a relatively short span of time.

Poverty has come to the open in economies in transition. A drastic drop in production, steep rises in prices and the new phenomenon of unemployment created a class of poor people hitherto absent in economies in transition.

High levels of unemployment and the decline in the demand for unskilled labour in developed countries permitted the emergence of a class of long-term poor in these economies. The persistence of poverty, especially in families with young children in some developed countries, has raised questions regarding the design and adequacy of policies for social security (see chapter 10).

Restraints on public sector expenditure has limited the capacity of Governments in all countries to provide short-term redress to people in poverty. The major emphasis has been on providing opportunities for people to earn their way out of poverty. That approach requires both opportunities to acquire skills and a rapid expansion of employment opportunities. Special efforts need to be made in ensuring disadvantaged groups access to productive employment. Credit and extension services to women in developing countries are examples of such policies. In developed countries, policies have been adopted to encourage and enable mothers with dependent children to find adequately paying employment.

## C. ECONOMIC GROWTH AND SOCIAL DEVELOPMENT

The previous section has related economic growth with two major social problems: unemployment and poverty. Rapid economic growth is necessary to expand employment opportunities and to alleviate poverty in the long term. But rapid growth by itself may not be sufficient to do either. Annual growth rates of GDP of 9 per cent in Brazil and 7 per cent in Egypt and Thailand from 1965 to 1980 were not sufficient to reduce low productivity employment and unemployment to satisfactory levels or significantly alleviate poverty in those countries. Patterns of growth are decisive.

Across countries, there is an association of low income per capita with higher infant mortality and illiteracy, especially among women. Countries in which the infant mortality rate exceeded 100 per thousand and female adult illiteracy rates were over 40 per cent in 1989 were at the low scale of per capita GNP. At the other end of the scale were those countries whose annual per capita GNP exceeded $10,000 and whose infant mortality rate was characteristically lower than 10 per thousand and which had virtually no illiteracy. However, there were significant exceptions. Sri Lanka, for instance, whose annual per capita GNP was about $450 in 1989, had a relatively low infant mortality ratio of 20 per thousand. The infant mortality rate in Barbados is as low as that observed in the USA.

Despite the observable links between economic growth and improvements in social conditions there were no countries, regardless of what happened to their income per capita from 1956 to 1989, where infant mortality rates rose during the same period (see chapter 7). In 22 developing countries for which there were data, GNP per capita fell between 1965 and 1989 at the same time as infant mortality rates fell. There were 14 countries in which GNP per capita grew by less than 1 per cent per annum during 1965-1989 and infant mortality rates fell over the entire period. There were remarkable achievements in Costa Rica and Oman where infant mortality rates fell by a factor of five, as well as in Botswana, China, Mauritius, Singapore, Sri Lanka and Thailand where infant mortality rates fell by a factor of three over the same period.

A part of that success has been due to a growth in knowledge and technology. The value of nutrition, sanitation and primary health care in reducing infant mortality has come to be better appreciated. Developments in technology permitting oral rehydration therapy at little cost and successful vaccination against childhood diseases in areas without refrigeration facilities have helped reduce infectious diseases.

The increase in resources brought about by economic growth permits improvements in social conditions. Whether such improvements actually take place depends on patterns of growth and the economic and social policies of Governments. Even in developed economies, improvements in living standards have often been the direct result of social intervention rather than of simple economic growth.[3]

The extent to which Governments can intervene depends on their ability to collect in tax revenue sufficient resources for the Government to provide services to improve social conditions. The ability of Governments to mobilize resources in this fashion ultimately is determined by the public who pay taxes. Whether Governments do actually provide the necessary services depends on patterns of public expenditure. Expenditure to provide food entitlements, primary health care and primary education will improve social conditions, in contrast with public expenditure on the military or programmes and projects benefiting a privileged few. Policies and their efficient implementation do matter.


## D.  HUMAN RESOURCE DEVELOPMENT

Among recent insights into factors determining long-term growth, the most significant in the present context is the role of education and a "knowledge industry" in generating, adapting and adopting technology.[4] In that light, recent emphasis on human resources development is clearly appropriate.

However, human resources development can mean several things, each of them leading to different policy initiatives. There is for one a focus on human development, which is a broad approach to development. For another, the centre of attention is education and training, which are essential whether for the adoption of prevailing technology or the development of new technology. In a period of rapid technological change the capacity of an economy to gain from these changes would depend on the development of its human resources. Then there is entrepreneurship. Whatever else may take place in an economy, it is entrepreneurs who put together production processes. The importance of each of these concepts to economies will vary depending on initial conditions, and so will the policy responses.

Human resources development is the product of policies in a wide range of areas. Nutrition, housing, health and education (see chapters 6, 7, 8 and 9) all play mutually supporting roles in raising the quality of labour. Education, especially of women, is an essential condition for improving nutrition and sanitation. It is less clear what sorts of policies can contribute to the development of entrepreneurial talent. Institutional arrangements which reward entrepreneurship permit and encourage the exercise of such talent.

Worsening unemployment and poverty conditions have made problems of hunger and malnutrition more severe than earlier in some instances (see chapter 6). Flood, drought and other natural disasters brought about conditions of acute hunger and famine in several countries in both Asia and Africa. Civil wars and other strife contributed to these dire conditions in a number of countries in Africa. Some 550 million people, mostly in developing countries, were afflicted by chronic hunger. The sudden collapse of income-earning opportunities and rapid price increases have been major causes reducing food supplies to certain sections of the population in economies in transition. In developed countries the major problems in nutrition were those of consuming the wrong kinds of food in excessive quantities.

Health conditions have improved the world over, as shown by the rise in the average expectation of life from 60 years in 1975-1980 to 64 years in 1985-1990 (see chapter 7). In 1990 for the first time, 80 per cent of all young children were immunized against diphtheria, pertussis, tetanus, measles, poliomyelitis and tuberculosis. Yet public health policy was confronted with new and continuing challenges. Nearly half the world's population remain exposed to malaria. Nearly a third were infected with tuberculosis and some 20 million people suffered from the disease. New strains of drug-resistant bacteria appeared and, among those infected in large cities in developed countries, some 1.5 million were estimated to be suffering from AIDS in 1992. Twelve to thirteen million people were estimated to be infected with HIV and the number by some calculations, was projected to grow to 40 million by the year 2000.

AIDS which seemed concentrated among homosexual men and intravenous drug users mostly in developed countries has spread to other groups and places. In 1992, about 40 per cent of those infected were in Africa, of which about 50 per cent were women. In 1988 the proportion of the population infected by heterosexual contact in the Caribbean region was estimated at 65 per cent. Children infected with the virus and orphaned by the death of their parents became a major concern.

The main parameters of a sound health policy came to be seen in broader terms. The significance of education for women, adequate nutrition, safe drinking water and the sanitary disposal of sewage were increasingly recognized for their value in improving health conditions. In most developing countries it became evident that much could be gained by directing more resources from curative services to preventative health care.

In health care, equitable access to services remains a major problem in almost all countries. In developing countries, resource constraints have been a principal limiting factor in extending health care services to all population groups. In economies in transition, serious shortcomings in the delivery of services and the change-over to new institutions created major problems of health care. Rising costs of health care posed major challenges to policy makers in developed countries, especially in the United States. Means of financing health care came under scrutiny mainly from the point of view of equity.

Primary school enrolment increased in all countries during the 1980s, although at a much slower rate than during the previous decade (see chapter 8). Yet the proportion of school children in the relevant age group enrolled in primary schools did not exceed 60 per cent in Africa as compared to 92 per cent in developed countries in 1990. The access of women to education at all levels remains a major concern in all countries, although in developed countries this was more pronounced in respect of science and technology education at the tertiary level than at other levels. Nearly 1,000 million people, two thirds of them women, remain illiterate.

## E.  NEW CHALLENGES IN THE PROVISION OF SOCIAL SERVICES

The provision of social services has had to face several challenges during the last two years (see chapter 10). The demand for social services in developed countries increased on account of continued high levels of unemployment, population ageing and the growth of one parent families earning low or no incomes. In the economies in transition, the change-over to a new system disrupted old arrangements where the government and government-owned enterprises provided cradle-to-grave social services. In developing countries, deteriorating conditions of economic well-being in some countries, rapidly growing populations in most, and conditions of often widespread poverty placed heavy burdens on these services.

In many developing countries, payment of interest on debt, both domestic and foreign, and expenditure for military purposes reduced public sector resources available for social services. In the more heavily indebted countries, interest payments on the foreign debt abroad siphoned off 2 per cent to 5 per cent of GDP. In several developing countries, government expenditure for military purposes exceeded that of social services. With subsiding interest rates, reduced government debt and the general abatement of military conflicts, improvements were recorded in most of those countries in 1990 and 1991.

In this general atmosphere of scarcity, some attention has been paid to limiting expenditure and raising the effectiveness of such expenditure by targeting social service expenditure to the more needy. Several problems have surfaced in the process. First, identifying the "more needy" can be costly in societies where there is little economic and social information and the skilled personnel to generate such information are few. Further, where information is available on the population, government authorities often make use of the knowledge to subject the public to controls which have little or nothing to do with the provision of social services. When public officials are given discretion in identifying persons eligible for benefits and determining the extent of those benefits, the exercise of such discretion can become a source of illegal emoluments to the officers concerned. Finally, the extension of benefits to influential and vocal groups who do not need government assistance may be a political price a Government must pay to obtain sufficient popular support to assist the poorest and most vulnerable members of society.

In all groups of countries there has been dissatisfaction with social services provided by the public sector. One major reason for the poor quality of services has been the lack of incentives to improve their quality. Attempts have been made in several countries to introduce elements of competition with a view to raising the quality of services and reducing their cost (see chapters 10 and 12). Decentralizing control over institutions and providing clients with opportunities to seek alternative sources of services have helped subject services providers to greater competition.

## F.  SOCIAL CONSEQUENCES OF ADVANCES IN TECHNOLOGY

The pace of technological change sharply accelerated during the last two decades. These changes were in three main areas: information technology, biotechnology and material sciences (see chapter 14). These changes have affected virtually all aspects of everyday life and are therefore in parallel with the series of changes which brought about the Industrial Revolution some two hundred years ago. Like that earlier wave of changes, these advances will spread among countries differentially. This is mostly because the new technology is closely associated with advances in science and engineering. Since change is rapid, they can be adopted only where investment is high. For the same reason it is also necessary to train workers continually. Therefore, the spread of the technology will be mainly limited to developed countries and a few developing countries that have the requisite scientific and engineering capacity and investment potential. However, the use of equipment embodying the technology is already quite widespread.

The new technology has enabled the rapid dissemination of information, including news. It has also helped to connect financial markets and to increase the number and volume of transactions. With the new technology, work is beginning to be decentralized in contrast to the factory system which came with the Industrial Revolution and which brought a large number of people to work in one place. By extension, some work such as accounting and record keeping are being performed in distant economies connected by communication systems. Computer-assisted designing has permitted both reductions in inventories and quick responses to consumers' choices in designs and materials. Managerial and clerical work in offices has been deeply affected by the innovations. The advancement of knowledge has been furthered by the new capacity for processing at high speed massive volumes of data at low cost. The rapid diffusion of news, especially via television, has created opportunities for bringing the world closer together, as demonstrated by the response most recently to the disasters in Somalia and elsewhere.

The advent of numerically controlled machine tools has de-skilled some of the best-paid workers in manufacturing. The new technology has mechanized several functions usually performed by women while creating others tasks for them. The nature of work in some professions has begun to change as expert systems take over many routine functions now performed by skilled professionals.

Biotechnology has deep implications for agriculture, the pharmaceutical industry, the practice of medicine and many other areas. These arise from a new capacity to alter and otherwise affect genes. The new technology can raise yields, reduce dependency on chemical fertilizers, pesticides and herbicides and modify plant and animal characteristics to suit given conditions. There is a danger that these techniques may make it feasible to write society's preferences into the evolution of humans, challenging deeply held humanistic views about equality among humans. New pharmaceutical products produced with the new technology have been on the market for several years with promise of many more to come. Interventions with human reproduction has posed challenges to long-held concepts of parentage and the related laws.

## G. ETHNIC CONFLICTS AND NATIONAL DISINTEGRATION

Civil wars and internal conflicts have become the principal causes of violence, destruction and the displacement of people as conflicts between nation-states and rivalry among major military powers subside (see chapter 13). In 1989-1990 there were 33 armed conflicts in the world, only one of which was between nation-states. Some two million people have fled the former Yugoslavia as refugees or displaced persons. Over a longer period of time, civil war, and other internal conflicts have destroyed opportunities for economic and social betterment in several countries, including Afghanistan, Angola, Ethiopia, Liberia, Somalia and Sudan.

The causes behind these conflicts are not clear since many nation-states have ethnic groups living in peace with each other. However, plentiful supplies of armaments at low prices has made conflicts more lethal than ever before in countries prone to ethnic violence. A lack of physical and social infrastructure that can bring people together and enlarge markets and opportunities for economic betterment may have contributed to divisiveness between communities. The collapse of a unifying authority, as in the former USSR and Yugoslavia, is another factor behind ethnic conflicts in these regions. A tendency to affirm one's identity by rejecting outside cultural influences is yet another possible factor. A failure to provide opportunities for minority groups actively to participate in the exercise of political power has also contributed to social divisions. Finally, is noteworthy that some nation-states are built up of several ethnic and religious groups who have historically been antagonistic to one another.

Although the conflicts have been internal in origin, they often became internationalized. People of the same ethnic origin and religious affiliation often live in several nation-states, especially those adjacent to one another. Those living abroad have supplied both moral and material support. Victims have fled to other countries. Refugees and displaced persons have become a major concern to host-country governments and international organizations. The United Nations, regional intergovernmental organizations and non-governmental organizations have all been involved in providing humanitarian assistance and in seeking to resolve such conflicts.

The assimilation of diverse groups in a culture shared by all, as has happened in much of Latin America and North America, is the best long-term solution to these problems. Increased mobility in an expanding economy can be enormously helpful in such processes. Wider means of transport and communications are an essential component of improved relations. Greater autonomy in political structures and ample opportunities for consultation and participation can significantly contribute to defusing violence as a means of obtaining access to power.

## H.  COVERAGE AND STATISTICAL INFORMATION

The statistical data available for this book suffer from severe limitations and should be interpreted with caution. Data were frequently incomplete, not up to date and often non-comparable among countries. For instance, with respect to indicators of general mortality such as life expectancy at birth fewer than 40 developing countries — mostly in Latin America — have vital registration systems recording 90 per cent or more of deaths.[5] For several countries in Asia and all countries in continental sub-Saharan Africa, mortality estimates are based on indirect techniques, using model life tables, that take advantage of data collected in surveys and censuses. In 18 countries, averages of neighbouring countries were used to generate mortality rates. Measurements of literacy and education are based on infrequent surveys and censuses, with short-term changes interpolated. Changes reported in mortality and education are as much derived from short-cut estimates, assumed model changes, and the introduction of data based on new censuses and surveys, as they are from any actual changes in the social situation.

However, in order to assess general trends in social development and the efficacy of different development policies, utilizing the best available estimates is better than making no estimates at all. In the present volume no attempt was made to refine the data in published sources. Yet, one cannot overemphasize the need for reliable and timely data on social development. Moreover, the widespread use of data based on estimates and other indirect approaches should be a matter of concern to the extent that such data may give the false impression the data needed are already being gathered in all developing and developed countries. Such estimates, in a sense, devalue a host of efforts to obtain real and timely information on social variables in developing countries. Empirical data remain now, as before, essential for the identification of problems in social development, the formulation of social policies and the evaluation of their efficacy.

## I. ORGANIZATION OF THE REPORT

The present report is organized as follows. Part I examines the recent changes in output and income distribution among and within countries. Current issues of unemployment low productivity employment and poverty are also presented and discussed here. The assessment of social conditions is found mainly in Part II. Chapters are sectorally divided in terms of demographic changes, hunger, malnutrition and food supplies, health care, education, shelter and social security, and their relationship to the satisfaction of basic needs and the improvement in the quality of life. Part III discusses selected problems of social development which have emerged as concerns of major significance in today's world.

## Notes

[1] Much of this compensated for losses in terms of trade. In 1991 losses on account of the fall in terms of trade amounted to half the value of net inflows of financial resources.

[2] Taylor, Lance, *Foreign Resource Flows and Developing Country Growth*, WIDER, Hesinki, 1991, p. 9.

[3] See Drèze, Jean and Amartya Sen, Public Action for Social Security: Foundations and Strategy, in Eds. Ahmed, Ehtisham, Jean Drèze, John Hills and Amartya Sen, Social Security in Developing Countries, Oxford University Press: New York, 1991, p. 11.

[4] Helpman, Ephanan, "Endogenous macro-economic growth theory, *European Economic Review* 36, 1992, pp. 238-267.

[5] See C. Murray, "A critical review of international mortality data", *Social Science and Medicine Review*, vol. 27, no. 7, 1987, pp. 773-781.

# PART I

Income, employment and poverty

# 2

# Income distribution and inequality

GREATER inequality between rich and poor countries and between rich and poor people occurred in the 1980s. The increasing disparity was the result of the slowing of the world economy and the new economic policies that were put in place all over the world. The polarization has been growing but it is not uniform. Rapid economic progress in many Asian countries, notably China, has reduced measures of inequality among countries in the world and lessened the incidence of poverty in Asia.

Keep in mind, however, the inadequacy of the statistical evidence. Even where official statistics about income distribution exist, illegal and unreported economic activities may make for a quite different situation. Household surveys exist in only a few countries. But even after such caveats, the available information confirms the impression that income distribution became more inequitable in most of the countries where national income declined or stagnated in the 1980s. In other cases, it is relevant to ask which policies have proved successful in maintaining an equitable distribution of income and what has been the experience of sacrificing equity for efficiency.

## A. DISTRIBUTION OF WORLD OUTPUT BY REGION

Even a cursory look at world output (and thus income) and population immediately illustrates the disparities between rich and poor countries. In 1981 the developed market economies, with 17 per cent of world population, generated 72 per cent of world output. Developing countries had 74 per cent of the world's population and 15 per cent of world output (see table 2.1). These figures suggest that the average per capita output in the developed countries was 20 times higher than in the developing countries. The share of output for the developed market economies in 1993 had grown, and the share of population for the developing countries had also grown. In the course of the decade the ratio of the average per capita output in developed countries to that in developing countries had risen to 22.

*Table 2.1*
Share of country groups in population and world GDP

| Country group | Share of GDP[a] | | Share of population | |
|---|---|---|---|---|
| | 1981 | 1993[b] | 1981 | 1993 |
| Developed market economies | 71.7 | 74.6 | 17.2 | 15.3 |
| G-3[c] | 44.8 | 48.1 | 9.1 | 8.3 |
| Developing countries | 15.2 | 18.5 | 74.3 | 77.3 |
| Africa | 1.7 | 1.7 | 10.1 | 11.9 |
| Mediterranean | 0.7 | 0.6 | 1.6 | 1.5 |
| South and East Asia | 5.4 | 9.4 | 53.3 | 54.1 |
| Western Asia | 2.6 | 2.4 | 1.2 | 1.4 |
| Western hemisphere | 4.8 | 4.5 | 8.2 | 8.4 |
| Economies in transition[d] | 13.1 | 6.9 | 8.4 | 6.9 |
| Soviet Union | 9.5 | 4.9 | 6.0 | 5.1 |
| Memorandum items: | | | | |
| 15 heavily-indebted[e] | 5.3 | 5.0 | 11.1 | 11.6 |
| 4 NICs[f] | 1.3 | 2.4 | - | - |
| China | 1.3 | 3.2 | 22.4 | 21.6 |
| Least developed countries | 0.5 | 0.5 | 7.7 | 8.5 |
| Sub-Saharan Africa (excl. Nigeria) | 0.6 | 0.6 | 7.0 | 7.0 |
| India | 1.2 | 1.7 | 15.9 | 16.1 |

Source: United Nations/Department of Economic Information and Social Policy Analysis.

a   Based on 122 countries. GDP estimates at constant US dollars of 1988.
b   Preliminary estimates.
c   Germany, Japan and the United States of America.
d   In Europe, not including Yugoslavia. Data concerning the former German Democratic Republic were included in the economies in transition up to 1989. Beginning in 1990 the data were transferred to the developed market economies group, reflecting German reunification.
e   Argentina, Bolivia, Brazil, Chile, Colombia, Côte d'Ivoire, Ecuador, Mexico, Morocco, Nigeria, Peru, Philippines, Uruguay, Venezuela, Yugoslavia.
f   Hong Kong, Republic of Korea, Singapore, Taiwan Province of China.

Major changes in the international economy during the 1980s constrained the growth of many developing countries. A persistent drop in the prices of exports and in international terms of trade, a massive net transfer of resources to developed countries from developing countries, and the restrained expansion of exports of manufactures, because of slow growth and market protection policies in developed countries, contributed to the slow growth of the developing economies.

Domestic policies aimed at providing unsustainable rates of growth produced domestic price instability and repeated devaluation, resulting in capital flight. Policies of taxation, producer and consumer subsidies, the protection of domestic industrial activity and complex regulations impaired flexibility in the economy, reduced productivity and stifled enterprise. The painful stabilization policies and structural adjustment programmes were designed to correct these imbalances in the economy, establish price stability, promote flexibility, raise productivity and, in the long term, increase income and welfare of the people. To raise capacity utilization and investment, it would have been essential to release restrictions on import capacity, given the current structure of these economies. That, in turn, would have required both an expansion in the demand for their exports at higher prices and an augmented flow of capital into those economies.

Developing countries also grew apart during the 1980s (see figure 2.1). Other countries experienced a sharp deceleration while countries in South and East Asia maintained the growth momentum of the previous decade. This productivity growth has been variously attributed to technological progress, availability of adequate infrastructure, the education and skills of the labour force, its capacity to absorb new technology, managerial flexibility and government policies. Moreover, when compared to other developing regions, South and East Asia suffered relatively milder external shocks and had to deal with less severe macroeconomic imbalances.

Investment declined in the 1980s in both Latin America and Africa in contrast with South and East Asia where investment rates

*Figure 2.1*

Indices of real GDP in developing countries, 1970-1993[a]

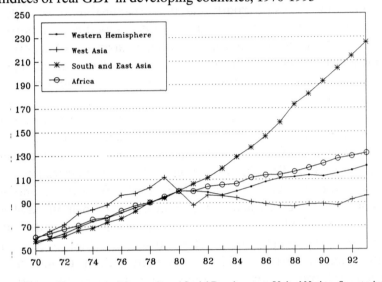

Source: Department of Economic and Social Development, United Nations Secretariat.

Note: 1980 = 100.

a   Preliminary estimates.

were maintained or rose.[1] Many countries in Africa and Latin America had to cut imports because of foreign exchange constraints. The result was reduced access to both new technology and more efficient production processes. A decline in employment, especially in the more productive sectors of the economy, also contributed to slow growth. In contrast, with higher investment and higher employment, there was also higher growth in total factor productivity (the changes in output per unit of all inputs, such as labour and capital, combined) in the newly industrializing countries of Asia.

The economies of Eastern Europe and the former Soviet Union accounted for 8 per cent of the world population in 1981 and generated 13 per cent of world output in that year but only 7 per cent in 1993. Dramatic changes took place in the political and economic environment in these countries. Industrial production was severely hit, as the old trading arrangements collapsed. Severe disruptions in the system of distribution affected the supply of fuel and other essential inputs. The dissolution of the former USSR in 1991 compounded the region's economic problems. Regional GDP contracted by 9 per cent in that year and by 17 per cent in 1992.

## B.  INTERCOUNTRY DISTRIBUTION OF INCOME IN THE 1980s

Table 2.2 presents some indicators of the distribution of world output and income among countries. Three measures were used: gross domestic product (GDP), gross national product (GNP — i.e., the GDP adjusted for net factor payments abroad[2]), and gross national

*Table 2.2*
Estimates of inequality in the distribution of world[a] income, 1981, 1985 and 1989

|  | 1981 | 1985 | 1989 |
|---|---|---|---|
| GDP per capita |  |  |  |
| Coefficient of variation | 1.69 | 1.73 | 1.78 |
| GINI | 0.7285 | 0.7288 | 0.7324 |
| THEIL | 0.7906 | 0.7965 | 0.7993 |
| GNP per capita |  |  |  |
| Coefficient of variation | 1.72 | 1.76 | 1.81 |
| GINI | 0.7321 | 0.7328 | 0.7361 |
| THEIL | 0.7994 | 0.8048 | 0.8081 |
| GNI per capita |  |  |  |
| Coefficient of variation | 1.71 | 1.75 | 1.80 |
| GINI | 0.7298 | 0.7305 | 0.7357 |
| THEIL | 0.7875 | 0.8007 | 0.8064 |

Source: Department of Economic and Social Development, United Nations Secretariat, based on international and national sources.

Notes: The co-efficient of variation is obtained by dividing the standard deviation of the distribution by the mean.
The Gini co-efficient varies between 0 and 1. The lower the co-efficient, the closer the distribution is to equality.
The Theil (T) index varies from 0, when incomes are distributed equally to the logarithm of the number of income recipients when all incomes accrue to one the logarithm of the number of income recipients when all incomes accrue to one recipient and none to others.

a     Based on a sample of 97 countries

income (GNI — i.e., the GNP adjusted for changes in terms of trade). These alternative measures were used to verify whether factor payments and terms of trade losses had a significant impact on the world distribution of income. For instance, one might expect that the distribution of GNP and gross national income would be more uneven than the distribution of world GDP and GNP, respectively, since debt service payments increased and the relative prices of developing countries' exports deteriorated during the last decade.

A sample of 97 countries was constructed and includes both market economies and economies in transition. Estimates of income per capita in national currency were converted into United States dollars using official exchange rates. The use of official exchange rates may distort the outcome somewhat but it is unlikely to affect the direction of change in the indicators.[3] Deciles of world population were ranked by per capita GDP.[4] Where the population of one country exceeded a decile, the balance was carried over to the next higher decile. Lorenz curves were constructed for the resulting cumulative distributions and the coefficients of variation and Theil and Gini indices calculated. This exercise does differ from that of estimating income inequality within a country: GDP is not conceptually the same as household or personal income used in those estimates.

The Gini and Theil coefficients, whichever output concept was used, increased over the past decade, as did the coefficient of variation. (Contrary to what was expected, the indicators of inequality did not deteriorate significantly as factor income and terms of trade adjustments were made to GDP. This may be due to the fact that per capita income in China and India, hosting more than 40 per cent of the world's population, was about the same whichever concept was used.) However, the changes are small, and these results were not confirmed by shifts in the Lorenz curves. As shown in figure 2.2, the Lorenz curves of distribution of output in 1981 and 1989 crossed each other and did not uniformly lie one above the other. Changes in the distribution, however, evidently took place during the decade.

*Figure 2.2*

Lorenz curves of distribution of world GDP, GNP and GNI among countries, 1981, 1991

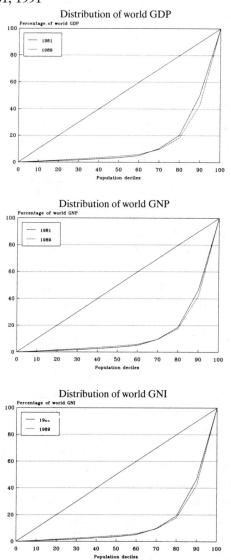

Source: Department of Economic and Social Development, United Nations Secretariat.

Table 2.3 shows the changes in income shares of population deciles in 1981, 1985 and 1989. The bottom five deciles, when considered as a block, consistently increased their income share during the period, largely due to fast growth in China and India. Given the weight of its population, the influence of Chinese economic growth on this distribution is considerable. As China moves out of the first decile into higher deciles, the rate at which the first population decile gains in output share decelerates. In fact, from 1985 to 1989, the output share of the lowest population decile either stagnated or was slightly reduced (see table 2.3).[5] This decile was dominated in 1989 by people in sub-Saharan Africa and Bangladesh.

The top population decile increased its share of world output significantly during the period. This share increased from about 53 per cent to 58 per cent from 1981 to 1989. Relatively strong economic growth in the United States of America and Japan accounted for most of the gain.

Population deciles 6-9 lost output shares. All deciles in those groups lost at least 10 per cent of their respective share in the total world output. The seventh decile lost the most in relative terms: about 20 per cent during the period. This decile contains the population of middle-income developing countries, mainly in Latin America. In some of them, economic difficulties were compounded by civil strife. Population in the ninth decile had their share of output fall from about 27 per cent in 1981 to 24 per cent in 1989. Output losses in this decile were due to the drastic fall in per capita income in oil-exporting countries and the relatively slow growth in developed countries in the decile.

In sum, some of the bottom and top deciles gained output shares, leaving the middle deciles squeezed. Income disparities within deciles remained substantial. Despite impressive growth in China and India, the five bottom population deciles continued to have an average per capita output no more than 10 per cent of the world average per capita output and 1.25 per cent of the per capita output of the top decile (see figure 2.3).

*Table 2.3*

Distribution of world output, 1981, 1985, and 1989

| Population deciles | 1981 Income shares | 1981 Cumulative share | 1985 Income shares | 1985 Cumulative share | 1989 Income shares | 1989 Cumulative share |
|---|---|---|---|---|---|---|
| | *Gross domestic product* | | | | | |
| 1 | 0.54 | 0.54 | 0.66 | 0.66 | 0.66 | 0.66 |
| 2 | 0.56 | 1.10 | 0.77 | 1.43 | 0.91 | 1.57 |
| 3 | 0.62 | 1.72 | 0.78 | 2.21 | 0.91 | 2.48 |
| 4 | 0.89 | 2.61 | 0.93 | 3.14 | 1.00 | 3.48 |
| 5 | 0.90 | 3.51 | 0.96 | 4.10 | 1.02 | 4.50 |
| 6 | 1.54 | 5.05 | 1.43 | 5.53 | 1.39 | 5.89 |
| 7 | 4.73 | 9.78 | 4.25 | 9.78 | 3.82 | 9.71 |
| 8 | 9.67 | 19.45 | 9.39 | 19.17 | 8.54 | 18.25 |
| 9 | 27.67 | 47.12 | 25.90 | 45.07 | 24.71 | 42.96 |
| 10 | 52.88 | 100.00 | 54.93 | 100.00 | 57.04 | 100.00 |
| | *Gross national product* | | | | | |
| 1 | 0.56 | 0.55 | 0.65 | 0.65 | 0.64 | 0.64 |
| 2 | 0.56 | 1.11 | 0.78 | 1.43 | 0.92 | 1.56 |
| 3 | 0.63 | 1.74 | 0.78 | 2.21 | 0.92 | 2.48 |
| 4 | 0.90 | 2.64 | 0.94 | 3.15 | 1.00 | 3.48 |
| 5 | 0.93 | 3.57 | 0.96 | 4.11 | 1.02 | 4.50 |
| 6 | 1.46 | 5.03 | 1.37 | 5.48 | 1.37 | 5.87 |
| 7 | 4.59 | 9.62 | 4.10 | 9.58 | 3.69 | 9.56 |
| 8 | 9.12 | 18.74 | 8.87 | 18.45 | 8.16 | 17.72 |
| 9 | 27.62 | 46.36 | 25.60 | 44.05 | 24.28 | 42.00 |
| 10 | 53.64 | 100.00 | 55.95 | 100.00 | 58.00 | 100.00 |
| | *Gross national income* | | | | | |
| 1 | 0.56 | 0.56 | 0.67 | 0.67 | 0.64 | 0.64 |
| 2 | 0.58 | 1.14 | 0.78 | 1.45 | 0.93 | 1.57 |
| 3 | 0.64 | 1.78 | 0.80 | 2.25 | 0.92 | 2.49 |
| 4 | 0.90 | 2.68 | 0.96 | 3.21 | 1.00 | 3.49 |
| 5 | 0.94 | 3.62 | 0.97 | 4.18 | 1.02 | 4.51 |
| 6 | 1.62 | 5.24 | 1.42 | 5.60 | 1.36 | 5.87 |
| 7 | 4.56 | 9.80 | 4.10 | 9.70 | 3.69 | 9.56 |
| 8 | 9.33 | 19.13 | 8.99 | 18.69 | 8.19 | 17.75 |
| 9 | 27.36 | 46.49 | 25.73 | 44.42 | 24.34 | 42.09 |
| 10 | 53.51 | 100.00 | 55.58 | 100.00 | 57.91 | 100.00 |

Source: Department of Economic and Social Development, United Nations Secretariat, based on international and national sources.

*Figure 2.3*

Decile average per capita income as a percentage of world average per capita income, 1981, 1985, 1991

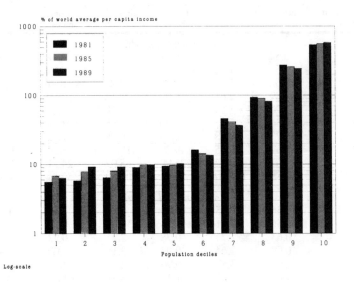

Source: Department of Economic and Social Development, United Nations Secretariat.

## C.  INCOME DISTRIBUTION WITHIN THE DEVELOPED MARKET ECONOMIES

During the first two decades after the Second World War, economic and social conditions improved at an historically unprecedented pace. This performance was accompanied in most OECD countries by a movement towards greater equality in household incomes and a rapid expansion in public expenditure on education, health, housing, social security and welfare. Starting with the second half of the 1970s, however, economic growth slowed sharply throughout the industrialized world.

Household incomes were particularly affected and this growth decelerated quite markedly in the 1980s. The decline is especially noticeable for income from employment and self-employment rather than from rent, interest and dividends. In fact, the average annual rate of growth of real wages and salaries was well below that of GDP during the period 1979-1988.

The slower growth of household incomes has been accompanied by an increasing inequality of earnings. The gap between the average earnings of skilled and educated workers and those of uneducated and less skilled labour is growing. Among many of the developed market economies, increased earnings inequality is one of the major factors responsible for the deterioration in the distribution of income among households (see figure 2.4). Such phenomenon is not restricted to the United States but also took place in Canada, the United Kingdom, Australia, France, the Netherlands and Sweden.[6] The extent of increased earnings inequality is larger the less strongly administered the salaries. It was especially large in

*Figure 2.4*
Changes in income distribution in selected developed countries

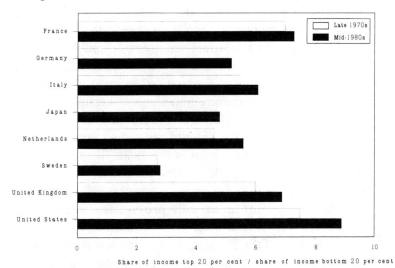

Share of income top 20 per cent / share of income bottom 20 per cent

Source: Boltho, A."Growth, income distribution and household welfare in the industrialized countries since the first oil shock". Innocenti occasional papers, Economic policy series, number 26, April 1992.

Note: The figures are not comparable across countries.

the United States and the United Kingdom. Labour supply conditions also had an impact on increasing earnings inequality. In the former Federal Republic of Germany, for example, inequality in earnings actually decreased during the last decade because of the larger
number of more educated workers joining the labour force during
that period.[7] Changes in the household composition in the 1980s also
had an impact on the distribution of income. For instance, in the
United States, the increase in the number of households headed by
females, many of them single mothers earning low incomes, contributed to the deterioration of the income distribution.

Not less relevant to increased inequality of household income
in developed market economies is the change in government taxes
and transfer policies. In some countries (Canada, for example),
increased income transfers could offset the negative impact of
enlarged earning differentials on the distribution of income. In
other countries, however, changes in the fiscal policy reinforced the
growing earnings inequality. The United Kingdom is an example.[8]

Increasing fiscal deficits and the acceleration of inflation in
many industrialized countries led to a revision in their fiscal policies. Pressure increased to restrain the growth of public expenditures. Moreover, in the quest for greater efficiency in their
economies, policy orientation was changed so as to allow private
initiative to flourish by removing impediments brought about by
the Government through regulation and taxation.

The growth of transfer payments and public expenditure on
social services suffered a slowdown in the 1980s. Tax revenues, on
the other hand, increased quickly during the decade. The increasing taxation was especially hard on the poorer households as some
countries moved away from broadly progressive income taxes
toward the more regressive indirect taxes. Furthermore, the income
tax schedule in many OECD countries became less progressive as
well. The most striking change was a cut in the top marginal
income tax rate; 21 OECD countries took this course. For the 12
countries that raised their lowest marginal rate, the tax structure
became a great deal more compact.[9]

## D.  INCOME DISTRIBUTION WITHIN DEVELOPING COUNTRIES

The distribution of income of a country can be thought of as being linked to the structure of the economy and the distribution of the labour force within the various productive sectors. Also linked to the distribution of income are the way access to productive assets (land, physical and human capital) is distributed within economic agents and the particular growth path followed by that country. The growth path stresses the role of the development strategy in determining the structural transformation a country undergoes. The extent of government participation in this process also points up the role of the development strategy, as does its interference in the income distribution — by, say, an agrarian reform and distributive fiscal policies — and the vulnerability of the economy to external shocks and the policy response they generate.

The capacity of an economy to grow and consequently to generate employment (and the quality of employment generated) has, therefore, a direct impact on the distribution of income of that country. The growth performance of many developing countries was disappointing, to understate the case, during the last decade. With the exception of the South and East Asian region, all developing regions showed a marked deceleration in their rate of growth, with per capita income failing to grow at all in many of them (see table 2.4).

Adjustment was necessary. A series of policy responses were formulated to face the new economic realities. Production emphasis was to be shifted from non-tradeable to tradeable and resources were to be allocated to ensure a pattern of production that would be viable at international prices.[10] Price distortions were to be eliminated.[11] Equilibrium in the balance of payments was to be restored via a reduction in domestic absorption. Wage repression, limited credit supply and cuts in government expenditure played an important role in reducing the aggregate domestic demand. Output fell in many countries. In the absence of higher growth that would

*Table 2.4*

Rate of population and output growth, 1972-1991

|  | Population | | Real GDP | | Real GDP per capita | |
|---|---|---|---|---|---|---|
|  | 1972-<br>1981 | 1982-<br>1991 | 1972-<br>1981 | 1982-<br>1991 | 1972-<br>1981 | 1982-<br>1991 |
| Developing economies | 2.2 | 2.1 | 4.9 | 3.6 | 2.7 | 1.5 |
| Latin America | 2.4 | 2.1 | 5.2 | 1.5 | 2.8 | -0.6 |
| Africa | 2.9 | 3.1 | 4.5 | 2.4 | 1.6 | -0.7 |
| Sub-Saharan Africa | 2.9 | 3.2 | 2.4 | 1.6 | -0.5 | -1.6 |
| West Asia | 3.6 | 3.5 | 3.4 | 0.2 | -0.2 | -3.3 |
| South and East Asia | 2.3 | 2.3 | 5.9 | 5.9 | 3.6 | 3.6 |
| China | 1.7 | 1.4 | 5.6 | 8.9 | 3.9 | 7.5 |

Source: Department of Economic and Social Development, United Nations Secretariat.

bring about greater savings, debt-servicing obligations were met at the expense of investment. This not only had a negative impact on the short-term performance of these economies but also compromised their future growth prospects.

A redistribution of incomes results from a reallocation of resources and the resulting changes in the productive structure of a given economy. The direction that redistribution will take depends on the outcome of the complex relationship of a series of factors. Some we have just reviewed. All in all, for many countries the adjustment process of the 1980s resulted in an increase in inequality.

## 1. *Latin America and the Caribbean*

The slow-down in output growth in Latin America was reflected mostly in the labour market. Urban unemployment increased, reaching about 10 per cent in 1989 after being at 7.5 per cent in 1980 and 11 per cent in 1985. This increase was accompanied by a sharp drop in real wages, particularly the urban minimum wage. In Brazil, Ecuador, Mexico, Peru and Venezuela, urban minimum wages, after deducting for inflation, were at least 40 per cent lower in 1990 than in 1980.[12]

Manufacturing activities were badly hit, mainly during the early 1980s. Facing lower domestic and international demand and input constraints due to the unavailability of foreign currency, output declined and employment opportunities were reduced. Output in manufacturing recovered somewhat from 1984 onwards, most likely because of the end of the recession in industrial countries and the resulting growth in international trade. Yet employment in manufacturing failed to grow; it actually decreased further. To increase competitiveness, most large industries cut labour costs by laying off personnel and hiring the services of small enterprises instead.[13] In fact, one of the characteristics of the last decade was the decrease of the relative importance of manufacturing in particular, and of the formal economy in general, in generating employment. Most of the new jobs in the region during the 1980s were located in the lower productivity, low-paid sectors. Reduced economic opportunities help to explain the increase of migration abroad among skilled labour, especially in some of the Caribbean countries.

Many low-paid jobs in the region were filled by people who had been laid off from the relatively higher paying sectors of the economy. As middle-income generating jobs were lost, incomes became more polarized. Furthermore, unemployment increased, expanding the number of people without access to any source of income. Income distribution, therefore, deteriorated.

The relative importance of the informal sector increased in many Latin American countries during the 1980s. Its share in total non-agricultural employment expanded from 26 per cent in 1980 to about 33 per cent in 1987. But while the "escape" to the informal sector gave displaced workers a favourable alternative to unemployment, it did not prevent a fall in their incomes. The fall occurred not only because of the sector's relatively lower average, but mainly because the average incomes fell by more than 40 per cent in real terms in this sector between 1980 and 1987. Real wage losses in the organized sectors of the economy ranged from 10 per cent in manufacturing to 16 per cent in construction during the same period.[14]

The impact of the crisis was felt mostly by the urban poorer groups, i.e., those earning minimum wages and those in the informal sector. The segments of the middle class whose incomes depend mostly on salaried employment suffered a relative impoverishment. This was caused not only by fewer employment opportunities in the formal sector of the economy and the decline in salary levels, but also by a decline in the supply of public goods provided by the state to the urban population.[15] Nothing could better illustrate the consequences of the decline of public spending on social services and basic infrastructure in the region than the 1990 outbreak of cholera in Peru.

Employment in the public sector continued to grow in Latin America despite the economic crisis; adjustment came in the form of lower wages and salaries, affecting the middle income classes particularly. From 1980 to 1987, emloyment in the public sector expanded by 32 per cent, while wages declined by 17 per cent in real terms.[16] Wage repression in the public sector was used many times as a specific policy instrument. For instance, in some of the various economic shocks applied in Brazil and Peru during the past decade, civil servant employees had their wages either frozen or adjusted at rates lower than the ones applied to other economic sectors. A combination of wage repression and emphasis on unskilled job generation (mostly public works) to mitigate the negative effects of adjustments on the poor, led the regional share of the wage bill in the total expenditures of central Government to fall from 21 per cent in 1980 to about 13 per cent in 1987.[17] Some countries of the region, however, did experience deep cuts in public sector jobs that were more pronounced than those in manufacturing.

With the lower- and middle-income strata of the population losing their relative share in total income, distribution became more polarized, The income gap between the rich and the rest of the population increased. Indeed, amongst the seven Latin American countries for which there is available information, the share of the top quartile (urban areas only) in total income increased to the detriment of all other quartiles in six of them: Argentina, Brazil, Costa Rica, Uruguay and Venezuela. Colombia is the only country in the sample where inequality decreased. This country is also the only one that experienced continuous growth during the decade and one of the few in Latin America where workers, particularly those earning minimum wages, did not suffer real income losses.

This process of income dispersion in favour of the urban elite can be partially explained by the acceleration of inflation, repeated devaluation and capital flight. The vicious circle of inflation and the resulting devaluation because of the need to maintain the competitiveness of exports gave people with access to funds abroad tremendous opportunities to increase their wealth in local currency.[18] Moreover, even without resort to capital flight, the richer segments of the population usually have ways to safeguard their income from inflation. It should be remembered that as one advances on the income scale, the income dependence on wage earnings decreases. Therefore, even if wages and salaries are indexed below the inflation rate, the earnings from financial investments usually are not, especially in a situation where high real interest rates are maintained because of the need to finance the public deficit and support the exchange rate. In some countries the mechanisms of domestic public debt financing provided for full indexation *and* attractive interest rates, thus resulting in a transfer of wealth to those holding government papers from the other segments of the society.

Rural groups did relatively better in the region than the urban population, and yet inequality may have increased in the rural areas.

Agriculture did relatively better than the rest of the economy due to a combination of factors. Among them were the lesser vulnerability to external constraints and the adoption of policies aimed at increasing agricultural output and/or at shielding domestic agriculture from the price oscillations in the external markets. But it was the large and medium-sized farmers who most likely took advantage of these factors. They had easier access to credit and to the required imported inputs such as fertilizers and pesticides. Moreover, the wages of agricultural landless workers fell by 20 per cent in real terms and most of the Latin American rural

population is landless. Such a reduction in the cost of labour benefits the large capitalist farmers. The limited data available seems to
support these hypotheses. In the rural areas of both Brazil and
Venezuela, the share of the top quartile in income expanded to the
detriment of all three bottom quartiles. The Gini coefficient of
income distribution in the rural area worsened sharply in both
countries. In Brazil it increased to 0.47 in 1987 from 0.41 in 1979,
while in Venezuela it jumped to 0.37 in 1986 from 0.29 in 1981.[19]

### 2. *Africa*

Urban groups in Africa, particularly wage earners and workers
in the informal sector, carried the brunt of adjustment burdens. In
addition, some evidence indicates that the steep decline in urban
incomes led to a reduction in the rural/urban income gap. However, African economic problems were not touched off by the
world economic recession of the early 1980s and the debt crisis.
Economic decay had been present since the mid-1970s with declining exports, food production per capita, terms of trade and a negative growth in per capita output. However, the situation undoubt-
edly worsened in the 1980s.

Unemployment increased in many African countries. Output
fell in many industries and the workforce was reduced accordingly.
For instance, by 1986-1987, Nigerian manufacturing industries were
operating at 35 per cent of their capacity and in branches of manufacturing particularly dependent on imported inputs, capacity utilization was at 20 per cent. Unemployment among skilled workers,
uncommon during the boom years of the Nigerian economy,
became acute.[20] Government-sector employment continued to
grow, at least during the first half of the decade. Adjustment came
in the form of lower wages.

Even if employment in the public sector was not drastically
reduced, the same is not true for the supply of public services. A
number of services previously provided by the State at zero or minimum cost to consumers have been privatized or otherwise charged
for. In many countries the quality of public services deteriorated.

Services at public hospitals in Morocco now need to be paid for, and the decay of public schools has led to the emergence of private schools with high fees, beyond the reach of the majority of the population.[21] Cuts in government consumer subsidies also adversely affected urban incomes. In sum, reductions in the quality and quantity of the services provided by the State entailed losses in standards of living of urban populations in addition to the more readily accounted for losses in real wage incomes.

Urban wage earners are a small minority in many African countries. About 70 per cent of the African labour force are smallholder farmers producing food (most of it for subsistence) or cash crops. Some measures were adopted in the 1980s to reduce biases against agriculture, so it has been argued that the rural sector was less adversely affected by adjustment policies than the urban economy. Therefore, income distribution may have become less unequal in African countries as urban incomes fell steeply and rural incomes stagnated.

However, there is evidence that adjustment measures did have an adverse impact on rural incomes in some countries and that in others, income inequality in the countryside increased. Rural household incomes are not exclusively derived from farming. Complementing them are earnings from wage labour, rural non-farm activities, occasional work in the informal urban sector and remittances from the urban sector.[22] About 20 per cent of crops produced in subsistence farming are traded for cash or for products from cities. As a result, one may expect declining economic activity in urban areas to affect rural incomes adversely.

### 3. *South Asia and South-East Asia*

Output grew faster in South Asia and South-East Asia during the 1980s. Unemployment was lower and real wages increased in several countries. However, agricultural products, fuels and other minerals still account for a considerable share of exports of a number of countries. These countries had to contend with low prices and stagnant demand. Other countries — India, Pakistan, the

Philippines and Sri Lanka and Thailand — had to adjust to a declining supply of foreign exchange and a lower demand for contract labour, a problem that was aggravated by the Persian Gulf conflict. Balance of payments problems temporarily affected other countries in the region as well. Adjustments were made, however, without major output losses. The first reason for this is that external shocks were milder in Asia than elsewhere. Secondly, macroeconomic disequilibria were also relatively smaller. Consequently, adjustment in the region did not require sustained cuts in demand as in most of Latin America and Africa.[23]

Distributive policies deliberately implemented by Government and growth patterns providing widespread employment were also important in reducing inequality. Land reforms in China, including Taiwan Province and the Republic of Korea in the late 1940s and early 1950s secured reasonable equality in asset distribution in rural areas. Income distribution improved during the 1960s and the 1970s. Recently, some signs have appeared suggesting a slight increase in inequality.

Inequality probably increased after 1987 in Malaysia. The Malaysian economy had been cushioned from the global recession of the early 1980s by an increase in government expenditure. As the public sector deficit increased, especially after the fall in oil prices reduced government revenue, expenditure was cut back. The construction boom subsided and unemployment increased, reaching 9 per cent in 1987, up from less than 5 per cent in 1982.

In Hong Kong, the tax structure is highly progressive, and government expenditure favours low-income groups. The post-tax distribution of income in Singapore is less unequal than the pre-tax one as the result of progressive taxation and government expenditure on housing and education. Income inequality also declined during the 1970s with the massive creation of low-skilled jobs in the labour-intensive export manufacturing sector. But income inequality may have increased in the first half of the 1980s as the economy underwent rapid changes. In the fast-growing financial, business service and construction sectors, wages were higher than in other sectors.[24]

In Indonesia, government policies were successful in improving the distribution of income during a programme of stabilization and structural change. Income distribution became slightly less uneven. The Government had established a social infrastructure to provide health and education facilities, especially in rural areas and to women, before the new policies came into effect. The budget deficit was reduced mainly by cutting capital outlays and by freezing civil servants' salaries from 1985 to 1988. Adjustment costs were mostly borne by the urban population, specifically government employees and educated youths. The heaviest burden fell on protected sectors with rental incomes.[25]

### 4. China

Income distribution in China changed after the reforms introduced in 1978. The reforms themselves were the result of a change in the government development strategy. The goal of equality as an end in itself was abandoned. Some income differentiation was perceived as a means to stimulate individual initiative. With the disbanding of the communes, the introduction of the household responsibility system and other related measures to stimulate agriculture production and diversification, total output grew quite fast in China. The annual average growth rate during the 1980s was about 9 per cent. But income disparities increased among both households and regions.[26]

Although access to land is guaranteed to every rural household, the yield from that land depends on the quality of the land and the working capacity of each household. Families with young children, elderly persons and/or disabled persons receive lower incomes. One objective of the reforms was to raise procurement prices for agricultural products as an incentive to increase output. The increases penalized net purchasers of these products. But with the emergence of township and peasant enterprises (collectively or individually owned), some of the rural labour force found jobs in non-farm activities where productivity and incomes were higher than in the farm sector.

Income disparity is believed to have widened at the regional level as well. Regions with access to irrigation programmes appear to have benefited more than others from the reform. Fast growth in the special economic zones has also provided wages at much higher levels than in the rest of the economy.

Immigration to the cities reappeared after controls were relaxed. Some migrant workers did particularly well and succeeded economically, while others were less fortunate. This so-called "floating" population is usually engaged in services, mostly in the informal sector, and has no access to subsidized housing or cheaper goods provided through coupons for rationed goods. The acceleration of inflation compounded their difficulties. Registered urban residents, on the other hand, were cushioned from the impact of higher prices because of their access to more stable prices via the coupon system and subsidies from the Government.[27] Since the introduction of reforms, however, the importance of coupons to the welfare of the people has been diminishing as both the range of products offered and the price differential between the state-owned stores and the free market have declined. Only a restricted number of goods, usually basic staples, are still rationed and their prices are just below the free prices.

### 5. *Eastern Europe and the former Soviet Union*

Income distribution under socialism differed significantly from that in market economies. A minimum income was guaranteed to everyone by maintaining full employment.[28] Wages and salaries were controlled by the State, the dominant employer in the economy. The tax system played a marginal role, except where there was a private sector. Money incomes were established at relatively low levels, sufficient, however, to support modest living standards. They were generously supplemented by numerous welfare benefits, consisting of transfers in cash, transfers-in-kind, and subsidized housing and consumer goods. Transfer payments were unrelated to income levels and were equally distributed among households, except for family allowances.[29]

Although the ratio of expenditure on social benefits to national income was not, in general, larger than in market economies, the structure and character of social expenditure was very different. Transfer payments played a more important role in supporting the average income.

Transfers-in-kind and subsidies satisfied many social needs. They were delivered directly from the central budget or through enterprises. A full account of the effects on household income distribution cannot be made; there are no precise data on social services dispensed through the workplace.

The impact of consumer subsidies and benefits acquired through the workplace on living standards was substantial. State enterprises contributed to various social funds to defray the costs of those services.[30] The division of responsibilities between the government budget and enterprises varied among countries. In Poland and Bulgaria, sickness benefits were entirely borne by enterprises. In general, the provision of many important benefits, including housing, cafeterias, child care facilities, health clinics and vacation resorts, were tied to the workplace.

During the first two decades after the Second World War, inequality as measured by access to opportunities and the distribution of money income decreased substantially. The virtual abolition of income from the ownership of wealth[31] eliminated the most powerful source of income inequality. Equal access to opportunities was sought through job security and State-provided education. Wages allowed only a narrow differential to account for differences in skill, priority of the branch of industry and its location. As a result, the ratio of non-manual employees' income to that of manual employees was significantly reduced in all countries in the region, especially as compared to the conditions before the war.

Privileges for the Party nomenclatura and the emergence of a second and parallel economy grew to meet unsatisfied demands and to circumvent increasing inefficiency in the State sector.[32] In the former Soviet Union and all the countries of Eastern Europe, the second economy included a large variety of activities, ranging from fictional cooperative activities between individuals and State enterprises, private production of consumer goods and services and arbitrage to bribes and illegal trading of foreign currency.[33]

The shadow economy, which was a "free", or "black" market, constituted a powerful channel of income distribution outside the plan. It was a source of additional income — most often from a second or third job possible due to the undemanding pace of work in the State sector[34] and tips — and a source of supply outside the plan of many scarce goods, including apartments, cars and services, such as repairs and maintenance, and medical care. Prices were usually much higher than for similar items within the State sector.

Bonuses, paid in kind and in cash — in particular, coupons for cars, washing machines or television sets for fulfilment of norms in piece-work, premiums for innovations[35] and the payment of a thirteenth month's wage — proliferated in the 1970s and 1980s as work incentives.[36] However, these bonuses could not work as planned in the absence of work-related evaluation criteria. At the enterprise level it was impossible to distinguish profit-making enterprises. Thus, bonuses to higher management and, to some extent, to workers, could not reward productive work. The distribution of bonuses was in effect unrelated to work performance and was guided, depending on circumstances, by the principle of equality or by the wish to reward political loyalty. In either case the bonus system lost its value as an incentive and added to the perception of an "unfair" system.

In the "unfair" system, consumer goods and housing were cheap[37] but most often inaccessible on a regular basis. Job security was maintained, but wages were low, failing especially in the 1980s to support even moderate living standards. Unemployment practically did not exist, yet demoralizing "unemployment on the job" enabled workers to take second or third jobs performed during regular working hours at State enterprises. In some professions, as in the State retail distribution system of health care, tips were prevalent and they became *quasi* official compensation to supplement low official wages and salaries. Social benefits of better quality were accessible only through privileges or bribes. Equality of money incomes became limited to official incomes in the State sector. Equality of opportunity and upward mobility were restricted to the Party nomenclatura. Executive positions and professional career opportunities, including access to lucrative privileges, became practically inaccessible to outsiders, regardless of their qualifications. At the same time, rapidly increasing distortions and the inefficiency of the centrally planned system resulted in declining growth rates, structural imbalances and distribution problems. The gap between the economic capabilities of the system and the expectations of better living conditions was stretched during the past two decades.

## 6. Distribution of income among households

Income distribution in Eastern Europe and the former Soviet Union was highly egalitarian in comparison with other countries.[38] At the end of the 1980s, Gini coefficients of the distribution of household income were systematically lower than in other countries.[39] They ranged, except in Yugoslavia, from 0.2 to 0.3, compared to 0.3 to 0.4 and above in other regions.

The lowest income inequality in the region was in Czechoslovakia and the highest in Yugoslavia. The differences among countries could be explained by the size of the private sector, especially in agriculture, and by regional differences in income. The development of the private sector in urban areas and mixed ownership in agriculture contributed to the higher Gini coefficient in Hungary. The large share of private agriculture in the Polish economy and significant income differences among republics in the former Soviet Union and Yugoslavia contributed to higher income inequality in those countries.

In general the differences between the wages of more and less educated and skilled workers were lower in these economies than elsewhere. High technical qualifications and the social status of some professions — doctors, lawyers or teachers — were combined with low wages. A part of the explanation for low differentials is ideological.[40] The relatively high wages of blue-collar workers probably were due to the disproportionally high demand for their labour sustained by archaic economic structures.[41] Until 1990 the average wage of manual workers was almost equal to or even slightly above the average salary in industry (see table 2.5). The premium paid to engineers and technicians was decreasing, except in Czechoslovakia where the ratio was stable. The position of other white-collar work-

*Table 2.5*
Wages and salaries of blue collar workers, engineers and technicians, and other white collar workers relative to average industrial wages and salaries[a]

|  | 1960 | 1970 | 1980 | 1984 | 1990 |
|---|---|---|---|---|---|
| Bulgaria[b] | | | | | |
| Blue collar | 0.99 | 0.98 | 1.01 | 1.01 | .. |
| Engineers, technicians | 1.41 | 1.37 | 1.23 | 1.24 | .: |
| Other white collar | 0.93 | 1.00 | 0.96 | 0.99 | :: |
| Czechoslovakia | | | | | |
| Blue collar | 0.98 | 0.97 | 0.97 | 0.98 | 0.97 |
| Engineers, technicians[c] | 1.14 | 1.17 | 1.14 | 1.15 | 1.13 |
| German Democratic Republic | | | | | |
| Blue collar | 0.99 | 0.97 | 0.98 | 0.98 | |
| Hungary | | | | | |
| Blue collar | 0.97 | 0.95 | 0.94 | 0.94 | 0.88[d] |
| Engineers, technicians | 1.52 | 1.47 | 1.20 | - | 1.38[d,e] |
| Poland | | | | | |
| Blue collar | 0.96 | 0.96 | 1.00 | 1.01 | 0.96 |
| Engineers, technicians | 1.54 | 1.43 | 1.23 | 1.18 | 1.15 |
| Other white collar | 1.00 | 0.98 | 0.84 | 0.84 | |
| Soviet Union | | | | | |
| Blue collar | 0.98 | 0.98 | 1.00 | 1.00 | 0.96 |
| Engineers, technicians | 1.48 | 1.34 | 1.15 | 1.11 | 1.16 |
| Other white collar | 0.81 | 0.84 | 0.79 | 0.78 | |

Source: Department of Economic and Social Development, United Nations Secretariat, based on national statistics.

a   Average wage and salary in the so-called socialized industry (state and cooperative enterprises).
b   State enterprises only.
c   Engineers and planners.
d   1989.
e   Persons in the learned professions. The ratio for 1990 is not fully comparable with previous years due to the inclusion of income tax since 1 January 1988.

ers deteriorated in all countries except Bulgaria. Data for 1990 indicate that the relative wages of blue-collar workers were beginning to decline in all countries and that those of white-collar workers were on the rise. The trend is especially marked in Hungary. In some countries — Bulgaria, Poland and Czechoslovakia — farmers were better off than workers (see figure 2.5).[42]

*Figure 2.5*
Relative per capita income in 1989 in selected Eastern European countries (*average = 100*)

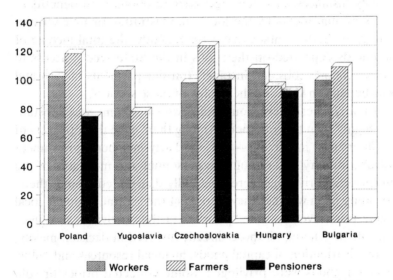

Workers    Farmers    Pensioners

Source: Branko Milanovic, "Poverty in Eastern Europe in the years of the crisis, 1978-1987: Poland, Hungary and Yugoslavia", World Bank Economic Review, vol 5, No. 2 (1991), pp. 187-205.

Notes: Estimates are based on national household surveys. For Czechoslovakia data refer to 1988.

Most incomes within the second economy came from second jobs and tips. Typically, one retained a job in the State sector to secure basic wages and social benefits and worked elsewhere for higher incomes.[43] Sometimes, as in Hungary until 1988, the second job was conducted on the same premises as the first, under "business partnerships" with public enterprise. In other cases it was done illegally. Plumbers and other craftsmen employed in State enterprises offered their services during working hours using factory equipment and stolen spare parts. Doctors performed surgery on private patients in State hospitals, and teachers gave private lessons to their pupils in State schools or universities.

The non-targeted welfare system proved to be particularly vulnerable to abuse. A large number of benefits, especially those of higher quality, were distributed outside the formal channels as political privileges, political and personal rewards, gifts and bribes. In many instances, tips were necessary to obtain such benefits as repairs of apartments by the local administration or timely treatment at the State dental clinic. Consequently, the total income of households depended on their jobs in the State sector, access to second economy jobs and incomes, transfer payments in cash and social benefits in kind and the quality of those services.

Clearly, there were households whose income was substantially higher than that of others. Among them were the top layers of the Communist hierarchy — selected Party members, government officials, military and diplomatic personnel and managers of big enterprises.[44] Privileges were unequally distributed among them, depending upon whether they worked at the central, regional, local or enterprise level, and the "priority" of their activities at a given moment. In general, all those directly involved in decision-making and the distribution of capital goods, financial resources and public consumer goods were privileged. Some collected bribes or sold goods and services stolen from the State. Others were rewarded for genuine entrepreneurial talent or professional knowledge. Small-scale businessmen or farmers producing fruits, vegetables and flowers around big cities, representatives of the intelligentsia, such as doctors or lawyers with easy access to second jobs within the State sector, earned high incomes. The overvalued exchange rates of hard currencies and black market operations offered huge gains to those who had foreign currency.

# Notes

[1] The average level of investment per worker — measured in thousands of 1980 dollars — doubled from $0.2 to $0.4 in South and East Asia from the period 1976-1980 to the period 1986-1990. It declined in Africa from $0.5 to $0.3 and in Latin America from $1.5 to $0.9 during the same periods. See *World Economic Survey, 1992* (United Nations publication, Sales No. E.92.II.C.1), pp. 67-69.

[2] Net factor payments abroad are the balance of flows of compensation of employees, property and entrepreneurial income and other current transfers that the domestic economy receives from and sends to the rest of the world.

[3] For a parallel exercise using purchasing power parity rates of exchange, see Ronald V. A. Sprout and James H. Weaver, "International distribution of income", *Kyklos*, vol. 45 (1992), pp. 237-258. The results derived are not entirely different. It had been shown that the main inequality measures and the Lorenz curves of world distribution of income are not very sensitive to the different exchange rates. See A. Berry and others, "The world distribution of income: evolution over the recent period and effects of population growth," paper presented at the United Nations Expert Group Meeting on the Consequences of Rapid Population Growth in Developing Countries (IESA/PAC.26, August 1988).

[4] This ignores the distribution of income within each country. Lack of data is the obvious reason.

[5] Chinese per capita output grew at an average annual rate of about 9 per cent during the period 1981-1985 and about 6 per cent in the period 1985-1988, whichever the output concept used. India's performance was less formidable at around 3 per cent a year during the periods considered.

[6] Gottschalk, P., Changes in inequality of family income in seven industrialized countries in *American Economic Review* (AEA Paper and Proceedings), vol. 83, No. 2, May 1993, pp. 136-142.

[7] Abraham, K.G., and Housman, S.N., Earnings inequality in Germany, NBER Working Paper No. 4541, November 1993.

[8] P. Johnson and S. Webb, Explaining growth in U.K. income inequality, 1979-1988 in *The Economic Journal*, 103, March 1993.

[9] A. Boltho, Growth, income distribution and household welfare in the industrialized countries since the first oil shock, Innocenti Occasional papers, Economic Policy Series, number 26, April 1992.

[10] See report of the Secretary-General on the state of international economic cooperation, in particular the revitalization of economic growth and development of developing countries to the special session of the General Assembly (A/AC.233/5).

[11] See the report of the Secretary-General on economic stabilization programmes in developing countries to the forty-sixth session of the General Assembly (A/46/385).

[12] ECLAC, Balance preliminar de la economia de America Latina y el Caribe 1990. (Documento informativo de 19 de diciembre de 1990).

[13] ECLAC, Notas sobre el disarrollo social in America Latina (Notes sobre la economia y el disarollo); No 511/512 (July 1991), p. 9.

[14] ILO, World Labour Report 1989, volume 4, pp. 31-32.

[15] Ghai, D. and de Alcantara, C. H., "The crisis of the 1980s in Africa, Latin America and the Caribbean: an overview", in Ghai, D. (ed), "The IMF and the South: the social impact of crisis and adjustment", United Nations Research Institute for Social Development (Geneva, 1991).

[16] ILO, World Labour Report 1989, op. cit.

[17] van Ginneken, W., "Labour adjustment in the public sector: policy issues for developing countries", in *International Labour Review*, vol. 129, 1990, No. 4, pp. 441-457.

[18]Ghai, D. and de Alencar, C. H., "The crisis of the 1980s . . .", p. 26.

[19]Data obtained from ECLAC, "Panorama Social de America Latina", (LC/G.1688), October 1991, table no. 4, p. 46.

[20]T. Fashoyin, "Economic recession and employment security in Nigeria", *International Labour Review*, vol. 129, no. 5 (1990), pp. 649-663.

[21]Z. Daoud, "La frustration des classes moyennes au Maghreb", *Le Monde Diplomatique*, No. 452, 38ème année (Novembre 1991).

[22]In Ghana, for instance, about 70 per cent of rural income originated in farming, with the rest coming from self-employment (16 per cent) and wage employment (11 per cent). See Ghana Statistical Service (Accra), and World Bank, "Ghana living standards survey: preliminary results 1988", (mimeo), October 1988, p. 86.

[23]See World Bank, *World Development Report*, 1990, (Oxford and New York, Oxford University Press, 1990), pp. 106-107.

[24]L. Lim and others, "The political economy of poverty, equity and growth: Singapore", in Findlay, R. and Willisz, S. (ed), "The political economy of poverty, equity and growth; five small open economies", (unpublished World Bank study), November 1988.

[25]S. Ahmed and R. K. Peters, Jr., "Adjustment with poverty alleviation: Indonesia's experience", background paper for *World Development Report*, 1990 (mimeo, December 1989), and Hall Hill, "Regional development in a boom and bust economy: Indonesia since 1970", *Economic Development and Cultural Change*, vol. 40, no. 2 (January 1992), pp. 351-379.

[26]For a summary on the Chinese reforms see S. Mukhopadhyay, "Rural poverty and inequality in post-reform China" (New Dehli, ILO/Asian Employment Programme, March 1990).

[27]Ahmad, E. and Wang, Y., "Inequality and poverty in China: institutional change and public policy, 1978-1988", (background paper for the 1990 World Development Report), December 1989, (mimeo).

[28]"All that is required is that they (workers) should work equally — do their proper share of work — and get paid equally". V. I. Lenin, "The state and revolution" in *Essential Works of Lenin*, Henry M. Christian, ed. (New York, Bantam, 1966), p. 348.

[29]Family allowances were the only source of income that had a strong pro-poor bias. Households in lower deciles received more, not only in comparison to their incomes but also in absolute amounts. With a guaranteed minimum income, high family allowances and pensions related to previous earnings, there was no need for target cash transfers. Poverty should have been limited to isolated cases such as the disabled and alcoholics.

[30]The social funds of enterprises were also expected to play a role in providing incentives. However, due to the "soft budget constraint", ultimately, all enterprise losses were financed from the central budget.

[31]In all countries of the region, private-sector activities were severely restricted and incomes controlled by tax policy (unpredictable and often acting retroactively) in order to prevent an accumulation of wealth.

[32]The second, or shadow, economy is used to cover all activities outside the plan.

[33]The formal status of the second economy under socialism was not easy to define, and the distinction between legal and illegal activities was ambiguous. In general, there were three broad kinds of activities: those that evolved in support of activities within the planning system; those that met personal consumer demands for goods and services; and arbitrage and rent-seeking behaviour.

[34]In that way the workers in State enterprises captured a fraction of dissipated rent in the form of non-pecuniary benefits ("leisure on the job").

[35]The lack of entrepreneurship was one of the major deficiencies of the centrally planned economies. Efforts to stimulate innovations within the past two decades through material incentives brought poor results, spurring "fake" innovations. For further discussion, see chap. VII of *World Economic Survey, 1992*.

[36]They also served to "buy" social peace and reverse declining support for the Communist party in the 1970s and 1980s. Party officials, in particular in Poland, negotiating with workers of big industrial units on strike, often promised additional allocations of scarce goods to local shops, car "vouchers" and other bonuses.

[37]These prices were not cheap, measured in terms of the amount of labour required to buy them. In 1988, the average Polish employee had to work twice as long as his counterpart in the former Federal Republic of Germany to buy a given quantity of meat, seven times longer to buy an egg, nine times longer to buy a comparable motor car and 13 times longer to buy a colour television set. See *Economic Survey of Europe, 1988-1989* (United Nations publication, Sales No. E.89.II.E.1), p. 121.

[38]See Abram Bergson, "Income inequality under Soviet socialism", *Journal of Economic Literature*, vol. XII (September 1984); Henryk Flakierski, loc. cit.; Alan H. Gelb and Ceryl W. Gray, *The Transformation of Economics in Central and Eastern Europe. Issues, Progress, and Prospects*, Washington, D. C., World Bank, 1991; Alistair McAuley, "The economic transition in Eastern Europe: Employment, income distribution, and the social security net", *Oxford Review of Economic Policy*, vol. 7, no. 4 (Winter 1991); Christian Morrisson, "Income distribution in East European and Western countries", *Journal of Comparative Economics*, no. 8 (1984).

[39]Gini coefficients were calculated using national household sample surveys. Hungary has conducted these surveys every five years since 1962 and every two years since 1983; Poland and Yugoslavia, every five years since 1963. In 1980, Poland began to conduct the surveys annually, as did Yugoslavia in 1984. Czechoslovakia conducted household surveys in 1970, 1977 and 1988. Their results are not widely distributed. Data for Bulgaria, Romania and the Soviet Union are not readily available and are based on occasional surveys and estimates.

[40]The basic wage in Socialist ideology was close to a monetary equivalent of a right to work.

[41]See Jan Winiecki, "Narrow wage differentials between blue-collar and white-collar workers and excess demand for manual labour in the CPEs: casually linked system-specific phenomenon", *Osteuropa-Wirtschaft*, no. 3 (1988).

[42]In Czechoslovakia, farmers benefited from large subsidies to agriculture. Gains in farmer's incomes in Poland in the 1980s resulted mostly from strong lobbying, including that of "Rural Solidarity". Full-time private agriculture in Poland was not included in household surveys. Income differentials within this social group, as shown in several studies, have always been significant. See Eugeniusz Gorzelak, "Incomes of farmers' households in Poland", *Oeconomica Polona*, No. 5 (1987).

[43]P. G. Hare, "The assessment: microeconomics of transition in Eastern Europe", *Oxford Review of Economic Policy*, vol. 7, no. 4, p. 8.

[44]Some have suggested that the Communist nomenclatura had, in fact, many characteristics of a new class with specific property rights to the nation's resources. See Jan Winiecki, *Resistance to Change in the Soviet Economic System: A Property Rights Approach* (London, Routledge, 1991).

# 3

## Unemployment and low productivity employment

EMPLOYMENT, the main source of income for most people, determines a person's income and social status. Unemployment, especially when long-term, leads to poverty and to feelings of worthlessness. For society as a whole, unemployment and underemployment signify the waste of potentially productive human resources.

The implications and perceptions of unemployment differ from country to country depending upon the traditions and values of the specific society in which it occurs. In developed countries, support systems reduce the danger of destitution, but always the loss of work leads to a reduced income for the individual. In developing countries, prolonged unemployment for the main or sole income earner is not feasible for the vast majority of the population because of the lack of unemployment insurance. To survive, an unemployed person must find some way of making a living.

Definitions of unemployment vary because of social and accounting differences between countries. In general, a person is unemployed if without employment or self-employment, currently available for work, and actively seeking work. Variations occur with regard to age limits, reference periods, criteria for seeking work, treatment of persons temporarily out of work, and persons looking for work for the first time. In the developing countries, for example, unemployment estimates are based on labour force sample surveys made in the urban areas; it is assumed that the rural population is employed, however unemployed most may be.

Worldwide, the numbers of unemployed are substantial. At the beginning of the 1990s, unemployment was affecting about 28 million people in the developed market economies, 7.5 million in eastern Europe and the former Soviet Union and at least 70 million in developing countries. Arresting as these numbers are, they reveal little of the problem. They do not include discouraged workers, whose numbers tend to grow as unemployment increases, or involuntary part-timers, nor do they cover rural unemployment and underemployment or those working long hours for meagre wages in the informal urban sector.

Productive employment has not grown nearly enough in the developing countries to absorb the large increase in the labour force following rapid population growth in the 1960s to the 1970s. In the economies in transition, the process of change has been accompanied by drastic falls in output and employment. Continued high levels of unemployment have persisted in developed countries despite policy initiatives to reduce it.

Women still experience higher rates of unemployment than men, despite improvement in the developed market economies. This problem is also present in developing countries, where women are usually less educated than men and have limited access to land tenure, credit and training. Their chances to find productive jobs are therefore considerably slimmer than those for men. In the economies in transition, many of the displaced workers are women.

## A. DEVELOPED COUNTRIES

In the second half of this century, employment in the developed countries was stable in the 1950s and 1960s but then became uneven. Until 1973 most developed market economies experienced low unemployment rates of about 1.5 to 3.5 per cent. But decline in economic performance and structural changes affecting both demand and supply factors caused a sharp rise in unemployment rates; between 1973 and the early 1980s they increased about threefold in many developed countries. In the second half of the 1980s, those rates declined but in 1990 started to increase again in the

United States, where they reached 7.4 per cent in 1992. A similar
pattern occured in the Western European countries (see figure 3.1).

*Figure 3.1*
Unemployment rates in the developed market
economies, 1970-1992

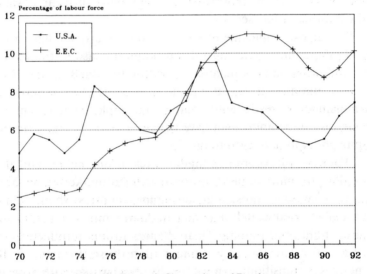

Source: Organisation for Economic Cooperation and Development.

The recent increase in unemployment in the developed market
economies has been caused by a combination of cyclical and structural factors. Despite the economic recovery during 1983-1989,
unemployment rates were still higher than they were in 1979. A
comparison of the growth in GDP and employment in industrial
countries during 1960-1973 and 1973-1987 shows that employment
has consistently lagged behind economic growth. The GDP growth
rates were fairly respectable, but few new jobs were created. In fact,
between 1973 and 1987 employment in countries like France, Germany and the United Kingdom actually fell.

Statistics point up the special problem of unemployment in Western Europe. According to Organisation for Economic Cooperation and Development (OECD) figures, the 12 countries of the European Union have created only around 3 million jobs since the mid-1970s, most of them in the public sector. In the United States during the same period, more than 30 million jobs were created, the majority in the private sector. Moreover, more than 17 million people were estimated to be unemployed in the member countries of the European Union in 1993, up from 12.7 million in 1990. Part of the problem has been the high cost of money because of German interest rates. This has delayed economic recovery and the creation of jobs; however, more fundamental structural problems suggest that many of the jobs lost in the slump may never come back. Now that capital and exchange controls have been largely removed and communication is more or less instantaneous, investment is going increasingly to countries offering the best combination of labour costs, productivity and growing markets. Low-wage manufacturing jobs are more and more being moved to countries where labour costs are low. Only jobs involving mainly skilled labour and high value-added content are being preserved.

Concern is mounting that the overall burden of tax, pension, social security and health insurance payments are driving wage costs too high. According to OECD estimates, these costs add up to about 41 per cent of the total output of goods and services in Western Europe, compared to about 30 per cent in Japan and the United States. This burden is especially marked in countries where shifts in the exchange rate have increased the value of the national currency in international markets, thereby making even wage rates alone high by international standards. Wage costs in Germany, for instance, are about 35 per cent higher than in Japan, 50 per cent higher than in the United States and much higher yet relative to Eastern Europe or the developing countries. Such statistics suggest that unemployment may become endemic in Western Europe, as entrepreneurial activity becomes stunted by the heavy costs to employers of the direct wages and various benefits they must provide to workers.

Unemployment is now affecting a wider range of occupations. In previous recessions, most job losses were concentrated in manufacturing and construction. The services were able to expand the number of jobs, acting as a buffer. In the latest recession, although manufacturing continued to be the hardest hit, services were also affected. This was largely owing to a more efficient and wider use of computer technology in many branches of the services sector and the need to increase productivity within the industry. As companies revise their working methods, lower level jobs are more affected than higher level ones.

Nonetheless, services continue to dominate the world economy. They generate about 60 per cent of the GDP and two thirds of the employment opportunities in the industrial countries. Manufacturing's share will continue to dwindle as more low-technology factories move to countries where labour-intensive assembly or other operations can be performed more cheaply.

## 1. *Long-term unemployment*

Unemployment might seem to be increasing from business cycle to business cycle as labour markets fail to overcome the difficulties in adjusting to the structural changes in the economy. Indications of the latter are the co-existence of unemployment with sectoral labour shortages and the increasing incidence of long-term unemployment (LTU).[1] LTU usually has a lagged response to the overall fall in unemployment when economic activity picks up. The fact that LTU failed to recede during the last recovery points up the gravity of the problem.

The early 1980s were characterized by an increasing share of the long-term unemployed in total unemployment. When the unemployment rate reached its peak in OECD in 1983, more than 60 per cent of the unemployed were out of work for more than six months in all European OECD countries except Austria, Luxembourg and Scandinavia. Another set of numbers illustrates the trend. In 1980 the number of people who were unemployed for 12 months or more amounted to about 27 per cent of the labour force; by 1989 this number had reached about 34 per cent (see figure 3.2).

*Figure 3.2*
Developed market economies: Incidence of long-term unemployment[a] (*percentage of total unemployment*)

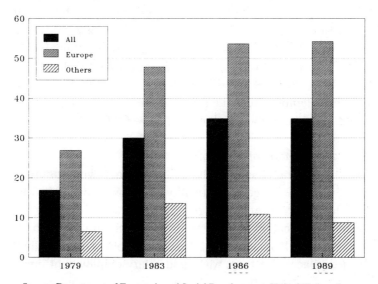

Source: Department of Economic and Social Development, United Nations Secretariat, based on Organisation for Economic Cooperation and Development.

Note: Based on a sample of 14 countries.

a    12 months and over.

Persistence of this problem is partly a result of inherent dynamics, since even if inflow and outflow cancel each other out and the unemployment rate remains unchanged, the share of long-term unemployment is likely to increase. In addition, the longer persons stay unemployed, the lower the exit probability, owing to declining skills and capabilities, decreasing intensity of job search and lesser likelihood of being hired. Some of the policies employed during the 1980s were aimed at remedying these difficulties. Results were mixed.

Long-term unemployment is not exclusive to people who lose their jobs. It also affects many entrants to the job market. In fact, a persistent problem in many OECD economies is the high unemployment of their younger people. Young persons who enter the labour force in these countries have found it especially difficult to keep or find a job. In almost all these countries, young persons are considerably more affected than adults by unemployment. In 1989 the ratio of the rate of youth unemployment to that of total unemployment ranged from 1.1 in Germany to 2.8 in Italy. Since 1989, youth unemployment rates have increased in those countries that have been in recession — Australia, Canada, Finland, New Zealand, Sweden, the United Kingdom and the United States. In 1991, youth unemployment rates were still more than 30 per cent in Australia, Canada, France, Ireland and New Zealand.

2. *The changing nature of employment*

A fundamental change in the nature of employment seems to be taking place, a change in the quality of the work available. Many of the recently created jobs are temporary, part-time or self-employment, indicating an increase in instability in job tenure and reduced benefits. Part of the so-called "new" jobs were actually the result of displacement from wage and salary employment, mainly within the self-employed.

Most of the new jobs created are filled by workers who are hired under short-term contracts or as part-time, temporary or casual workers. In the United Kingdom by the early 1990s, almost 40 per cent of jobs did not involve regular full-time wages or employment. Others among these workers may be self-employed individuals working at home. But a large number will be engaged through subcontractors. The problem exists in industrial countries but it is even more pronounced in the developing countries.

Subcontracting and hiring of freelancers are common practices in services, and it is becoming more conventional in manufacturing as well. The change in the nature of employment results from changes in the nature of the enterprises. Reduced product cycles, changes in technology and increased international competition implies that firms have to respond quickly to fluctuations in demand and changes in consumer taste. Manufacturing companies have therefore changed their working methods by becoming more flexible. Production units have been reduced. According to the International Labour Organisation (ILO), "they are now composed of a secure group of core workers surrounded by a precarious periphery of temporary wage workers, outworkers and subcontractors. This allows them to adjust to production peaks and troughs without having to bear the costs of a permanent labour force".[2] As large companies shed their working force, the smaller units become the most dynamic element in the labour markets.

Changes in the nature of employment had an impact on the organization of labour movements. Trade union membership has been falling in most industrial countries in recent years. In the Netherlands, membership in unions fell from 39 per cent of the labour force in 1978 to 24 per cent in 1991. And the United States has seen a three-decade slide in union membership from 30 per cent to about 15 per cent.

Trade unions in industrial countries have been undermined from different directions. Unemployment has reduced the number of workers and strengthened the hand of employers. Futhermore, enterprises and capital have moved from countries with powerful trade unions to low-wage, non-unionized countries. But a more fundamental problem is the fragmenting of the labour force. It is now much more difficult to organize. The shift to services and the growing numbers of part-time workers, or those adopting flexible working patterns, puts them beyond the reach of traditional methods of organization. Workers doing different jobs feel much less solidarity. As they move out of manufacturing, their aspirations change and they tend to be even more individually oriented.

## 3. *Unemployment compensation*

Unemployment compensation programmes guarantee an income to unemployed people with a previous record of employment. Recipients are expected to return to work within a relatively short time. Most often, the basic benefit is supplemented by another amount which varies with the worker's past income. Unemployment benefits are usually paid for a year or less. In France and Germany the period is longer for older workers; in Canada it varies with the length of previous employment; in the Netherlands it may be extended to two years. The level of unemployment benefits is reduced after a specified period.

Since the early 1970s, total expenditure on unemployment compensation has risen in the developed market economy countries as a result of both higher unemployment levels and increases in benefits. Benefits increased primarily because more high-income employees lost their jobs and were paid higher earnings-related benefits. On the other hand, unemployment coverage since the early 1980s has tended to fall as a result of new labour market conditions, as was mentioned earlier. Youth unemployment and long-term unemployment have risen in many countries, but many youths lack a previous employment record and cannot claim unemployment compensation, while many long-term unemployed have exhausted their claims to benefits. Married women also represent a rising proportion of the unemployed and are often inadequately covered by unemployment insurance because of incomplete or part-time employment records.

Some countries have responded to these problems. The period of unemployment needed for youths to qualify for unemployment benefits has been reduced in Australia and Belgium. Several countries, including Australia, France, Ireland and the United Kingdom, have emphasized training programmes to raise skills and improve information in labour markets.

## B. DEVELOPING COUNTRIES

Developed and developing countries are somewhat similar with respect to employment conditions, in particular the growth of low-paying, part-time jobs lacking security and other benefits. However, high rates of fertility combined with improvements in infant mortality have led to a rapid increase in the labour force in developing countries. The increase has far surpassed the formal employment creating capacity of most developing countries. The differences, therefore, are greater than the similiarities. In the majority of these countries, the workers engaged in regular, stable employment with adequate working conditions and social protection represent only a small proportion of the total labour force.

Underemployment is higher than open unemployment, but unemployment is present. It is high in many countries and disturbing because many countries lack safety nets such as unemployment benefits. According to ILO, "Latin America has the highest proportion of workers in the formal sector and only seven countries there provide any kind of unemployment benefits. Even in those countries the programmes cover only a narrow section of the population and have quite restrictive benefits".[3]

Unemployment rates exceeded 10 per cent in most African countries during the 1980s; in the Niger the rate was about 50 per cent. Per capita gross domestic product (GDP) declined and wage employment stagnated in many sub-Saharan countries. The average urban unemployment rate in these countries increased to about 18 per cent. ILO estimates that 9 million were unemployed in sub-Saharan Africa in 1990 and that this number will increase to 28 million during the 1990s. Urban unemployment is expected to rise to 31 per cent.[4]

In Latin America and the Caribbean region, unemployment increased during most of the last decade. Only a few countries witnessed declining unemployment rates in the early 1990s (Chile, Colombia, Costa Rica and Jamaica). Unemployment increased substantially in Barbados, Bolivia, Colombia, Nicaragua, Trinidad and Tobago, Uruguay and Venezuela.

Unemployment rates in Asia often decreased during the 1980s and were mostly lower than those in Africa and Latin America. Since several Asian countries have large populations, the number of unemployed is large. In India, more than 34 million people were registered as looking for work in 1990, 10 million more than in all OECD countries combined. Urban open unemployment rates were below 3 per cent in a few countries (China, Hong Kong, Singapore and the Republic of Korea). Moreover, countries with high unemployment rates also experienced rising rates during the 1980s.

Unemployment and underemployment are expected to increase in developing countries in the next few years. The world labour force in 1993 was estimated to be 2.4 billion people; 1.8 billion (75 per cent) were in developing countries. An increasing proportion of labour force growth is taking place in developing countries — 82 per cent in the 1970s, 88 per cent in the 1980s and 92 per cent in the 1990s. An additional 38 million persons each year will seek employment in developing countries during the decade of the 1990s, well beyond the number of new jobs to be created if current economic conditions persist in these countries.

The labour force in developing countries will grow at the rate of about 3 per cent per annum, increasing from 3 to 3.5 per cent in Africa. Since roughly 50 per cent of all output accrues to labour, developing economies will need to grow at the rate of 6 per cent per annum (and 7 per cent in Africa) during the present decade to absorb the growing labour force at current levels of income. Considering the already large numbers of unemployed persons, rates of economic growth will need to be in the order of 8 to 9 per cent over a decade or more to provide adequate opportunities for employment in developing countries. Growth rates of this magnitude are extremely unlikely in almost all of the countries.

## 1. The young and the educated

Two pressing problems in many developing countries are high unemployment among the young and high unemployment among the educated. Unemployment rates are often highest among those who have completed secondary education (see table 3.1). Unemployment among persons with third-level education is, in several countries, higher than among those without any education whatsoever. In Africa, on average, the share in the unemployed population of people with secondary education doubled between the mid-1970s and the mid-1980s to approximately 50 per cent and has not changed much since then.[5]

In 32 developing countries for which data were available, more than 2.3 million people who had been previously employed as professional, technical, administrative or managerial workers and had most likely benefited from a tertiary education were unemployed at

*Table 3.1*

Unemployment rate by age and level of education, developing countries, 1989/1990

| | Total unemployment | Age | | | | Level of education | | | |
|---|---|---|---|---|---|---|---|---|---|
| | | Youth (15-24) | | Adult (25+) | | None | First | Second | Third |
| | | Male | Female | Male | Female | | | | |
| Algeria | . | . | . | . | . | 9 | 24 | 29 | 6 |
| Tunisia | 13.4 | . | . | . | . | 11 | 20 | 17 | 5 |
| Brazil | : | 6 | 8 | 2 | 2 | 1 | 3 | . | . |
| Chile | 5.6 | 13 | 12 | 3 | - | . | . | . | . |
| Colombia | 10.2 | . | . | 5 | 8 | 8 | 8 | 13 | 8 |
| Costa Rica | 4.6 | 8 | 10 | 3 | . | 5 | 4 | 6 | 3 |
| Guatemala | 7.2 | 3 | 6 | 1 | 1 | - | 2 | 7 | 2 |
| Honduras | 7.7 | . | . | . | . | 2 | 4 | 8 | 6 |
| Jamaica | 16.8 | 34 | 99 | 6 | 21 | . | . | . | . |
| Mexico | 2.6 | 3 | 7 | 2 | 3 | . | . | . | . |
| Panama | 16.3 | 29 | 44 | 10 | 15 | - | 2 | 6 | 6 |
| Paraguay | 6.6 | . | . | . | . | . | 5 | 8 | 4 |
| Trinidad & Tobago | 22.0 | 37 | 46 | 9 | 14 | 11 | 21 | 25 | 5 |
| Uruguay | 9.2 | . | . | . | . | 3 | 6 | 11 | 7 |
| Venezuela | 8.7 | 17 | 16 | 7 | 5 | 6 | 12 | 13 | 6 |
| Hong Kong | 1.3 | 4 | 3 | 1 | 1 | 1 | 1 | 2 | 1 |
| India | . | . | . | . | . | 2 | 3 | 9 | 12 |
| Indonesia | 2.8 | 14 | 11 | 1 | - | 1 | 1 | 10 | 10 |
| Korea, Rep. of | 2.3 | 9 | 6 | 1 | - | 1 | 3 | 4 | |
| Pakistan | 3.1 | . | . | . | . | 2 | 3 | 6 | 4 |
| Singapore | 1.8 | 3 | 3 | 2 | 1 | 2 | 2 | 2 | 2 |
| Syria | . | . | . | . | . | 3 | 7 | 8 | 8 |
| Thailand | . | 5 | 6 | 1 | 1 | 1 | 3 | 6 | . |

Source: World Labour Report 1992 (ILO, Geneva).

the end of the 1980s.[6] They represented 5.7 per cent of all unemployed in those countries. In 24 out of the 32 countries, the percentage of educated unemployed increased at the end of the decade, compared with the beginning. These were the people who had made the greatest investment in their education and whose skills were the most marketable internationally. In the absence of work opportunities at home, they would look for work in other countries.

Unemployment rates among persons younger than 25 years are often two to four times as high as among persons older than 25. In 15 sub-Saharan countries in the mid-1980s, youth unemployment rates were on average three times higher than those for adult unemployment. Youth unemployment rates of 30 per cent or more are not uncommon in sub-Saharan Africa and the Caribbean (see table 2.1). In many countries, the educated youth were disproportionally affected by unemployment. In India, young people accounted for about 80 per cent of long-term unemployment among males. Young people with secondary- or higher-level schooling, who made up 12 per cent of the labour force, accounted for almost one third of all unemployed at the end of the 1980s. In Egypt, 80 per cent of the unemployed were new entrants to the labour force and 75 per cent of those new entrants had received an education at the secondary level or above.[7]

## 2. *Low-productivity employment*

Notwithstanding the above, the employment problem of developing countries is not open unemployment. Rather, it is precarious, low-productivity and low-income employment in which workers are deprived of any form of social protection beyond that provided by their extended families or sometimes by local communities. This is especially the case in developing countries where the majority of the population live in rural areas in disguised unemployment or seasonal employment.

Unemployment rates do not include those in disguised unemployment and the underemployed, caricatured in the image of the young man waiting by the roadside to inflate bicycle tyres. The total number is quite large in many developing countries and it increased during the 1980s. In the Philippines, urban and rural underemployment in 1991 was estimated to be about 20 and 41 per cent respectively, compared with an official unemployment rate of 8 per cent. In 1990 in China, the number of unemployed, underemployed and casually employed persons may have been as high as 50 million, compared with 3.8 million, the figure for the officially unemployed.[8] Underemployed persons typically earning lower incomes than others are common in the informal and agricultural sectors. The sizes of these two sectors indicate the underutilization of labour in several countries. The share of the labour force employed in agriculture is about 60 per cent in sub-Saharan Africa, 70 per cent in South and East Asia and between 20 and 33 per cent in other developing regions. The problem for the rural poor is not so much a lack of work as low productivity and therefore little reward for often arduous work.

Estimates of the share of the informal sector in urban or non-agricultural employment vary between 20 and 60 per cent. In general, the size of the informal sector is inversely related to the level of development and the size of the manufacturing sector. The informal sector in Africa employs about 61 per cent of the urban labour force; in the newly industrialized countries of Asia, the figure lies between 10 and 20 per cent.[9] During the 1980s, as the result of declining economic activity and the slow or negative growth of wage employment in the manufacturing and public sectors, the informal sector increased in many countries in Latin America and Africa and in some countries in Asia.

The inverse relation between the size of the informal sector and economic development does not imply that earnings in the informal sector are generally lower than elsewhere or that employment in the informal sector is always temporary, involuntary, isolated from the rest of the economy and chosen as a last resort. The average income of entrepreneurs in the informal sector is usually many times the official minimum wage or earnings in the agricultural sector, and may be significantly higher than the average wage in the formal sector. However, incomes are far more insecure. Employees within the informal sector, excluding apprentices and family workers, earn on average between one and two times the minimum wage. The informal sector is in many cases not the employer of last resort. Many migrants from rural areas start in the formal sector and use the skills and money acquired there to set up their own enterprise within the informal sector. [10]

Many have argued that the informal sector can contribute significantly to the solution of the unemployment problem in developing countries if constraints to its development are removed. This will not be enough. The sector is most dynamic where it has links with the larger companies in the formal economy through subcontracting. Incomes generated in the sector are usually the result of a trickle-down from the formal economy. Furthermore, part of the increase in employment in the sector was due to job sharing and not to productive job creation. Although having an important role to play, the informal sector has limits to its capacity to absorb labour productively. Growth has to be led by the formal economy. [11]

### 3. Migration: escaping unemployment

Rising unemployment and declining income prospects have driven many people from developing countries to migrate abroad to work. Illegal migration has increased markedly, especially to the developed market-economy countries. Often, however, moving has not solved the unemployment problem for the migrant.

Unemployment among the foreign population is usually higher than among the local population. In Germany, during the economic recession of the early 1980s, unemployment among Germans increased from 3.1 per cent in 1980 to 7.5 per cent in 1983, and among foreigners from 4.7 per cent in 1980 to 12.3 per cent in 1983.[12] In the Netherlands, unemployment of young people from Morocco, Suriname and Turkey increased from 1983 to 1990, while among the young Dutch it contracted.[13]

The reasons for higher unemployment among immigrants are

many. Most are unskilled or semi-skilled workers, usually concentrated in ailing sectors of the economy. The restructurings of these sectors were postponed due to the use of relatively cheap migrant labour. When changes in technology and production structure finally arrived in those sectors, factories were shut down and unemployment soared. Immigrants lacking skills could not move into the more dynamic areas of the economy.

It has been argued that immigrants do not in general harm the prospects of the local population in the labour market, although particular groups may be temporarily adversely affected.[14] Foreign workers are typically employed in activities that are low paid, require few skills, are physically demanding, and employ outdated technology. They are generally concentrated in what nationals consider low-status occupations that do not correspond to their aspirations. The substitution of nationals for foreigners is limited, therefore, and labour shortages in particular sectors of the economy may coexist with unemployment elsewhere owing to segmentation and rigidities in labour markets.[15] In other cases, generous social security benefits may contribute to make unemployment more attractive than moving backwards on the social ladder by accepting a low-status job.

The recent deterioration of economic opportunities in many developing countries has also led to an increase in illegal migration. Additionally, many of the undocumented migrants end up working in the underground economies of the industrialized countries. There they suffer at the hands of their employers from mistreatment and exploitation such as denial of minimum wages and overtime pay and hazardous working conditions. The combination of cost-cutting needs of employers during economic slow-downs and structural change, rising anti-immigrant sentiments among the public and, paradoxically, tightened immigration laws have worsened this exploitation. Illegal immigrants are more and more unwilling to complain about abuses for fear of being turned over to immigration authorities and being deported. With many developing countries losing young, energetic and better educated persons through emigration, valuable human resources are being lost. Despite the hard-currency remittances they generate, this loss complicates the prospects of eventual economic recovery and growth in some of those countries.

## C. ECONOMIES IN TRANSITION

Growing mass unemployment has become a major social issue in all economies in transition. Between 1988 and the first half of 1992, industrial production fell more than 40 per cent. In 1992 alone, output in Eastern Europe fell an estimated 10 per cent, with much of the decline in defence industries.

In many of these countries a sharp fall in output has been paralleled by a fall in labour productivity, suggesting that massive lay-offs are yet to take place. And as the process of privatization gains momentum and provisions for pushing firms into bankruptcy become more widespread, increased unemployment can be expected.[16]

Both internal and external factors were responsible for the serious cut-backs in output. On the external side there was a collapse in foreign trade following the demise of the Council for Mutual Economic Assistance (CMEA). Poland, Hungary and the former Czechoslovakia have been fighting hard to get access to markets in OECD countries, but so far these markets have been inadequate to offset in full the loss of traditional ones. Some prices were liberalized, but a workable pricing system has yet to emerge. Several economic stabilization programmes were accompanied by a set of anti-inflation measures that reduced demand and cut down employment. The reduction of fiscal subsidies to balance the government budget and the tightening of monetary policy brought additional pressure on enterprises to shed some labour.

During the two-year period 1990-1991 there was a 40-fold increase in unemployment in Central and Eastern Europe, albeit from a small base. By March 1992 there were over 4 million registered unemployed, up from less than 100,000 at the beginning of

1990.[17] In Hungary the rate of unemployment increased fourfold and in Bulgaria and Czechoslovakia, sixfold; in Poland the number of unemployed doubled, from 1.1 million in 1990 to 2.2 million in 1991[18] (see table 3.2).

The issue of joblessness also carries a heavy psychological and emotional load. Under central planning, employment was guaranteed by the State to every able-bodied citizen of working age. Workers were accustomed to almost unlimited job security. Before the transition began in Eastern Europe and the former USSR, the utilization of labour had nearly reached its demographic limit. Female participation rates were particularly high everywhere. There was persistent excess demand in labour markets. During the current transition, people are not psychologically prepared for the possibility of unemployment. Negative public reactions to rising unemployment and the subsequent decline in income and status are potentially harmful to the process of economic and political reform.

## 1. Profile of unemployment

Most job losses in 1990-1991 in Central and Eastern Europe occurred in manufacturing, but there were also sizeable declines in agriculture (900,000 jobs) and construction (800,000 jobs).[19] Until now, the hope that the disproportionately underdeveloped service

*Table 3.2*
Open unemployment in Central and Eastern Europe *(thousands)*

|  | January 1990 | June 1990 | January 1991 | June 1991 | January 1992 | March 1992 |
|---|---|---|---|---|---|---|
| Bulgaria |  | 22 | 74 | 248 | 426 | 453 |
| Czechoslovakia |  | 13 | 119 | 301 | 523 | 503 |
| Hungary | 23 | 42 | 101 | 186 | 442 | 478 |
| Poland | 56 | 568 | 1 196 | 1 574 | 2 230 | 2 238 |
| Romania |  |  |  | 104 | 386 | 461 |
| Total | 79 | 645 | 1 490 | 2 413 | 3 893 | 4 133 |

Source: Department of Economic and Social Development of the United Nations Secretariat, based on OECD, Employment Outlook, July 1992 (Paris, OECD, 1992).

sector in all former centrally-planned economies would become a major source of new jobs has not materialized. However, although the labour-absorbing capability of the service sector has been limited, the share of services in total employment has increased in all countries.

Table 3.2 provides information on open unemployment in transition economies. The actual numbers, reflecting lack of registration among those who lost their right to unemployment compensation because of changes in laws or other administrative action regarding eligibility criteria, may differ from the ones provided in the table. The information on unemployment is largely based on the officially registered.

At the first stages of transition, new entrants to the labour market, mainly recent school-leavers, represented a larger proportion of unemployed than those released by enterprises. In the former Czechoslovakia, in mid-1991, the number of jobless school-leavers was estimated to be 10 per cent of the 300,800 unemployed. Recent increases in the ranks of the unemployed can be largely attributed to the growing number of people losing their jobs. In Poland, for instance, mass lay-offs accounted for about 23 per cent of the unemployed at the end of 1991.[20]

Unemployment varied significantly according to skill level. Unskilled workers and women were among the first to lose their jobs. As the transition progressed, unemployment became common among other skill categories. However, unemployment remained higher among unskilled (31 per cent) than skilled and semi-skilled workers (9 per cent). With the exception of Bulgaria and Romania, unemployment rates among people with vocational training are higher than among those with elementary or secondary education.[21]

In Russia, particularly in major urban centres such as Moscow and St. Petersburg, a recent rise in unemployment among clerical and other white-collar workers has occurred. There was an obvious mismatch between the skills of released workers and those in demand. In Moscow, at the end of 1991, more than 90 per cent of the city's unemployed were white-collar workers while 85 per cent of the job openings were for blue-collar workers.[22] Yet as a rule, white-collar workers have had a better chance of finding employment in a short period than blue-collar workers, particularly if they have been willing to undergo additional training. The growing number of redundant workers with higher education and with certain vocational skills has become a feature of unemployment in economies in transition.

Women have been especially vulnerable to unemployment in the economies in transition. In Bulgaria, two thirds of the unemployed in 1991 were female. In the former Soviet Union, among those who lost their jobs in the period 1989-1991 the share of women was 60 per cent. When the state bureaucracy was streamlined from 1985-1987, more than 80 per cent of those dismissed were women.[23] In Moscow, about three quarters of those laid off in the industrial sector were women.

Unemployment is also rising sharply among minority groups. In Slovakia in 1992, the official unemployment rate for gypsies was 30 per cent, more than four times the rate for the rest of the population. In Bulgaria, there are reports of unemployment of 50 per cent for the Turkish minority and more than 80 per cent for gypsies. These minorities tend to be either overrepresented in jobs that are eliminated or to suffer direct discrimination in new recruitment.

## 2. Policy response to unemployment

Institutions to cushion the effects of unemployment were created immediately after major changes occurred in social and political systems.[24] In Poland in December 1989, Parliament adopted an Employment Act in which it recognized unemployment as a legitimate employment category. In Hungary in February 1991, Parliament passed the New Employment Act providing for unemployment compensation through unemployment insurance. Unemployment compensation schemes have also been set up in several other countries. In Poland, a law was adopted in 1990 introducing an unemployment benefit scheme that would pay 70 per cent of the previous wage for three months, and then fall to 50 per cent for another six months and to 40 per cent thereafter without limit on duration.

In the Russian Federation, workers who are dismissed from work are entitled to severance pay equal to three months salary. Unemployment benefits accrue after the expiration of three months but only if the employment centre has been unable in that time to find the individuals employment appropriate to their skills and education. Persons are not entitled to unemployment benefits if they leave their employment voluntarily or were dismissed for disciplinary reasons, or if they reject two suitable employment vacancies proposed by the employment centre.

Finding adequate regular employment for the unemployed has become the primary concern of labour centres. In most countries those offices have been transformed into employment agencies and given additional functions beyond those related to their traditional information services. Major new tasks include help in retraining, administration of the new system of unemployment benefits and provision of legal assistance. In Hungary and Poland, among the responsibilities assigned to the labour offices was the creation of temporary employment in local community projects.[25]

## D. WOMEN'S PARTICIPATION IN THE WORKFORCE AND UNEMPLOYMENT

Unemployment among women was mostly higher than among men in developing countries for which there were data. The phenomenon is also present in developed market economies where the unemployment rate for women is sometimes twice as much as for men (e.g., Belgium, Italy, Portugal and Spain). In several countries, including Israel, Mexico, Pakistan and the Philippines, the female-to-male unemployment ratio declined during the 1980s, indicating a relative improvement in the employment situation of women.

Participation rates of women in the workforce rose in many

regions of the world between 1970 and 1990. The exceptions were sub-Saharan Africa, South Asia, South-East Asia and Oceania. Participation of women in all age groups declined in sub-Saharan Africa. In 1990, participation rates were below 25 per cent in South and West Asia and North Africa.

Participation rates of women in the workforce are particularly sensitive to economic conditions. "Women generally continue to be the last to benefit from job expansion and the first to suffer from job contraction".[26] In OECD countries the participation rate of women increased from 48.3 per cent in 1973 to 60 per cent in 1990. Participation rates increased during the 1970s and 1980s in all OECD countries, except Turkey, although the rate of increase declined in most countries.

Within the developed market economies the rise of female participation was especially pronounced among women with children. In the United States, 50 per cent of mothers were working or actively seeking employment within a year of giving birth in 1987 (the figure was up from 31 per cent in 1976). The incentive to stay in the job market was higher for women who had had their first child after turning 30 years of age and for those with more education. Such women could earn higher incomes than younger and less well-educated ones and could pay more for child care. More intense economic necessity was often a motive for early return to the labour force. Sixty-six per cent of widowed, divorced and separated mothers were in the workforce; the figures for married women and single mothers were similar — 49.8 and 49.5 per cent respectively.[27]

Women fill over half of all clerical, sales and service jobs in the developed countries and Latin America, and more than one third of such jobs in Africa and Asia. Women account for a larger share of the labour force in the informal sector and subsistence agriculture, and they are largely excluded from most jobs in transport and management. In manufacturing, women are concentrated in the textile, clothing, leather, footware, electronics and food-processing sectors. These jobs often involve assembly line work and are at the lower end of the pay scale. In developed countries, occupational segregation is slowly changing. In Canada, Sweden and the United States, in particular, women have been taking a larger share of professional, management and administrative jobs.[28]

Working women in all regions of the world receive lower pay than men. The figure for women's earnings expressed as a percentage of men's earnings ranges from about 50 per cent in Japan and the Republic of Korea to about 90 per cent in France, Iceland and Sweden. Women have often received less or a different type of education, usually have less work experience when compared with men and are mostly confined to low-paying occupations. The earnings gap has declined in many developed countries over the last decades.[29] Yet there is some residual gap that can only be attributed to discrimination.

## Notes

[1] The average unemployment rate for the period 1983-1989 was 7.6 per cent, while it was only 4.9 per cent during the period 1974-1979. Long-term unemployment (LTU) affected 27 per cent of those without jobs in 1979, whereas it touched 34 per cent of them in 1989. LTU is more of a problem in European countries than in the United States and Canada. See OECD, "Employment Outlook 1991", Paris, 1991, pp. 37-40, and OECD, "Labour force statistics 1970-1990", OECD, Paris, 1992.

[2] International Labour Organisation (ILO), World Labour Report 1992, Geneva, 1992, p. 33.

[3] ILO, *World Labour Report 1993*, (Geneva, ILO, 1993), p. 60.

[4] International Labour Organisation/Jobs and Skills Programme for Africa (JASPA), *African Employment Report, 1991* (Addis Ababa, JASPA, 1991), p. 50.

[5] ILO/JASPA, op. cit., pp. 28-29.

[6] Calculations of the Department of Economic and Social Development of the United Nations Secretariat, based on ILO, *Yearbook of Labour Statistics, 1991*, (Geneva, ILO, 1991).

[7] ILO, *World Labour Report, 1989* (Geneva, ILO, 1989); ILO/JASPA, op. cit., pp. 25-28; and Susan Horton, Ravi Kanbur and Dipak Mazumdar, "Labour markets in an era of adjustment: evidence from 12 developing countries", *International Labour Review*, vol. 130, nos. 5-6 (1991), p. 536.

[8] Economic and Social Commission for Asia and the Pacific (ESCAP), "Economic and Social Survey of Asia and the Pacific", United Nations, New York (Sales No. E.92.II.F.4), 1992, p. 107.

[9] Jacques Charmes, " A critical review: concepts, definitions and studies in the informal sector", in *The Informal Sector Revisited*, David Turnham, Bernard Salome and Antoine Schwarz, eds. (Paris, Organisation for Economic Cooperation and Development (OECD) 1990), pp. 10-48; and ILO, *World Labour Report, 1992*, (Geneva, ILO, 1992), pp. 39 and 44.

[10] Jacques Charmes, op. cit., pp. 25-39; and Harold Lubell, *The Informal Sector in the 1980s and 1990s* (Paris, OECD, 1991).

[11] See B. Roberts, "The changing nature of informal employment: the case of Mexico", in G. Standing and V. Tokman, op. cit., pp. 115-135; ECLAC, "Social equity and changing production patterns: an integrated approach", ECLAC, Santiago,

1992, (LC/G. 1701 (SES. 24/3)) and B. Salome (ed.), "Fighting urban unemployment in developing countries", OECD, Paris, 1989.

[12] P. Gans, "Changes in the structure of the foreign population of West Germany since 1980", *Migration*, no. 7 (1990), pp. 25-50.

[13] P. Muus, "Employment and vocational training", paper presented at the International Conference on Migration, Rome, 13-15 March 1991 (Paris, Organisation for Economic Cooperation and Development).

[14] Julian N. Simon, *The Economic Consequences of Immigration* (Oxford, Basil Blackwell, 1989), appendix A.

[15] D. Maillat, "Long-term aspects of international migration flows: the experience of European receiving countries", in *The Future of Migration* (Paris, Organisation for Economic Cooperation and Development, 1987), pp. 38-63.

[16] UN/ECE, "Economic Survey for Europe 1992-1993", p. 97.

[17] *Zycie Gospodarcze* (Warszwa), 23 February 1992, p. 15.

[18] OECD, *Employment Outlook, July 1992* (Paris, OECD, 1992), p. 26.

[19] OECD, *Employment Outlook, July 1992* (Paris, OECD, 1992), p. 243.

[20] OECD, *OECD Economic Surveys, Poland 1992* (Paris, OECD, 1992), p. 26.

[21] OECD, *Employment Outlook, July 1992*, July1992), p. 253.

[22] I. Zaslavskyi, "O pol'ze rynka truda" ("About the usefulness of the labour market"), *Voprosy Economiki* (Moscow), no. 9 (1991), pp. 33-34.

[23] Pravitel' svennyui Vestnik (Moscow), no. 40 (September 1991), p. 14.

[24] In Hungary, the first system of unemployment compensation was established in 1986; the law on unemployment and the right to compensation became effective in January 1989, in the last month of the former regime.

[25] A. Chilosi, "The impact on employment of institutional transformation in Eastern Europe and the tasks of social policy, with particular reference to the Polish case", *MOCT-MOST* (Bologna, Italy), no. 3 (1991), p. 84.

[26] *The World's Women, 1970-1990, Trends and Statistics* (United Nations publication, Sales No. E.90.XVII.3), p. 83.

[27] *The New York Times*, 16 June 1988.

[28] ILO, *World Labour Report, 1992* (Geneva, ILO, 1992).

[29] Morley Gunderson, "Male-female wage differentials and policy responses", *Journal of Economic Literature*, vol. 27, no. 1 (March 1989), pp. 46-72; and *The World's Women* . . . .

# 4

# Poverty

AN estimated 1,100 million people in the world live in poverty (see table 4.1). More than 600 million are considered
extremely poor.[1] Of these 600 million, two thirds live in Asia, where
they are concentrated in rural areas with high population densities.
In sub-Saharan Africa, 120 million people are estimated to be
extremely poor. As in Asia, extreme poverty in sub-Saharan Africa
is largely a rural phenomenon, concentrated in areas where soils
are poor and farming techniques underdeveloped. The incidence of
extreme poverty is smaller in other developing regions. In

*Table 4.1*
Poverty estimates and projections by regions for low and
middle-income countries, 1985-2000

| | Percentage of population below the poverty line[a] | | | Number of poor (millions) | | |
|---|---|---|---|---|---|---|
| | 1985 | 1990 | 2000 | 1985 | 1990 | 2000 |
| South Asia | 51.8 | 49.0 | 36.9 | 532 | 562 | 511 |
| East Asia | 13.2 | 11.3 | 4.2 | 182 | 169 | 73 |
| Middle East and North Africa | 30.6 | 33.1 | 30.6 | 60 | 73 | 89 |
| Sub-Saharan Africa | 47.6 | 47.8 | 49.7 | 184 | 216 | 304 |
| Latin America and the Caribbean | 22.4 | 25.5 | 24.9 | 87 | 108 | 126 |
| Eastern Europe[b] | 7.1 | 7.1 | 5.8 | 5 | 5 | 4 |
| All low- and middle-income countries[c] | 30.5 | 29.7 | 24.1 | 1 051 | 1 133 | 1 107 |

Source: World Bank, *World Development Report 1992; Development and the
Environment*, Oxford University Press, 1992, table 1.1.

a    The poverty line used here is based on $370 annual income per capita in 1985
     purchasing power parity dollars.
b    Does not include the former Soviet Union
c    Does not include the former Soviet Union and the Economic Union (EU)
     middle-income countries, Greece and Portugal.

Latin America, extreme poverty encompasses 50 million and is concentrated in the Andean highlands, sizeable urban slum and squatter areas and among rural households made landless as a result of
inequalities in landholding. The extremely poor amount to 40 million people in North Africa and the Near East. For the most part,
they are dispersed in smaller, less visible pockets of poverty in rural
and urban areas.

Incomes and consumption expenditures are the criteria most
commonly used for distinguishing between the extremely poor, the
poor, and the non-poor. The main difference between the first two
groups is that for the extremely poor, nutritional needs far out-
weigh all other considerations, whereas the poor have a low consumption level relative to the general society but have sufficient
incomes to eat adequately. As a group the extremely poor are disproportionately made up of underfed children and adults who have
limited physical and educational assets. They live predominantly in
rural areas. Being landless or near landless, they are highly prone
to unemployment, disguised or not, and are especially vulnerable to
seasonal variations in caloric adequacy. The extremely poor tend to
have large numbers of children as a form of social insurance,
although eventual family size is restrained by illness and mortality
associated with severe anthropometric shortfalls.[2]

## A. DEVELOPING COUNTRIES

Table 4.1 shows the fight on poverty is far from over. Efforts to
reduce poverty have produced mixed results. Poverty is believed to
have increased in Africa and in Latin America in both absolute and
relative terms. On the other hand, both the share and the number
of Asian people living in poverty is supposed to have declined during the 1980s. But when China is excluded from this group, poverty
is thought to have affected a larger number of people in the 1980s
than in the 1970s due to the rapid increase of population growth.

In Latin America many of the benefits the years of rapid
growth brought to poverty alleviation during the 1970s were lost in

the 1980s. The region entered the 1980s with an estimated 35 per cent of its households living in poverty, down from 40 per cent in 1970. It closed the decade experiencing an increase in poverty, reaching 37 per cent of its households in 1989, i.e., about 44 per cent of its total population.

The increase in poverty in the region was mainly the result of the changes that took place in the labour market during the past decade. Those changes were due to the overall slow-down of economic activity associated with the adverse external economic conditions, particularly in the early 1980s, and the policy measures adopted as a result of the slow-down.[3] Urban unemployment increased, wages declined in real terms, and the economy lost its capacity to generate employment in the most productive branches of economic activity. In fact, employment generated during the decade was concentrated on the less productive, more unstable, low-paid jobs.

With the urban economy adversely affected by the economic crisis and the agricultural sector doing relatively better, the increase of poverty was basically an *urban* phenomenon. Reversing an old trend in the region, the urban poor — about 94 million people — are now more numerous than the rural poor. The number of the latter reached 76 million in 1986. And with few exceptions the share of households in poverty in the rural areas was maintained or even continued to decrease despite the sluggish economic growth overall. Yet the rural areas continued to host the vast majority of the extremely poor, people whose incomes are insufficient to purchase the minimum basket of food.

According to ECLAC, the increase in poverty in the 1980s was not the result of an increase in structural poverty but rather a new phenomenon as other social groups, the so-called "new poor", were also affected by it. These are people whose incomes were originally somewhat higher than the level established by the poverty line, had access to housing, education and health services and had a stable source of income that however was lost with the crisis. The increase in inequality also led to more poverty in the region. In countries where the brunt of adjustment was reasonably shared by all social groups, poverty increased moderately.

The decline of real wages and the growing income disparity implied that a greater number of people moved down in the social scale, thus increasing the number of people living around the poverty line. In all metropolitan areas in the region where information is available, with the exception of Colombia, the number of households with per capita income around the poverty line has increased.[4] This suggests that more people are now vulnerable to new adverse external shocks or, worse still, even to poor overall economic performance of their respective countries. For these people, a small decline in their per capita income means that they probably would no longer be able to satisfy their basic needs.

Few reliable statistics on the incidence of poverty are available for the African continent. It can be said, however, that poverty continued to increase in the region during the 1980s. African poverty is less a problem of landlessness than in other regions. Rather, it is the result of rapid population growth increasing the pressure on the limited fertile land and on the reduced supply of social services. It is also the product of inadequate growth of agricultural output failing to keep up with population growth,[5] of a continued deterioration in the region's terms of trade and of failed policies that attempted to promote (capital-intensive) industrialization at the expense of agriculture. As if this were not enough, the continent has also been subject to drought, locust infestation and other pests and civil strife. All of these misfortunes have imposed a heavy toll in output growth and development and left a considerable number of people — estimated at 30 million in 1991 — facing starvation. With no substantial change in this background in the past decade, the economic difficulties of the 1980s compounded the region's problems and led to growing urban unemployment (described in chapter 1), price increases and deteriorated social services. As rural incomes stagnated and urban earnings declined, the number of people living in poverty probably increased. Fortunately, this situation does not apply to all African countries. Some African economies, such as Morocco and Tunisia, experienced rapid growth in the last 15 to 20 years and could therefore improve the social welfare of their less favoured people.

South and East Asia were the only developing regions where previous gains in poverty alleviation were not lost during the past decade. Poverty is still considerable in some countries, but progress has been made in recent years. Individual countries' experiences varied, with certain countries being more successful than others in pulling people out of deprivation, while others had setbacks.

In many countries of the region, poverty alleviation is located in the generation of employment brought about by fast growth. Contributing as well are measures that allow the poor to have access to productive and remunerative activities either by the distribution of assets (such as agrarian reform) or by upgrading their skills through education and providing social services, or by the combination of both. In addition, reduced fertility rates have played an important role in lessening poverty as pressure is released from scarce land resources and the number of children and elderly to be supported by an adult decreases.

Government action in rural development has been considerably important in poverty reduction, as much of the poverty in these countries is located in the rural areas. The land reform programmes in the Republic of Korea and Taiwan, Province of China (POC) in combination with the extension of credit and infrastructure services had not only a positive impact on poverty alleviation in both countries but also created a domestic market for manufactured goods. Subsequent industrialization and urbanization produced the required demand for excess labour force from agriculture, while the development of a strong schooling system facilitated the absorption of labour by the modern sector of the economy. Later on, the emphasis on export-oriented industries generated fast and sustained growth and raised labour incomes.[6]

India, Pakistan, Sri Lanka and Bangladesh adopted a more direct approach in dealing with poverty. They started direct employment programmes (e.g., food-for-work programmes) aimed at the rural poor so that a supplementary source of income would be available during the dry months when there is little work in agriculture.

The local community also benefits from the provision of assets (such as roads, irrigation works, and the like) created by the programmes. Another common approach has been promoting self-employment for the poor through providing subsidized credit so they can start a business, usually on a small scale.[7] Some of these programmes have been criticized on the grounds of the inferior quality of the assets created or that they are not reaching the target population or even that they are not effective in generating additional revenue for the poor. Nevertheless, some of the poor have been reached and have benefited. The Jawahar Employment Programme, for example, provides jobs for about 10 per cent of the rural poor in India. Most of the problems that do exist can possibly be solved through a more careful design and more rigorous management and monitoring.[8]

In sum, the experience of the majority of developing countries in alleviating poverty has ranged from mixed to disappointing. Most countries, even those assisted by generous amounts of foreign aid, have not found the resources necessary for reducing poverty significantly. Many Governments have been too unstable and insecure, hamstrung by an inadequate command over resources, weak institutional capacity and insufficient social backing and consensus to wage war on poverty effectively. In addition, recent economic shocks and local exploitation and discrimination against the poor have undercut the ability of many Governments to eliminate poverty. Other Governments have chosen not to give much attention to poverty alleviation. Finally, for a number of countries, the benefits of rapid economic growth were distributed unequally so poverty was reduced less than should have been the case.

The weight of poverty falls heavily on women. Females in a poor household are often worse off than males because of gender-based differences in the distribution of food and other entitlements within the family.[9] In poor households they often shoulder more of the workload than men, are less educated and have no access to remunerative activities. On average, women in developed countries live six years longer than men, whereas in developing countries, the excess is two years. In some developing countries, including Bangladesh, Bhutan and Nepal, life expectancy at birth is higher for males than for females.

Low literacy levels of women go hand in hand with poverty, particularly in rural areas where low enrolment and high dropout rates result from the belief that it is more important to educate boys. Of the 960 million illiterate adults in the world in 1990, 640 million, or two thirds, are women. In 1990, in developing countries, the female illiteracy rate was 45 per cent, compared with 25 per cent for males. Female illiteracy rates in sub-Saharan Africa, North Africa, West Asia and South Asia were above 60 per cent, while the rate for males varied between 35 per cent and 41 per cent. If current trends continue, one female adult out of two will still be illiterate in these three regions in the year 2000.

About one third of all households in developing countries are headed by women. In some regions, as in rural Africa and the urban slums of Latin America, the figure is closer to half. A large proportion are landless, unskilled, illiterate, unemployed or under-employed. In most industrialized nations, households headed by women are also poorer than those headed by men. In the United States, almost half of all poor families are supported by a woman with no spouse present, and their average income is 77 per cent of the official poverty line.[10] Furthermore, nearly one in every four children under the age of six is currently brought up in poverty.[11]

Workloads and household responsibilities place a heavy physical and mental strain on poor women. The multiple roles of rural women, who have both domestic and agricultural responsibilities, impose a long working day. Most studies put the daily workload of rural women in developing nations at 15 to 16 hours. At seasonal peak periods, such as harvesting, it may be longer. Rudimentary utensils and procedures for food preparation and the lack of nearby sources of fuel and clean water make their household tasks even more time-consuming. Participation of women in economic development programmes is usually hampered by a lack of time and energy.

Women play a central role in producing food, generating income, bearing and raising children and in overall household production. They are a key force in reducing hunger and poverty, promoting family welfare and contributing to overall economic development. As labourers for hire and on the family farm, women play a major role in food production. They produce more than half the food in developing countries and as much as three quarters in Africa; they probably account for more than 90 per cent of all time spent processing and preparing it.[12] They play a substantial part in storing, processing and marketing food and cash crops, and they often take care of small livestock. In India, for example, women provide 75 per cent of the labour for transplanting and weeding rice, 60 per cent for harvesting and 33 per cent for threshing.[13] In Bangladesh, apart from harvesting activities, they are responsible for the post-harvest work, including the processing of rice. In addition, women are the primary collectors of fuel and water, which poor people generally must provide for themselves in the absence of public services. Moreover, women bear the major responsibility for ensuring the nutrition, health and cognitive development of children during pre-school years.

The adverse effects of the economic recession and remedial structural adjustment programmes should be added to the list of factors that have contributed to the impoverishment of women. As producers, women have been adversely affected by recession and demand restraint. There is some evidence that reduced employment and real wages in the formal sector affected women worse than men and that real earnings in the informal sector fell.[14] Reduced family income in many economies, often below subsistence levels, imposed increasing demands on women's time to shop more often, trying to stretch income to meet the subsistence needs of the family. The income women themselves control has fallen in countries undergoing adjustment. Women's health, nutrition and education has fallen along with that of the rest of society, especially in the worst affected counties.

## B.  THE DEVELOPED MARKET-ECONOMY COUNTRIES

Sometimes it is assumed that because poverty often takes a mild and subjective form in the OECD countries, it is not as serious for those countries compared with the low-income countries of the world. Certainly, much of the debate in the OECD countries has been concerned with relative rather than absolute poverty. Goods and services considered luxuries in the developing countries are defined as necessary for a minimum standard of living in the rich countries. However, the fact that poverty is relative does not mean that it is not visible and a social thorn. The French political philosopher, de Tocqueville, may have been half jesting when he asserted that it is only in rich countries that one finds poor people,[15] but it is true that the characterization of poverty as an undesirable abnormality better fits countries where the poor are a minority than where they represent the general condition of the majority.

Poverty in the OECD countries has been increasing and becoming much more visible since the 1970s: the growth of homelessness in cities in North America and much of Western Europe has provided a harsh face to the accumulating poverty in recent years.

According to the U.S. Census Bureau, poverty in the United States is increasing, even with the end of the latest recession. The number of poor people rose in 1992 for the third consecutive year, reaching 36.9 million, or 14.5 per cent of the population. In 1971, it stood at 12.5 per cent.

The standard of living for poor people in the United States is better in some ways than it was three decades ago, but in other ways it is worse. Low-income people have better access to health care, through Medicaid, created in 1965. Many have food stamps, under a programme created in the 1960s. And there has been a steady increase in the quality of the nation's housing stock.

The face of poverty today is much younger. Social Security, automatically increased each year to keep pace with inflation, and private pensions have sharply reduced poverty among the elderly. The poverty rate for the elderly fell below the rate for the nation as a whole in 1982, and it has been lower ever since. But the poverty rate for children under 18, after declining to a low of 14 per cent in 1969, rose to a peak of 22.3 per cent in 1983 and now stands at 21.9 per cent.

Poverty in industrial countries may be traced in part to the increasing bifurcation in the occupational structure which is segmenting the job market between highly skilled and well-paid jobs and low-skilled, low-paid and precarious work. One consequence has been the widening range of the population that is subject to economic insecurity. The risk of recurrent or long-term unemployment has grown for both laid-off workers and young people trying to enter the labour market. Faced with the prospects of long-term dependence on welfare benefits, many of the young, in particular, end up feeling they have little real stake in society. The rapid pace of structural change coupled with the diminished role of extended family and community security support systems has left many disadvantaged persons vulnerable to poverty. Disproportionately high numbers of single parent families and other sub-cultural changes taking place within many of these groups have further reinforced their sense of exclusion and their descent into hard-core poverty.

Policies adopted to alleviate poverty in developed market economies need to be revised and improved upon. Income support schemes centred primarily upon individuals' employment records are generally inadequate for young people with limited or no employment history. In many cases, moreover, social assistance benefits have reached levels approximating or improving on minimum wages for employment. The marginal tax rates produced in these cases provide little financial incentive to take a job, thus imprisoning many of the unemployed in the poverty trap of welfare dependency. With economic slow-down and the rise in long-term poverty, systems of social assistance are being made to bear a burden unprecedented in the post-war period.

Summing up, the incidence of poverty in the OECD countries is distributed as follows: The number of single parent families in poverty has grown; unemployment and insecure employment are increasing in significance as causes of poverty;[16] and the elderly form a declining proportion of the poverty population. As for the duration of poverty, it tends to be shortest among many of the young and longest among the elderly. On balance, however, given their economic means, welfare systems and low population growth rates, the developed market economies are relatively well situated appreciably to alleviate, if not eliminate, the poverty in their midst.

## C.  POVERTY IN THE ECONOMIES IN TRANSITION

Poverty had been practically eliminated in the centrally planned economies during the rapid pace of post-war industrialization. Nevertheless, poverty reemerged in the late 1970s. An estimated one half of the poor in developed countries — about 100 million — live in Eastern Europe and the former Soviet Union,[17] but there are ambiguities in defining poverty levels.[18] These problems notwithstanding, there is agreement that the number of people living in poverty rose in all countries in the region during the past two decades. The studies of the World Bank,[19] the Luxembourg Income Studies[20] and certain others are consistent in their conclusions. Between 1978 and 1987, poverty increased most in Poland and Yugoslavia, less or not at all in Hungary and Czechoslovakia.

Poverty is a major problem in the constituent republics of the former Soviet Union, although estimates vary. Some estimates claim there were about 41 million people below the subsistence minimum in 1990.[21] Others show that every third person in the former Soviet Republics had a monthly income below 75 roubles in 1989.[22] The incidence of poverty was also uneven among the constituent republics.

Impoverishment among workers increased most during the 1980s. The living standards of residents in urban centres deteriorated more than those of farmers. Late in the 1980s, homeless people and beggars — extinct social groups under socialism — slowly became a part of the city landscape in many countries in Eastern Europe and in the former Soviet Union.

## D. POLICY CONSIDERATIONS

Policies for the eradication of poverty vary greatly. Such policies have, however, certain common features. In the International Development Strategy for the Fourth United Nations Development Decade, the General Assembly recognized that "the absence of an adequate income through landlessness or the lack of opportunities for work is a prime cause of poverty".[23] Since poverty is usually associated with landlessness and malnutrition, attacks on poverty call for a more equitable distribution of land resources and a greater emphasis on agricultural development, particularly food production.

Some land reforms, such as those undertaken in China in the late 1940s and 1950s, have been remarkably successful in both reducing economic and social inequality and generating economic growth. Other attempts at land reform — in Peru in 1960, for example — had less effect on either poverty or inequality, mainly because there was no absorption of rural labour in agriculture after the reform.[24] Most land reforms have been timid and partial and have not been followed by complementary measures that allow new owners to exploit their new assets.[25] In many cases, powerful groups in whose hands most of the land — often idle — was concentrated, opposed re-distribution, and when implemented the reform covered only limited areas of land of poor quality. The impact on poverty alleviation was small.

Employment creation remains the most powerful instrument for reducing both inequality and poverty. For people to be employable they must be healthy, educated and skilled. The spread of health infrastructure into rural areas and among the poor in urban areas is thus a necessary part of social policy. For functional literacy in the workforce, primary and secondary education have to be made available to all. The role of education needs special emphasis. Publically financed education provides an income-earning asset to the poorest, and it does not have to be snatched from some other owner. Through education the poor can upgrade their skills and participate in and influence the economic and political system. Education increases mobility and reduces inequality, if there is demand for the skilled labour released by the educational system.

A reduction in the rate of population growth is an integral part of these strategies. A slower rate of growth of the labour force makes it easier to provide full employment. It means less pressure on land resources and less demand for social services.

An improvement in the condition of women in economic and social life is a necessary condition for reducing inequality and poverty. Educating women and opening employment opportunities for them is an essential part of that process. They need access to medical services. Access to nutrition, health care, education and legal rights on an equal footing with men will enable women to assume the positions of responsibility from which they are so far conspicuously absent.

Poverty reduction is not necessarily a long-term process. The rapid reduction and elimination of the worst forms of poverty in several countries, including China, Japan, the Republic of Korea, and Singapore since the Second World War show what can be done in a relatively short time. On the other hand, the speed with which sub-Saharan Africa fell into extreme poverty, and the emergence of poverty in the economies in transition show how rapidly conditions can deteriorate. Determined, well-defined and efficiently implemented policies are crucial to anti-poverty strategies. Governments have a powerful role to play here.

A reduction in poverty in developing countries, especially in Africa, cannot happen unless growth and development take root. Domestic policies will determine whether such development will contribute to the eradication of poverty. But international conditions also play a major role.

Expanding trade, open markets and net flows of resources of capital, knowledge and skills are indispensible.

Approaches to dealing with poverty in developed countries could seek to incorporate more elements that are potentially poverty reducing, thus compensating for a tendency that is too often heavily weighted toward social protection and contingency alleviation. For instance, unemployment compensation structures might be modified to include retraining and relocation programmes for structurally unemployed persons to integrate them into labour markets in accordance with their capacities and the requirements of the market. Similarly, with respect to public assistance to lone-parent families, an effective way to break the poverty trap cycle of welfare dependency that such relief has often fostered could be to adopt "workfare" approaches that incorporate training, work and welfare packages in a non-punitive way to help facilitate the parents' integration or reintegration in the workforce. More generally, as progress is made toward European unification, reformulation of the concept of the welfare state may be needed as the walls of national welfare systems come down and more heterogeneous forms of transnational poverty needs and requirements emerge.

## Notes

[1] See World Bank, *World Bank Development Report 1990: Poverty*, op. cit., table 2.1.

[2] For further details, see: M. Lipton, *The Poor and the Poorest: Some Interim Findings*, World Bank Discussion Paper No. 25, 1988.

[3] The Secretariat has extensively analysed the impact of the economic crisis and adjustment policies on poverty. Please consult the Report of the Secretary-General on international cooperation for the eradication of poverty in developing countries, (doc. no. A/44/467), 18 September 1989, pp. 6-14. See also report under the same title (doc. no. A/46/454) of 2 October 1991, pp. 10-20, and the 1989 Report on the World Social Situation (Sales No. E.89.IV.1), particularly chapter IV: Inequality and poverty, pp. 36-46 and the annex to the report: The critical social situation in Africa, pp. 113-126.

[4] ECLAC, "Panorama social de America Latina: edicion 1991", (doc no. LC/G.1688), 31 October 1991, pp. 23-24.

[5] Food production in the continent has been growing at an annual average of 1.6 per cent since 1965, while population grows at about 3 per cent per year.

[6] Chakravarty, S., "Development strategy for growth with equity: the South Asian experience", *Asian Development Review*, volume 8, no. 1, 1990, pp. 133-159.

[7] On the particular issue of programmes to assist informal sector enterprises, see Report of the Secretary General on International cooperation for eradication of poverty in developing countries, (A/44/467), 18 September 1989, pp. 17-20.

[8] Ahluwalia, M. "Policies for poverty . . .".

[9] See UNDP, *Human Development Report, 1990* (Oxford, Oxford University Press, 1990), pp. 31-32.

[10] See *A Survey of Childhood Hunger in the United States*, report of the Community Childhood Hunger Identification Project, (Washington, D.C., Food Research and Action Centre, March 1991).

[11] See National Center for Children in Poverty, *Five Million Children: A Statistical Profile of our Poorest Young Citizens* (New York, Columbia University, 1990), p. 27.

[12] "Poverty and the socio-economic attainment of women", *World Economic Survey, 1991* (United Nations publication, Sales No. E.91.II.C.1), pp. 189-195.

[13] Gerd Holmboe-Otteson, Ophelia Mascarenhas and Margareta Wandel, "Women's role in food production and nutrition: implications for their quality of life", *Food and Nutrition Bulletin*, vol. 10, no. 3 (September 1988), pp. 8-15.

[14] Haleh Afshar and Carolyn Dennis, eds., *Women and Adjustment Policies in the Third World* (New York, St. Martin's Press, 1992).

[15] A. de Toccqueville, "Memoir on Pauperism", 1835, as reprinted in English in *The Public Interest*, 1983, pp. 102-120.

[16] G. Room, "Poverty in the European Community: trends and debates", *Intereconomics*, vol. 23, July-August 1988, p. 160.

[17] UNDP, *Human Development Report, 1991*, (Oxford, Oxford University Press, 1991), p. 26.

[18] Poverty incomes are those below the subsistence minimum calculated by official institutions in each country as a percentage of the average income. That percentage varied between 40 per cent in Czechoslovakia to almost 60 per cent in Hungary. The subsistence minimum was not used as an elgibility criterion for assistance.

[19] Branco Milanovic, "Poverty in Eastern Europe in the years of the crisis, 1978 to 1987: Poland, Hungary and Yugoslavia", *World Bank Economic Review*, vol. 5, no. 2 (1991), pp. 187-205.

[20] Smedding and others, "Poverty in Eastern Europe: lessons from cross-national income comparisons from the Luxembourg Income Study", seminar paper prepared for the Conference on Poverty Measurement for Economies in Transition, 7-9 October 1991.

[21] N. Rimashevskaja, "Uzlovia problema perekhodnogo perioda", *Voprosy ekonomiki*, no. 1 (1990), pp. 33-36.

[22] L. Zubova and others, discuss the issue of poverty based on an all-union population poll conducted in September 1990 by the Center for Public Opinion and Market Research in Moscow. See "Bednost' v SSSR: toczka-zrenia naseleniia", *Voprosy ekonomiki*, no. 6 (1991), pp. 60-67.

[23] General Assembly resolution 45/199 of 21 December 1990.

[24] Karl Ove Moene, "Poverty and land ownership", *American Economic Review*, vol. 82, no. 1 (1992), pp. 52-64.

[25] Report of the Secretary-General on international cooperation . . . (A/46/454), p. 29.

# PART II

Human development, basic
needs and social services

# 5

# Population growth, urbanization, migration and refugees

THE rapid population growth in developing countries has been a cause of alarm for many decades. It has recently attracted renewed attention in two specific contexts. The discussions about sustainable development before and during the United Nations Conference on Environment and Development, which was held in Rio de Janeiro in June 1992, brought into sharp focus the ecological limits to growth and the dangers posed by large and growing populations driven by poverty to despoil the environment irrevocably. Migration, both within countries and across borders, is mounting. Political and economic disruption are important immediate causes of specific flows of migration, but demographic pressure and growing economic disparities create strong underlying forces for population movements which threaten to become a serious source of international conflict.

This chapter reviews recent developments in these areas.

## A. POPULATION GROWTH

### 1. *Size, growth and distribution*

The world population in mid-1991 was 5.4 billion. Its annual rate of growth is expected to drop from 1.7 per cent per year at present to 1.6 per cent in 1995-2000, 1.5 per cent in 2000-2005, 1.2 in 2010-2015 and 1.0 in 2020-2025 (see table 5.1). The world population is projected to reach 6.3 billion in 2000 and 8.5 billion in 2025.

Out of an annual average increment to the world population of 47 million in 1950-1955, 23 per cent originated in the developed

*Table 5.1*

Size, annual rate of increase, increment and distribution of population by major areas of the world, medium variant, 1950-2025

| Year | World | Developed | Developing | Least developed | Africa | Latin America | Northern America | Asia | Europe | Oceania | USSR |
|---|---|---|---|---|---|---|---|---|---|---|---|
| *Population (millions)* | | | | | | | | | | | |
| 1950 | 2516 | 832 | 1684 | 169 | 222 | 166 | 166 | 1378 | 393 | 13 | 180 |
| 1970 | 3698 | 1049 | 2649 | 263 | 362 | 286 | 226 | 2102 | 460 | 19 | 243 |
| 1990 | 5292 | 1207 | 4086 | 444 | 642 | 448 | 276 | 3113 | 499 | 26 | 289 |
| 2000 | 6260 | 1264 | 4997 | 595 | 866 | 538 | 295 | 3713 | 510 | 30 | 308 |
| 2025 | 8504 | 1354 | 7150 | 1039 | 1597 | 757 | 332 | 4912 | 515 | 38 | 352 |
| *Annual rate of increase (percentage)* | | | | | | | | | | | |
| 1950-1955 | 1.79 | 1.28 | 2.04 | 1.82 | 2.21 | 2.73 | 1.80 | 1.89 | 0.79 | 2.25 | 1.71 |
| 1965-1970 | 2.06 | 0.90 | 2.54 | 2.48 | 2.64 | 2.60 | 1.13 | 2.44 | 0.66 | 1.97 | 1.00 |
| 1985-1990 | 1.74 | 0.54 | 2.11 | 2.80 | 2.99 | 2.06 | 0.82 | 1.87 | 0.25 | 1.48 | 0.78 |
| 1995-2000 | 1.63 | 0.45 | 1.94 | 2.83 | 2.97 | 1.76 | 0.61 | 1.68 | 0.23 | 1.24 | 0.64 |
| 2000-2005 | 1.47 | 0.38 | 1.74 | 2.71 | 2.89 | 1.62 | 0.55 | 1.43 | 0.15 | 1.13 | 0.61 |
| 2020-2025 | 0.99 | 0.18 | 1.15 | 1.73 | 1.90 | 1.12 | 0.34 | 0.89 | -0.05 | 0.76 | 0.47 |
| *Average annual increment (millions)* | | | | | | | | | | | |
| 1950-1955 | 47.1 | 11.0 | 36.1 | 3.2 | 5.2 | 4.9 | 3.1 | 27.3 | 3.2 | 0.3 | 3.2 |
| 1965-1970 | 72.3 | 9.2 | 63.1 | 6.2 | 8.9 | 7.0 | 2.5 | 48.2 | 3.0 | 0.4 | 2.4 |
| 1985-1990 | 88.2 | 6.4 | 81.7 | 11.6 | 17.8 | 8.8 | 2.2 | 55.5 | 1.2 | 0.4 | 2.2 |
| 2000-2005 | 95.7 | 4.9 | 90.8 | 17.3 | 27.0 | 9.1 | 1.6 | 55.0 | 0.7 | 0.3 | 1.9 |
| 2020-2025 | 82.6 | 2.4 | 80.1 | 17.2 | 29.0 | 8.2 | 1.1 | 42.5 | -0.2 | 0.3 | 1.6 |
| *Percentage distribution* | | | | | | | | | | | |
| 1950 | 100 | 33.1 | 66.9 | 6.7 | 8.8 | 6.6 | 6.6 | 54.7 | 15.6 | 0.5 | 7.2 |
| 1970 | 100 | 28.4 | 71.6 | 7.1 | 9.8 | 7.7 | 6.1 | 56.8 | 12.5 | 0.5 | 6.5 |
| 1990 | 100 | 22.8 | 77.2 | 8.4 | 12.1 | 8.5 | 5.2 | 58.8 | 9.4 | 0.5 | 5.4 |
| 2000 | 100 | 20.2 | 79.8 | 9.5 | 13.8 | 8.6 | 4.7 | 59.3 | 8.1 | 0.5 | 4.9 |
| 2025 | 100 | 15.9 | 84.1 | 12.2 | 18.8 | 8.9 | 3.9 | 57.8 | 6.1 | 0.5 | 4.1 |

Source: World Population Prospects, 1990 (United Nations publication, Sales No.E.91.XIII.4).

countries and 77 per cent in the developing countries (7 per cent in the least developed countries and 70 per cent in other developing countries). Of the annual average addition of 88 million in 1985-1990, the share of developed countries was 7 per cent; 93 per cent of the growth occurred in developing regions (13 per cent in the least developed countries and 80 per cent in other developing countries). An increasing share of the increment to the world population will come from Africa: on present projections Africa, which is presently contributing 20 per cent to the growth of world population each year, is expected to contribute 35 per cent in 2020-2025. Africa is currently growing at 3 per cent a year, faster than any other region, and it is so far projected to be growing rapidly in the next century even though population growth in other regions will then have slowed down a great deal. However, if economic development takes off in Africa, this could change.

The distribution of the population among the different regions of the world is changing. Africa, as a proportion of a growing world population, increased from 8.8 per cent in 1950 to 12.1 in 1990 and the share of developed countries fell from 16 per cent in Europe in 1950 to 9 per cent in 1990, and may be 6 per cent in 2025 (see table 5.1).

The acceleration in world population growth from 1.8 per cent per year in 1950-1955 to 2.1 per cent in 1965-1970 resulted from a rapid decrease in mortality (the crude death rate declined from 20 to 13 deaths per 1,000 persons) and a slow decline in birth rate (from 37 to 34 births per 1,000). The rapid decline in the rate of population growth in subsequent years can be described as fertility-driven. By 1975-1980, the crude birth rate had fallen to 28 births per 1,000 population while the crude death rate was still 11 per 1,000 population. Between 1975-1980 and 1990-1995, the crude birth rate declined more slowly from 28 to 26 births per 1,000 (see table 5.2). Since 1975, population growth has been stable and is anticipated to remain so until 1995. A rapid deceleration of population growth is projected to begin after 1995, from 1.7 per cent in 1990-1995 to 1.0 per cent in 2020-2025.

*Table 5.2*
Crude birth rate and crude death rate by major area: 1975-2025 (per 1,000 population)

| Major area and region | Crude birth rate | | | | | | Crude death rate | | | | | |
|---|---|---|---|---|---|---|---|---|---|---|---|---|
| | 1975-1980 | 1980-1985 | 1985-1990 | 1990-1995 | 1995-2000 | 2020-2025 | 1975-1980 | 1980-1985 | 1985-1990 | 1990-1995 | 1995-2000 | 2020-2025 |
| World total | 28.3 | 27.6 | 27.1 | 26.4 | 24.9 | 17.5 | 11.1 | 10.4 | 9.8 | 9.2 | 8.6 | 7.6 |
| Developed countries | 15.6 | 15.2 | 14.5 | 13.9 | 13.4 | 11.9 | 9.4 | 9.6 | 9.8 | 9.6 | 9.5 | 10.6 |
| Developing countries | 32.8 | 31.7 | 31.0 | 30.0 | 27.9 | 18.6 | 11.7 | 10.6 | 9.8 | 9.1 | 8.4 | 7.1 |
| Africa | 46.1 | 45.3 | 44.7 | 43.5 | 41.6 | 26.0 | 17.6 | 16.4 | 14.7 | 13.2 | 11.9 | 7.0 |
| Asia | 29.7 | 28.4 | 27.8 | 26.9 | 24.7 | 16.1 | 10.7 | 9.7 | 9.0 | 8.4 | 7.8 | 7.2 |
| Latin America | 32.4 | 30.6 | 28.7 | 26.8 | 24.8 | 18.4 | 8.6 | 7.9 | 7.4 | 7.0 | 6.6 | 7.0 |
| Northern America | 15.1 | 15.6 | 15.0 | 13.9 | 13.1 | 11.7 | 8.5 | 8.5 | 8.7 | 8.7 | 8.8 | 9.9 |
| Europe | 14.4 | 13.4 | 12.9 | 12.8 | 12.4 | 10.9 | 10.4 | 10.5 | 10.7 | 10.6 | 10.3 | 11.5 |
| Oceania | 20.9 | 20.0 | 19.4 | 18.6 | 17.9 | 14.0 | 8.8 | 8.2 | 8.1 | 8.0 | 7.9 | 8.3 |
| Soviet Union | 18.3 | 19.1 | 18.4 | 16.7 | 15.9 | 14.1 | 10.0 | 10.7 | 10.6 | 9.9 | 9.5 | 9. |

Source: World Population Prospects, 1990 (United Nations publication, Sales No. E.91.XIII.4) tables 35 and 38.

## 2. *Fertility and family planning*

Historically, lower rates of population growth have come about with reductions in fertility preceded by reduced mortality. The total fertility rate (the average number of children born to a woman during her childbearing age) in the world fell from 3.84 in 1975-1980 to 3.45 in 1985-1990 (see table 5.3). Total fertility rates in developing countries remain well above those in developed countries, where the rate is about two. In Latin America, the total fertility rate fell from 4.4 in 1975-80 to 3.6 in 1985-1990 and in Asia from 4.1 to 3.5. In Africa, however, the total fertility rate remained in the range of 6.5 to 6.2 children per woman.

Many factors determine the level of fertility: infant and child mortality, education (especially of women), industrialization, urbanization, income level and distribution, status of women, labour force structure, religious and ethnic affiliation, modernization, family structure, old-age security, and the costs and benefits of raising children. Advances in social and economic development and organized family planning programmes play significant roles in bringing about changes in reproductive behaviour.

The availability of contraceptives is of paramount importance. The decline in fertility in developing countries has been attributable largely to the rapid spread of contraception. Age of first marriage and sexual activity outside marriage, the duration of breast-feeding of children (which delays the return of ovulation following a birth) and the practice of induced abortion are other important proximate determinants of fertility. Yet none of them seem more important than the use of contraceptives.[1] The percentage of married couples using contraceptives in the developing countries has grown from less than 10 per cent in the 1960s to 45 per cent in 1983 and to 48 per cent in 1987. In East Asia, where fertility rates have more than halved over the past 25 years, the use of contraceptives increased from 13 per cent in the 1960s to 74 per cent in 1987.

The status of women in society, especially their level of education and employment, affects their ability to choose contraception and other family planning methods.

There is a close connection between the level of mothers' edu-

Table 5.3
Crude birth rate and total fertility rate, world and major areas, medium variant, 1950-2025

| Period | World | Developed regions | Developing regions | Africa | Latin America | Northern America | Asia | Europe | Oceania | Soviet Union |
|---|---|---|---|---|---|---|---|---|---|---|
| | | | | *Total fertility rate* | | | | | | |
| | | | | (number or births per woman) | | | | | | |
| 1950-1955 | 5.00 | 2.84 | 6.19 | 6.65 | 5.87 | 3.47 | 5.92 | 2.59 | 3.83 | 2.82 |
| 1975-1980 | 3.84 | 2.03 | 4.54 | 6.54 | 4.36 | 1.91 | 4.06 | 1.98 | 2.79 | 2.34 |
| 1985-1990 | 3.45 | 1.89 | 3.94 | 6.24 | 3.55 | 1.81 | 3.48 | 1.72 | 2.51 | 2.38 |
| 1995-2000 | 3.14 | 1.90 | 3.47 | 5.70 | 3.00 | 1.86 | 3.02 | 1.74 | 2.34 | 2.25 |
| 2020-2025 | 2.27 | 1.94 | 2.32 | 3.04 | 2.39 | 1.94 | 2.06 | 1.85 | 2.02 | 2.10 |
| | | | | *Crude birth rate* | | | | | | |
| | | | | (per thousand) | | | | | | |
| 1950-1955 | 37.4 | 22.6 | 44.6 | 49.2 | 42.5 | 24.6 | 42.9 | 19.8 | 27.6 | 26.3 |
| 1975-1980 | 28.3 | 15.6 | 32.8 | 46.1 | 32.4 | 15.1 | 29.7 | 14.4 | 20.9 | 18.3 |
| 1985-1990 | 27.1 | 14.5 | 31.0 | 44.7 | 28.7 | 15.0 | 27.8 | 12.9 | 19.4 | 18.4 |
| 1995-2000 | 24.9 | 13.4 | 27.9 | 41.6 | 24.8 | 13.1 | 24.7 | 12.4 | 17.9 | 15.9 |
| 2020-2025 | 17.5 | 11.9 | 18.6 | 26.0 | 18.4 | 11.7 | 16.1 | 10.9 | 14.0 | 14.1 |

Source: World Population Prospects, 1990 (United Nations publication, Sales No. E.91.XIII.4).

cation and the size of her family. Education directly changes attitudes, values and beliefs toward a small family norm and toward a style of child-rearing that is relatively costly to the parents in time and money. In Thailand, the fewer the numbers of children in a family, the more likely a child was to stay in school.[2] In Liberia, women who had been to secondary school were 10 times more likely to be using family planning services than those who have never been to school. In four Latin American countries, education was responsible for between 40 and 60 per cent of the decline in fertility registered over the past decade. With education, women acquire upward social mobility and a capacity to earn incomes, all of which increases the opportunity cost of the time spent on child-rearing.

Education is also associated with reduced child mortality. Educated women are more likely to protect their children's health. For every year of mothers' education, child mortality is reduced 7 to 9 per cent. To the extent that education affects maternal and child health, breast-feeding, contraceptive use, familial relationships, labour force participation and the acquisition of education by women help further to reduce fertility.

## 3. Dependency ratio

In mid-1990, one out of every three persons in the world was a child, less than 15 years old, one out of five was a youth, 15 to 24 years old and one out of 16 was old, over 65.[3] There were 1,710 million children in the world in 1990 compared with 1,400 million in 1970. Their number will reach 2 billion a few years after the beginning of the next century, most of them will be living in developing countries.

The number of elderly in the world is considerably smaller than the number of children. However, the projected increase of the world's elderly population is substantially faster than that of the world's child population. In 1990, the number of persons aged 65 years and over was 328 million. It is projected to grow to 828 million in 2025, more than 2.5 times .

The number of persons under 15 and over 65 divided into the number of persons aged 15 to 64 years is termed the dependency ratio. The dependency ratio in the world as a whole was 63 per cent

Table 5.4

Dependency ratio, total, under 15 and 65 and over, by major area and region, 1980-2025 (percentage)

| Major area and region | 1980 | | | 1990 | | | 2000 | | | 2025 | | |
|---|---|---|---|---|---|---|---|---|---|---|---|---|
| | Total | Under age 15 | Age 65+ | Total | Under age 15 | Age 65+ | Total | Under age 15 | Age 65+ | Total | Under age 15 | Age 65+ |
| World | 69.9 | 59.8 | 10.1 | 62.6 | 52.6 | 10.1 | 61.8 | 50.8 | 11.0 | 52.1 | 37.3 | 14.8 |
| Developed countries | 53.0 | 35.4 | 17.6 | 50.1 | 32.0 | 18.1 | 50.7 | 30.1 | 20.6 | 58.2 | 28.2 | 30.0 |
| Developing countries | 76.6 | 69.5 | 7.1 | 66.7 | 59.3 | 7.4 | 64.9 | 56.6 | 8.3 | 51.0 | 38.9 | 12.1 |
| Africa | 91.6 | 85.8 | 5.8 | 92.5 | 86.7 | 5.8 | 90.3 | 84.4 | 5.8 | 63.7 | 57.0 | 6.7 |
| Asia | 72.5 | 64.9 | 7.6 | 61.0 | 52.9 | 8.0 | 59.8 | 50.5 | 9.3 | 47.4 | 33.3 | 14.1 |
| Latin America | 77.5 | 69.7 | 7.7 | 68.5 | 60.4 | 8.1 | 61.4 | 52.7 | 8.7 | 52.2 | 39.1 | 13.1 |
| Northern America | 50.8 | 34.0 | 16.8 | 51.2 | 32.4 | 18.8 | 48.9 | 29.9 | 19.1 | 60.4 | 28.5 | 31.9 |
| Europe | 54.9 | 34.6 | 20.3 | 49.2 | 29.2 | 20.0 | 50.2 | 27.8 | 22.4 | 57.7 | 26.0 | 31.7 |
| Oceania | 59.5 | 46.8 | 12.8 | 55.1 | 41.1 | 14.0 | 52.8 | 38.3 | 14.5 | 53.0 | 31.7 | 21.2 |
| Soviet Union | 53.9 | 38.1 | 15.8 | 54.0 | 39.2 | 14.8 | 54.5 | 36.5 | 18.0 | 55.4 | 32.4 | 23.0 |

Source: World Population Prospects, 1990 (United Nations publication, Sales No. E.91.XIII.4), table 46.

in 1990 (see table 5.4). It is expected to decline to 62 in 2000 and further to 52 in 2025. In 1990, the dependency ratio was about 33 per cent higher in developing countries than in developed countries, reflecting higher fertility in the former group.

## 4. *Pressures on land and employment opportunities*

One of the most prevalent concerns about population growth is that it will result in steadily increasing pressure on available land. Another one is that it will produce ever more workers in need of employment. But it must be remembered that a growing population also increases demand and that adaptation to increasing population was a part of the great upswing of the industrial revolution.

The pressure on the land leads to the creation of new arable

*Figure 5.1*
Projected average annual growth rates for age group 20-34,
1980-2025 (*percentages*)

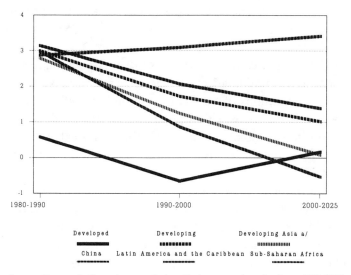

Source: Economically active population: Estimates and projections, 1950-2025, 3rd edition, ILO (Geneva, 1986).

a    Excluding China.

land, the adoption of new agricultural technologies and rural to urban migration. As a result, the change in the ratio of agricultural population to arable land usually presents a mixed experience.

The rapid growth of the labour force in developing countries means that more than a billion jobs have to be created in the course of the 1990s and this in turn means that development must accelerate. Once again, the situation in sub-Saharan Africa is especially disturbing (see figure 5.1). Levels of unemployment and underemployment are already high (see chapter 3), but there will be a need for 6 million new jobs a year in the 1990s and as many as 10 million new jobs each year at the beginning of the next century to absorb the new entrants into the workforce.

## 5. *Urbanization*

Towns and cities have grown beyond the capacity of local governments to deliver even basic essential services. In developed countries the urban population doubled from 448 million in 1950 to 875 million in 1990. The urban population in developing countries more than quintupled over the same period, from 285 million to 1.6 billion by 1990.

In 1990, 33 per cent of the world's urban population resided in agglomerations containing 1 million or more inhabitants and 13 per cent in agglomerations of 5 million or more.[4] In 1990 the number of urban agglomerations with a population over 5 million was 34, 22 of them in developing countries. By the year 2000, about three quarters of populations in urban agglomerations will be in developing countries.

Urbanization in developing countries gives rise to several concerns. Brazil, China, India, Mexico and the Republic of Korea are amongst the world's largest producers of many manufactured goods. Their manufacturing plants are concentrated in urban areas and all lack a safe means of waste disposal. In Thailand, a high proportion of all industry is located in Bangkok or its neighbouring provinces. This region has three quarters of all factories dealing with hazardous chemicals. Within Bangkok are five of Thailand's seven lead-smelting plants and over 90 per cent of its chemicals, dry-cell battery, paint, pharmaceutical and textile manufacturing, all of which are heavy pollutants.[5] Environmental pollution also emanates from activities other than industrial pollution. Large proportions of the population are not served by sewers and garbage disposal which adds greatly to land- and water-pollution problems.

Most cities in the developing world have also become loci for the most degrading poverty, with vast throngs of people living on the margins of survival. Of every 100 new households established in urban areas in developing countries during the second half of the 1980s, 72 were located in shanties and slums (92 out of every 100 in Africa).[6] Today, an estimated 1.2 billion people — almost 23 per cent of the world's population and 60 per cent of developing countries city-dwellers — live in squatter settlements, often shantytowns made from cardboard, plastic, canvas or whatever other material is freely available. The number of urban households in developing countries without safe water increased from 138 million in 1970 to 215 million by 1988, and those without adequate sanitation rose from 98 million to 340 million.[7] Rural environmental problems such as deforestation, soil erosion and water pollution are also linked to urban growth.[8] Deforestation takes place to satisfy the demand for fuelwood or charcoal from city inhabitants and enterprises.

Governments in developing countries are eager to slow down metropolitan growth, to promote the growth of small towns and intermediate cities and to develop rural areas in order to retain or attract rural populations. However, costlier population redistribution policies, such as the relocation of capital cities, the promotion of counter-magnet cities, the establishment of new towns and land colonization have been abandoned or cut back during adverse economic conditions. It has been realized that physical and spatial development policies alone will have little impact on changing patterns of urban development unless reinforced by other national economic and social policies.

## B.  INTERNATIONAL MIGRATION

1. *Changing immigration pressures*

Differential rates of growth of population and economic opportunities cause major movements of population among regions and countries. Such movements are not new. Until technology permitted people in large numbers to cross oceans, these movements were over land and over narrow stretches of sea. Large sailing vessels and later, steam ships with steel hulls, made it possible for large numbers of people to cross the oceans at little peril. In the twentieth century, air travel has made movement even cheaper and safer. The Americas came to be populated by people of European and African descent. Europeans also settled in parts of Africa, in Australia and New Zealand. Indians travelled to many parts including Fiji, Guyana, Mauritius and Trinidad and Tobago. Chinese, though in smaller numbers, travelled to many parts of the world. In the twentieth century, mass net migration until 1960 was from developed regions in the north to developing regions in the south. There was a dramatic change in the 1950s when the dominant flow originated in developing countries with developed countries in the north as their destination.

Economic betterment has been always a dominant objective in these mass movements.[9] Most European colonists in the Americas as well as Indians who migrated in search of work were moved by opportunities for economic betterment. Others, like the Irish who fled the "potato famine", were driven by desperate economic circumstances at home. They were economic refugees in modern terminology. Nonconformists and Jews fled persecution in Europe. Africans in North America were sold into slavery and Indians moved as indentured labour to Sri Lanka. Still others were penal offenders who were deported as far as Australia.

In recent years there have been several significant changes in mass migration between countries. After having stabilized — even declined as in the case of Germany — during the first half of the 1980s, immigration flows to some developed countries increased[10] during the last three years of the 1980s. The most dramatic flows were into the United States of America and Germany. There were new destinations such as Japan and Taiwan Province of China, to which migrants from other parts of Asia were attracted. Countries in southern Europe, such as Greece, Italy and Spain which had been countries of net emigration, became countries of net immigration. After the major upheaval in the Persian Gulf region in 1990-1991, labour migration to West Asia also slowed down. The size and composition of immigrant (foreign born) populations changed substantially. High unemployment in most developing countries made for increasing animosity towards immigrants.

Immigration into the former Federal Republic of Germany has increased since 1983. The largest gains were towards the end of the last decade. The number of immigrants rose to 900,000 in 1988 and exceeded 1.5 million in 1989, from 600,000 on average during 1986-1987. The bulk of them came from Eastern Europe and the former Soviet Union. Among them a large proportion were of German ancestry (Aussiedler), with a right to German citizenship, and Germans from the former German Democratic Republic (GDR). Together, these two groups accounted for about 50 per cent of all immigrants to the country in 1989, compared to 28 per cent the previous year. Immigrants from outside Eastern Europe and the former Soviet Union also increased but at significantly more modest rates. Non-European immigrants, including people from Turkey, totalled 213,000 in 1988 and 245,000 in 1989, representing 24 and 16 per cent, respectively, of all immigrants.

The continuing deterioration in economic conditions in Eastern European countries and the former Soviet Union, the uncertainties associated with the political and economic changes taking place in the region, and the relaxation of travel restrictions played a role in increasing these flows. But the much feared massive movements from Eastern Europe and the former Soviet Union have not occurred so far.

The number of immigrants admitted to the United States, refugees excluded, jumped from 640,000 in 1988 to 1.1 million in 1989 and reached a record high of 1.5 million in 1990, mainly consequent upon the implementation of the 1986 Immigration Reform and Control Act. The 1986 Act, among other things, provided for the legalization of the status of undocumented migrants who had entered the United States before January 1982 and agricultural labourers who had worked in the country during 1984-1986. These categories added an estimated 480,000 and 880,000, respectively, to the number of legal immigrants in 1989 and 1990. Without them, the flow of immigrants during these years would be roughly of the same magnitude as at the beginning of the 1980s, about 550,000 per year. Among the latter, family reunion is the major legal reason for admitting new arrivals in the United States.[11]

During the 1980s, Italy and to a less extent Spain and Greece emerged as labour importing countries. Descendants of former emigrants to Latin America were given the right to Italian or Spanish citizenship. The number of illegal immigrants entering these countries is believed to have increased significantly. Seasonal workers from the Maghreb countries (Morocco, Algeria and Tunisia) have for some time gone to work in Italian fishing ports and in agriculture, as have Poles and Yugoslavians. They have become more visible lately as they reach the big cities and become street vendors. There also was a highly visible inflow of Albanians in 1991. Albanians, particularly those of Greek descent, headed for Greece and more than 60,000 of them legally entered that country during the first nine months of 1991.[12] The relative economic prosperity of southern European countries as compared to the economies in transition and developing countries acted as a magnet.

Net flows of migrants to Japan have increased steadily since 1979. In the second half of the 1980s, the number rose substantially. The net flow of foreigners (arrivals less departures) was estimated at 50,000 in 1986 and rose to 150,000 in 1990. However, the number of illegal residents must also have increased substantially. In fact, the number arrested by the authorities in 1990 was five times that in 1985. Among those arrested, Asians, in particular from Bangladesh and Pakistan, figured prominently.

There are several reasons for the increase in the number of

illegal workers in Japan. The Japanese economy expanded considerably, raising labour demand. As the Japanese population became more educated, it became cheaper to employ immigrants in strenuous and menial work. The slow-down in the demand for immigrant labour in the oil-producing countries of West Asia also induced workers in emigrant countries to turn to Japan as a destination.

Migration to West Asia is estimated to have declined in the late 1980s as suggested by the smaller outflow of people from the major labour-sending countries of South Asia, particularly India and Pakistan.[13] The most dramatic development in a migrant population took place consequent upon the Iraqi invasion of Kuwait in August 1990. Some 2.5 million immigrant workers and dependants were forced to flee Iran, Iraq and Kuwait.[14] Most of them were from Egypt, Jordan and Yemen. Governments had to face a drop in the flow of labour remittances and bear the costs of repatriation, including outlay for the subsistence of returnees. The workers faced a prospect of prolonged unemployment. In Jordan the unemployment rate rose to over 25 per cent in 1991.[15] Costs related to the absorption and reintegration of the Jordanian/Palestinian refugees were estimated at $3 billion for the period 1992-1994.[16]

### 2. An increasing foreign population?

In the present climate of economic recession, objections to liberal immigration policies have risen to the top of the political agenda in many European countries. Immigrants are seen as competing with natives for employment, housing and welfare benefits, and strong feelings have been aroused by the insistence by new groups of immigrants on observing ethnic customs which run counter to the customs or even the laws of the host country.

The composition of the stock of foreigners living in European countries has changed during the last 15 to 20 years (see table 5.5). In the early 1970s, nationals of other European countries formed the vast majority of the foreign population living in European countries, ranging from 95 per cent in Sweden to 51 per cent in the Netherlands. At that time, immigrant labour came mainly from

*Table 5.5*

Composition of foreign population in selected European countries (*percentage*)

| Origin | Belgium | | France | | Germany | | Netherlands | | Sweden | | Switzerland | |
|---|---|---|---|---|---|---|---|---|---|---|---|---|
| | 1970 | 1989 | 1970 | 1985 | 1974 | 1989 | 1974 | 1990 | 1970 | 1989 | 1974 | 1989 |
| AFRICA | 8.0 | 20.0 | 34.6 | 44.5 | 1.7 | .. | 10.5 | 23.1 | 0.6 | 3.1 | .. | .. |
| Algeria | 0.9 | 1.2 | 20.7 | 23.7 | .. | 0.1 | .. | .. | .. | .. | .. | .. |
| Morocco | 5.6 | 15.7 | 7.6 | 5.9 | .. | 1.3 | 10.5 | 23.1 | 0.2 | 0.3 | .. | .. |
| AMERICAS | 2.5 | .. | 1.2 | .. | 2.4 | .. | 3.8 | 1.7 | 1.9 | 7.8 | 1.0 | .. |
| ASIA | 3.9 | .. | 3.0 | 4.2 | 27.7 | 41.3 | 23.6 | 32.8 | 2.0 | 19.7 | 2.5 | .. |
| Turkey | 2.9 | 9.3 | 1.5 | 4.2 | 24.9 | 33.3 | 19.8 | 29.8 | 1.0 | 5.3 | 2.5 | 5.7 |
| EUROPE | 83.5 | 63.6 | 61.1 | 37.4 | 66.2 | 48.0 | 50.9 | 25.7 | 94.5 | 66.9 | 88.5 | 89.3 |
| Non-EU | 6.7 | 2.2 | 4.8 | .. | 25.5 | 20.6 | 5.1 | 2.1 | 72.7 | 51.6 | 7.3 | 18.4 |
| Yugoslavia | 0.7 | 0.6 | 2.0 | .. | 17.2 | 12.6 | 4.1 | 2.0 | 9.0 | 8.7 | 3.3 | 11.2 |
| Poland | 2.6 | .. | 2.7 | .. | 1.1 | 4.5 | .. | .. | 1.0 | 3.2 | .. | 0.5 |
| EU | 76.7 | 61.4 | 52.8 | 37.4 | 40.8 | 27.4 | 45.8 | 23.7 | 21.9 | 15.3 | 81.2 | 70.9 |
| Italy | 35.8 | 27.3 | 13.5 | 8.0 | 15.3 | 10.7 | 6.2 | 2.6 | 1.9 | 0.9 | 52.1 | 36.5 |
| Greece | 3.2 | 2.4 | .. | .. | 9.8 | 6.1 | 1.3 | .. | 3.4 | 1.5 | 1.0 | 0.8 |
| Portugal | 0.1 | 1.7 | 22.1 | 21.7 | 2.9 | 1.5 | 2.5 | 1.2 | 0.4 | 0.3 | 0.0 | 6.6 |
| Spain | 9.7 | 6.0 | 14.5 | 7.7 | 6.6 | 2.6 | 9.9 | 2.7 | 1.0 | 0.6 | 11.4 | 11.0 |
| OTHERS | 2.2 | 7.0 | 0.0 | 13.9 | 2.0 | 9.3 | 11.3 | 16.7 | 1.0 | 2.5 | 8.0 | 7.5 |
| Total | 100.0 | 100.0 | 100.0 | 100.0 | 100.0 | 100.0 | 100.0 | 100.0 | 100.0 | 100.0 | 100.0 | 100.0 |
| MEMO ITEM: | | | | | | | | | | | | |
| Total foreigners (in thousands) | 696.3 | 880.8 | 3 442.4 | 3 462.2 | 4 127.4 | 4 845.9 | 316.3 | 642.0 | 411.3 | 456.0 | 1 064.5 | 1 040.3 |

Source: World Population Monitoring 1989 (United Nations publication, Sales No. E.89.XIII.12); and Organisation for Economic Cooperation and Development, Continuous Reporting System on Migration (SOPEMI) 1990, (Paris, 1991).

Greece, Italy, Portugal and Spain. During the 1980s, Europeans became a smaller proportion of the foreign population. The number of Greeks and Italians was halved in Sweden from 1970 to 1989 and so was the number of Spaniards in the former Federal Republic of Germany during the same period. The stock of Spanish and Italian immigrants was also considerably reduced in France. Yet Europeans formed the bulk of foreigners in many European countries including Belgium, Germany, Sweden and Switzerland. However, according to a survey conducted in the 12 country members of the then EEC in 1988, European immigrants were rarely perceived as the dominant foreign group.[17]

Changes in the composition of the foreign population may be one reason behind the recent increase in xenophobia in some of these countries. It is often claimed that immigrants from different racial, religious and cultural backgrounds present a threat to values of the native society, although similar concerns were voiced in the past when immigration was predominantly white and Christian.[18]

Antagonism towards foreigners usually intensifies in the face of deteriorating economic conditions. Immigrants are common scapegoats for the real or imaginary threats that recession and economic difficulties bring. Negative expectations of an uncertain and insecure future tend to exacerbate the problem. The issue is frequently exploited by extremist parties which single out foreigners as the root of economic and political difficulties.[19] Foreigners, for instance, are generally blamed for the increase in unemployment even if this is a concomitant part of swings in business activity or of adjustment to changing international economic conditions. Unemployment among the foreign population is usually higher than among the local population (see chapter 3).

## 3. *Outstanding problems*

The rapid growth of youthful populations without productive employment opportunities in developing countries, the political and economic disintegration in the former Soviet Union and in Eastern Europe, and the slow growth of the ageing populations in developed countries, all contribute to the continuing flow of migrants to developed countries. There is open hostility against migrant populations. These hostilities compound the serious difficulties immigrants face in integrating into the economic, social and political life of the host country. There are large numbers of undocumented workers whose rights need to be safeguarded.

Difficulties of integration and acceptance have their roots in the immigrants' lack of full legal rights in the country of residence. Immigrants with open rights to work would not accept wages lower than those of the local population in exchange for protection. Several countries have begun to award such rights. Others have intensified efforts to legalize the position of undocumented migrants and to impose severe punishments on those hiring illegal immigrants. Some developed countries see more economic assistance to countries from which potential immigrants may come as a means of preventing such flows. This is a rather long-term process whose impact on migrant inflows will not be felt for some time. The United Nations adopted in 1990 an International Convention on the Protection of the Rights of All Migrant Workers and Members of Their Families.[20] Very few countries have so far ratified or acceded to this Convention.

## C. REFUGEES

People have always moved across borders, some voluntarily seeking better lives, others pushed out as refugees by natural disasters, civil strife or expulsion by Governments. Another category of migrants are refugees in their own countries, victims of natural disaster or military conflicts. These immigrants and refugees, whether inland or across borders are of major economic and social concern both to individual governments and the international community at large: to individual governments because for humanitarian, health and economic reasons, it becomes necessary to divert resources to take care of these people; to the international community, in addition, because of threats to peace and security which arise from tensions between home and host governments and the rights and entitlements of immigrant workers. This section will contain a brief account of the magnitude of the problems of refugees and a survey of policies and programmes addressed to solve them.

## 1. A problem of growing magnitude

The world refugee population increased dramatically during the 1980s and grew further in 1991 and 1992. In 1990, there were 17 million refugees, compared to 9.6 million in 1980. The war in the Persian Gulf created a refugee population of 5 million and the conflict in the former Yugoslavia another 2 million. For the first time since the 1939-1945 Second World War, there are again large refugee populations in Europe. The conflicts in the former Soviet Union have also created a considerable number of refugees, although reliable estimates are yet hard to come by. There was also an outflow of 200,000 refugees from Myanmar in 1991. The situation improved remarkably in Central America with peace in Nicaragua, although Haiti continued to be a source of refugees. Agreements signed at the Paris Conference on Cambodia in October 1991 initiated a process for the return of refugees to that country. The fall of the Najbullah government in Afghanistan again opened prospects for a similar return. In Africa the refugee situation continued to worsen, especially in Angola, Ethiopia, Mali, Mozambique, Somalia and the Sudan. In Africa too, both famine and warfare drove people from their homes and productive activities and, as in Europe, parties to conflicts stood in the way of humanitarian relief to refugees. Desperate armed gangs regularly looted supplies meant for starving people. Resources of relief agencies, both intergovernmental and voluntary, were extended to their limits in handling problems which had increased vastly both in magnitude and complexity.

In 1990 there were 5.7 million refugees in Africa (see table 5.6). Eighty six per cent of them originated from Angola, Ethiopia, Mali, Mozambique, Rwanda, Somalia and the Sudan. They have been rendered refugees by two sets of circumstances: armed con-

## Table 5.6
## Refugee population in countries or areas of asylum

|  | Early 1985 | Early 1989 | 31 December 1990 |
|---|---|---|---|
| AFRICA, of which | 2 929 450 | 4 349 187 | 5 720 455 |
| Algeria | 167 000 | 170 000 | 169 100 |
| Burundi | 256 600 | 267 400 | 268 403 |
| Côte d'Ivoire | 0 | 500 | 300 000 |
| Ethiopia | 59 100 | 680 500 | 772 764 |
| Guinea | .. | .. | 325 000 |
| Malawi | .. | 628 000 | 927 000 |
| Sierra Leone | 200 | 80 | 125 000 |
| Somalia | 700 000 | 600 000 | 600 000 |
| Sudan | 690 000 | 745 000 | 780 000 |
| United Republic of Tanzania | 178 500 | 266 500 | 265 184 |
| Uganda | 151 000 | 95 000 | 142 400 |
| Zaire | 317 000 | 340 700 | 416 435 |
| Zambia | 96 500 | 143 500 | 138 044 |
| Zimbabwe | 46 440 | 174 500 | 122 302 |
| ASIA, of which | 5 023 781 | 7 051 860 | 7 973 764 |
| China | 279 750 | 284 018 | 287 000 |
| Hong Kong | 11 896 | 25 749 | 52 041 |
| Iran (Islamic Republic of) | 1 900 000 | 2 800 000 | 4 000 000 |
| Pakistan | 2 500 000 | 3 258 000 | 3 185 265 |
| Thailand | 128 439 | 108 634 | 101 347 |
| EUROPE of which | 674 400 | 766 500 | .. |
| France | 167 300 | 184 500 | .. |
| Sweden | 90 600 | 148 500 | 183 360 |
| Germany | 126 600 | 150 000 | 156 000 |
| United Kingdom | 135 000 | 101 300 | .. |
| LATIN AMERICA of which | 362 400 | 152 500 [a] | 135 561 [a] |
| Costa Rica | 16 800 | 28 600 | 42 433 |
| Mexico | 175 000 | 46 400 | 50 560 |
| South America | 22 200 | 23 400 | 20 985 |

*(continued)*

*Table 5.6 (continued)*

|  | Early 1985 | Early 1989 | 31 December 1990 |
|---|---|---|---|
| OTHERS | 1 446 500 | 1 475 000 | .. |
| Australia | 89 000 | 91 000 | 97 915 |
| Canada | 353 000 | 380 000 | .. |
| New Zealand | 4 500 | 4 000 | 5 424 |
| United States of America | 1 000 000 | 1 000 000 | .. |
| SUBTOTAL | 10 436 531 | 13 795 047 | .. |
| Palestinian refugees | 2 093 545 [b] | 2 334 637 [b] | 2 422 514 [b] |
| TOTAL | 12 530 076 | 16 129 684 | .. |

Sources: United Nations, *Population Newsletter, No. 51* (June 1991); Office of the United Nations High Commissioner for Refugees, "UNHCR activities financed by voluntary funds: report for 1990-1991 and proposed programmes and budget for 1992" (A/AC.96/774, parts I to VI; Report of the Commissioner-General of the United Nations Relief and Works Agency for Palestine Refugees in the Near East, 1 July 1990 to 30 June 1991, (Official Records of the General Assembly, Forty-sixth Session, Supplement 13 (A/46/13)).

a  Does not include displaced persons; if included, it is estimated that figures for the region would be 1,193,500 for early 1989 and 880,000 at the end of 1990.
b  Refers to the situation as of 30 June and includes only those people registered by the United Nations Relief and Works Agency for Palestine Refugees in the Near East, which is probably less than the recorded population.

flict and drought. Soldiers and armed bands have destroyed their lives, with drought conditions pushing further more people from a precarious living to helpless refugee status.

In Africa, several countries are both the source of and host to large refugee populations. Ethiopia, Somalia and the Sudan are outstanding examples.

Low income per capita in host countries, poor infrastructure and the scarcity of well-trained personnel have placed tremendous burdens on host countries. Refugees from Mozambique who fled to Malawi were mostly from rural areas and had ethnic ties with the Malawi population. Many were allowed to settle spontaneously in Malawi villages. By the end of 1990 there were 930,000 refugees in Malawi. Soon, there was no more land for them to cultivate. Health conditions of Mozambican refugees have deteriorated recently and diseases commonly associated with malnutrition have emerged, particularly in the refugee camps located in the south of the country.[21]

Similarly, refugees from Liberia were welcomed by host populations who showed enormous hospitality by sharing their meager food supplies, shelter and land for farming purposes. Liberian refugees were not put in camps. Two years later, tensions developed between the host population and refugees, particularly in Côte d'Ivoire and especially in villages and cities further from the border whose inhabitants did not have ethnic affinities with the refugees.

The situation became critical in Kenya where the refugee population has soared from 15,000 at the end of 1990 to 340,000 in mid-1992. Most refugees in Kenya suffer from acute malnutrition. Camps were overcrowded with deficient water supplies and insecure where they were close to the border. Kenya itself was under a severe drought and hard pressed to meet its own food needs.[22]

Armed conflict has obstructed the delivery of food, medical and other supplies to refugee camps. Some armed groups have prevented the flow of relief supplies lest they should feed opposing armies rather than refugees on the opposite side. In other instances, armed gangs have looted supplies as well as transport equipment.[23] Measles and dehydration caused by diarrhoea are common causes of death. Outbreaks of scurvy, pellagra, beri-beri and other deficiency diseases are common.

In Asia, there were some 7 million refugees, excluding 2.3 million Palestinian refugees. Five million of them were refugees from the war in Afghanistan. One third of the total population of Afghanistan were refugees, 2 million in Iran and about 3 million in Pakistan. They are well integrated in Iran, where only 3 per cent of them live in camps. They have settled in urban areas and have joined the local labour market. Since 1990 there has been some voluntary repatriation and about 200,000 refugees are estimated to have returned home. Fresh fighting in Kabul in August 1992 has reduced prospects of fast repatriation somewhat.

After signing the Comprehensive Political Settlement of the Cambodian Conflict agreed upon in Paris in October 1991, a major repatriation exercise was organized for the 350,000 Cambodian refugees and displaced people living in Thailand. However, the operation is beset with many problems. Many parts of the Cambodian territory are mined and casualties and accidents run high. A land-mine awareness programme was being implemented and some areas of the Cambodian territory were surveyed. There was a shortage of identified arable land on which the returnees could be settled. Access to water was another major constraint.[24]

As solutions were being found for some groups of refugees and displaced persons, new flows of refugees began in Myanmar and Iraq. Within a year beginning March 1991, there were 191,000 refugees from Myanmar in Bangladesh. Conditions in the camps were deplorable as only 54 per cent of refugees had shelter. Clean water was in short supply and there was a high incidence of disease.[25] The Persian Gulf conflict also created new flows of refugees and displaced persons. By the end of May 1991, the Iraqi refugee population reached 1.4 million in Iran and 400,000 in Turkey, up from 50,000 and 7,500, respectively, two months earlier. Many have since returned to Iraq.[26]

There was a sharp increase in the number of Vietnamese refugees, particularly of "boat people", after 1985. The number of Vietnamese refugees registered in UNHCR camps totalled 32,000 in 1986. In 1989, they amounted to more than 100,000. Most of them landed in Hong Kong. In June 1989, the International Conference on Indochinese Refugees (ICIR) adopted a Comprehensive Plan of Action (CPA) by which screening procedures were introduced in receiving countries in order to identify and separate genuine refugees who qualified for resettlement from economic migrants who were to be repatriated. Inflows of boat people fell off in 1990 and 1991. Some forced repatriation from Hong Kong to Hanoi took place at the end of 1991. Others returned spontaneously. Further, under the Orderly Departure Programme (ODP) in force, opportunities for legal migration were created.[27]

Trends in Latin America are more encouraging than those observed in Africa, Asia and Europe. A plan of action for voluntary repatriation of refugees and other displaced persons in Central America and for integration of those who opted for not returning to their home countries was set up by the International Conference on Central American Refugees (CIREFCA) convened by Costa Rica, El Salvador, Guatemala, Honduras, Mexico and Nicaragua in 1988. The end of the civil war in Nicaragua and the elections there in March 1990 contributed to the decrease in the number of refugees in Central America. With Nicaraguan refugees returning to their country, all camps in Honduras and Costa Rica are now closed. With the end of the civil conflict in El Salvador in December 1991, the number of returnees may have increased even further in 1992.[28] These successes in Central America were blighted by developments in Haiti in October 1991 with a new flow of refugees, most of them heading from Haiti to the United States. Some reached the Bahamas, Cuba and Jamaica. Others, with the assistance of UNHCR, were temporarily settled in Honduras, Suriname and Venezuela. From October 1991 to June 1992, some 37,000 Haitians reached the American naval base in Cuba. Approximately 30 per cent of them had their claims considered as legitimate and were given permanent asylum in the United States. The rest were repatriated.[29]

The number of asylum applications filed with the U.S. Immigration and Naturalization Service (INS) declined by almost 30 per cent from 191,000 in 1989 to 135,000 in 1990. People from the former Soviet Union constituted the largest group, followed by Vietnamese. During the period 1985-1990, a total of 554,000 people were accepted as refugees in the United States.[30] The number of people seeking asylum in Canada has increased substantially. In Canada, about 70 per cent of applicants are accepted as refugees.

Prior to the crisis in Yugoslavia, there were substantial increases in the number of applicants seeking asylum in Europe. Asylum seekers in Europe averaged 120,000 annually during the period 1980-1985. Their numbers jumped to 325,000 per year during the period 1986-1991, reaching 537,000 in 1991. That massive increase was mostly accounted for by asylum seekers from Eastern Europe. The increase, except from the former Yugoslavia and to a lesser extent Romania, was largely due to a relaxation of travel restrictions subsequent to political changes in the countries of that region.

Germany has been the country of choice for a high proportion of asylum seekers. There were 256,000 applicants in 1991, compared to 20,000 in 1983. Forty eight per cent of all asylum seekers in Europe did so in Germany in 1991, compared to 30 per cent in 1983.

Ethnic and religious conflicts in the former Yugoslavia have created the worst refugee crisis in Europe since the Second World War. Both the size of the problem as well as its nature evoke painful memories of that war. Processes of "ethnic cleansing" and detention camps for those persecuted reveal in some degree the barbarities in Europe in the 1930s and 1940s. In mid-1992 there were more than 2.3 million refugees, with about 1.8 million relocating themselves within the republics that formed the former Yugoslavia and 500,000 finding refuge abroad. This sudden exodus has tested the hosting capacity of receiving countries to the limits. Some countries are increasingly reluctant to accept more refugees in their territories, while others are raising border controls.

The potential for larger outflows of refugees from Eastern Europe and the former Soviet Union will remain strong for quite some time. As the old states are dismantled and new nation states are formed and claims for cultural homogeneity within each state are advanced, ethnic tolerance and co-habitation will come under severe strain. Their victims will escape as refugees.[31]

## 2. Is the status of refugees under threat?

The world refugee population doubled from 1980 to 1991. Most of the refugees originate in developing countries and are given temporary asylum in other developing countries. The increase of refugee inflows creates additional difficulties for receiving developing countries which usually lack resources to promote the well-being of their own populations. Although developed countries are better equipped than developing countries to deal with the inflows and the refugee populations they shelter are distinctly smaller than in developing countries, recent developments have been creating many problems for them and potential refugees.

Administrative costs and those for providing social security to asylum seekers have soared as their number increased. There has been a considerable buildup of unprocessed applications. The longer the period of waiting, the higher the costs become for providing housing, food and other services for asylum seekers. Costs incurred by the major industrial countries in dealing with asylum seekers reached $7 to $8 billion in 1991. This amounts to about 14 per cent of their development aid to developing countries in 1990.[32] The increase in the number of asylum seekers in Europe has coincided with persistent high unemployment and other economic and social difficulties in those countries, all of which contributed to the intensification of xenophobic sentiments within certain sectors of their populations.

There is an increasing feeling in developed countries that the principle of political asylum is being abused. Many asylum seekers from developing countries are seen as migrants looking for better economic conditions rather than as refugees with a well-founded fear of being persecuted. It is likely that restrictions on labour migration to many developed countries has contributed to the abuse of the refugee principle. Nationals of Eastern Europe and countries of the former Soviet Union have in the past enjoyed more generous treatment in developed countries because they were perceived to be fleeing totalitarianism. Until recently, their numbers were small as movement out of the region was tightly controlled, except on the occasion of political upheavals.[33] With political and economic reform in these regions and the rise in the number of refugees, several countries have questioned the validity of claims for asylum by applicants from Eastern Europe and the former Soviet Union.

Some countries have been changing their asylum-granting practices. Others have started to take measures to prevent people from reaching their territories. Visa requirements have been imposed on nationals from certain countries, fines imposed on airlines for bringing in passengers without proper documentation and surveillance increased at borders to prevent asylum seekers from crossing illegally.

In May 1992, the United States Coast Guard pushed boats full of potential Haitian refugees back to Haiti, preventing them from presenting their claims. While the aim was primarily to prevent potential migrants from landing, the process does affect refugees in need of protection. There is also a trend to keep asylum seekers in the region of their origin, making it more difficult for them to reach potential countries of refuge in other continents than their own.[34] It thus seems that the right to seek asylum is increasingly threatened by migratory pressures.

Most countries have also started to apply more strictly the definition of refugees contained in the 1951 Convention. The Convention defines a "refugee" as any person who "owing to well-founded fear of being persecuted for reasons of race, religion, nationality and is unable, or owing to such fear is unwilling to avail himself of the protection of that country;..."[35] Many people who have fled their countries of origin due to massive disrespect for human rights or other man-made disasters may not be able to prove that they have a well-founded reason to fear that their individual lives were in jeopardy. The percentage of people whose claims have been considered genuine has declined recently in many countries.

Despite declining approval rates, few have been forcefully repatriated. Many are allowed to stay on humanitarian grounds under a status not covered under the Convention. The number of applicants for asylum who have been permitted to stay on humanitarian grounds exceeds the number of people accepted as refugees under the 1951 Geneva Convention. Although this offers some minimum protection to refugees, it is unstable since Governments may withdraw permission to stay at any time.[36]

These new restrictions jeopardize the position of bona fide asylum seekers in two ways. Access to certain countries has become more difficult for them. Once in a country, access to full protection under the law has become more remote. To prevent the abuse of refugee status whilst regulating the flow of migrants for other reasons is an urgent challenge for the international community.

# Notes

[1] United Nations, "Levels and trends of contraceptive use as assessed in 1988", (United Nations publication, Sales No. E.89.XIII.4), (New York, 1989).

[2] Napaporn Havanon, John Knodal, and Werasit Sittitnal, "Family Size and Family Well Being in Thailand", Population Studies Centre Research Report No. 90-191, University of Michigan, August 1990.

[3] United Nations, "World Population Monitoring 1991", Population Studies No. 126, United Nations publication (Sales No. E.92.XIII.2, New York, 1992), p. 20.

[4] Defined as the combination of a city's urban core, the surrounding built-up area that is economically oriented to that core, without regard to administrative municipal boundaries.

[5] Dhira Phantumvanit and Wanai Liengcharernsit, "Coming to terms with Bangkok's environment problems", Environment and Urbanization, vol. 1, no. 1, April 1989, pp. 31-39.

[6] UNFPA, "Population, Resources and the Environment. The Critical Challenges", UNFPA (New York, 1991), p. 61.

[7] N. Sadik, "The State of World Population 1990", UNFPA (New York, 1990); and J. Hardoy and D. Satterthwaite, "Squatter Citizen: Life in the Urban Third World". Earthscan Publications Ltd., (London, U.K., 1989).

[8] HABITAT, "Urbanization and sustained development in the third world: an unrecognized global issue," United Nations Centre for Human Settlement (Habitat), (Nairobi, 1989), p. 39.

[9] See Stark, Oded and J. Edward Taylor, "Migration incentives, migration types: The role of relative deprivation", The Economic Journal, 101 (September 1991), pp. 1163-1178.

[10] Within the countries considered here, France is the exception in the period 1980-1985. International migration inflows actually increased in 1981 and 1982 due to the regularizations of illegal immigrants that took place during the period.

[11] During the period 1985-1989, about 70 per cent of the immigrants admitted to the United States were family members either of American citizens or of permanent residents. See United Nations, "World Population Monitoring 1991", (United Nations Sales Publication No. E.92.XIII.2), 1992, pp. 173-174.

[12] Financial Times, 26 September 1991.

[13] United Nations, "World Population Monitoring 1991", p. 181.

[14] Note by the United Nations Secretariat on the economic, social and environmental consequences of the situation between Iraq and Kuwait and its short-, medium- and long-term implications, (E/1991/102), 24 June 1991.

[15] United Nations, "World Economic Survey 1992", (United Nations Sales Publication No. 92.E.II.C.1), p. 41.

[16] ESCWA, "The return of Jordanians/Palestinians from Kuwait: economic and social implications for Jordan", (mimeo), September 1991.

[17] Lebon, A., "Ressortissants communautaires et étrangers originaires des pays tiers dans l'Europe des douze" in Revue Européenne des Migrations Internationales, vol. 6, no. 1, 1990, pp. 185-202.

[18] In France, for instance, there was strong resistance against Italian, Spanish and Polish immigrants reaching the country in the 1930s as well as against Belgians and Swiss who settled there at the end of the nineteenth century. Threats to the national identity were constantly mentioned and expulsion was demanded. For details, see Videlier, P. "Alerte: immigrés!" in Le Monde Diplomatique, September 1991, p. 15.

[19] Support for right-wing parties that have an explicit anti-migration platform has recently increased in Austria, France, Germany and Switzerland. The same trends were observed during the economic recession of the early 1980s and other periods of economic crisis.

[20] General Assembly resolutio119n 45/158.

[21] Report of the United Nations High Commissioner for Refugees, Assistance to refugees and displaced persons in Malawi (A/46/433), 11 September 1991.

[22] UNHCR, Information Bulletin on Kenya, 16 March 1992 and UNHCR, "Update on refugee developments in Africa: alarming death rate among new refugees from drought-stricken areas", 24 April 1992 (mimeo).

[23] See, for example, a part of the experience in Somalia in "The Situation in Somalia, Report of the Secretary-General, S/23829/Add.1, para. 32.

[24] UNHCR, Information Bulletin No. 4 on Cambodian Repatriation Operation, 14 April 1992; "De-mining", in *Refugees*, no. 88, January 1992, pp. 12-15; and Hovy, B., "Southeast Asian refugees: tide set to turn?", in *Population*, vol. 17, no. 12, December 1991, p. 2.

[25] UNHCR, Information Bulletin on Bangladesh, 7 April 1992.

[26] UNHCR, Information Bulletin No. 8 on Operations in the Persian Gulf Region, 27 January 1992.

[27] UNHCR, "Report of the United Nations High Commissioner For Refugees", ECOSOC substantive session of 1992 (E/1992/59), June 1992.

[28] UNHCR, "UNHCR activities financed by voluntary funds: report for 1990-91 and proposed programmes and budget for 1992", Executive Committee of the High Commissioner's Programme, forty-second session, 26 July 1991 (A/AC.96/774 (Part IV)).

[29] *The New York Times*, 2 July 1992, p. A9.

[30] United States, Immigration and Naturalization Service, *1990 Statistical Yearbook of the Immigration and Naturalization Service*, Washington, D.C., 1991.

[31] The process of state formation within the former Soviet Union, for instance, may result in further refugee movements, particularly of Russian minorities living outside Russia. Blaschke, J., "East-West migration in Europe and international aid as a means to reduce the need for emigration", Joint ILO-UNHCR meeting on international aid as a means to reduce the need for emigration, Geneva, May 1992.

[32] *Financial Times*, 4 March 1992.

[33] For instance, Hungary in 1956 and the former Czechoslovakia in 1968. Economic Commission for Europe, "Economic Survey for Europe 1992", chapter 7, pp. 259-262.

[34] "Continuity and change" in *Refugees*, no. 81, December 1990, pp. 27-29.

[35] Convention relating to the status of refugees, signed at Geneva, on 28 July 1951, in United Nations Treaty Series, vol. 189, 1954, p. 152.

[36] According to one author, in 1987, Germany granted Convention status to only 2 per cent of asylum applicants, while almost 70 per cent received de facto refugee status. In Norway, 80 per cent were given de facto refugee status while only 2 per cent received Convention status. See Loescher, G., "The European . . .", p. 625.

# 6

# Hunger, malnutrition
# and food supplies

MANY millions of people in the world go hungry, although the global supply of food is sufficient to feed them adequately. Innovations such as the "green revolution", large investments in agricultural infrastructure and extension services, and improvements in markets, ensure a global output of food adequate to meet nutritional needs. However, the results of these initiatives have been uneven. The nutritional situation has shown signs of improvement in Asia, long-term deterioration in Africa, and stagnation or some worsening in Latin America.[1] In the economies in transition, the collapse of economic institutions has reduced output during the past few years.

Famine and hunger are caused primarily by a lack of purchasing power on the part of either individuals and families wanting to buy food or of entire countries wanting to import food they do not produce.

A lack of purchasing power is characteristic of poverty. The poor have neither an adequate income nor assets that can be exchanged or sold. Food distribution within poor families often denies adequate supplies to the weaker members — women and children. In many countries, inefficient distribution systems raise the price of food beyond the capacity of the poor to feed themselves.

Man-made and natural disasters also create conditions of famine and hunger. In 1991 there were 40 million people around the world for whom emergency food aid was the only lifeline.[2] Natural disasters destroyed crops, infrastructure, and opportunities for employment. The absence of infrastructure for flood control, irrigation and transport and the incapacity of Governments to provide urgent assistance worsened the destruction caused by natural disasters. Man-made disasters, mainly in the form of civil war and other internal conflicts, destroyed both crops and employment opportunities and obstructed the flow of food supplies. Violence and villainy in such countries as Somalia and the former Yugoslavia also kept food from the hungry.

## A.  INCIDENCE OF HUNGER AND MALNUTRITION

An estimated 550 million people were hungry in the world in 1990. About 300 million, almost 60 per cent, lived in Asia; about 30 per cent lived in Africa and about 10 per cent in West Asia, Latin America and the Caribbean. The largest increase in the number of chronically hungry people in the 1980s was in Africa, a result of high population growth, poor economic performance and man-made and natural disasters. The situation also deteriorated in Latin America and the Caribbean;[3] it improved in East and South Asia.

The short-term prognosis is not promising. In sub-Saharan Africa, the number of hungry people is projected to increase to 165 million. The largest concentration of the hungry will continue to be in Asia, mainly in South Asia and overwhelmingly in rural areas.[4] In Latin America and the Caribbean, the share of the population remaining poor will be stable, and the absolute number will rise to 296 million.

In developing countries in 1987-1989 the dietary energy supply, or supply of calories, was 72 per cent of that in developed countries. It had risen two percentage points since 1979-1981. By the end of the 1980s, the average person was deficient in daily per capita supply of calories in 38 out of 103 developing countries. The national aggregate figures mask wide variations in daily per capita intake within the same country. For instance, in China undernutrition is reported in the western and central provinces and in minority autonomous regions. In the Philippines, undernutrition was worst in rural areas, especially among children of tenant farmers and agricultural labourers. Many children in urban areas also suffered from malnutrition.[5]

Hunger and malnutrition in India were most heavily concentrated in the poorest regions in the eastern and central states. Undernutrition was worse among women than among men and more common in northern than in southern India. In Latin America and the Caribbean, earlier improvements in nutritional status were reversed in some countries during the 1980s. Only Colombia, Costa Rica and Cuba were able to reduce poverty and hunger.

Hunger and undernutrition are widespread in Africa. The incidence of hunger is more severe in rural areas and among children and women. Undernutrition among children is highest in southern Egypt. The prevalence of hunger and undernutrition increased throughout the continent during the 1980s.

## B.  UNDERNOURISHED CHILDREN

Despite the increased food aid, hunger among children remains an agonizing problem. The visible signs of protein-energy malnutrition or protein-calorie malnutrition among children are stunting (below-normal height for a given age), wasting (below-normal weight for a given height) and being underweight (below-normal weight for a given age, a measure usually used for children under five years). Malnutrition intensifies the duration and severity of such diseases as diarrhoea and measles.

Underweight children are serious problems in most developing countries, as table 6.1 indicates.[6] The total number rose from 167 million in 1980 to 188 million in 1990. The largest increases were in sub-Saharan Africa and in South Asia. The largest majority (78 per cent) live in Asia. The proportion of underweight children to all children increased in sub-Saharan Africa.

A number of examples illustrate the unfortunate situation. The prevalence of stunted or underweight children in the Philippines was worst in rural areas, among children of tenant farmers and agricultural labourers. In Pakistan between 1985 and 1987, 52

*Table 6.1*

Underweight children[a] in developing countries, 1980 and 1990

| Region | 1980 Millions | 1980 Percentage | 1990 Millions | 1990 Percentage |
|---|---|---|---|---|
| Sub-Saharan Africa | 21.0 | 29.1 | 30.2 | 30.8 |
| Near East/North Africa | 5.0 | 17.2 | 4.8 | 13.3 |
| South Asia | 89.9 | 63.6 | 101.1 | 58.6 |
| South-East Asia | 23.4 | 42.8 | 22.4 | 37.7 |
| China | 20.4 | 23.8 | 23.6 | 21.0 |
| Central America and Caribbean | 3.1 | 17.7 | 3.0 | 15.3 |
| South America | 4.4 | 13.2 | 3.0 | 8.2 |
| Developing countries | 167.0 | 38.1 | 188.0 | 34.8 |

Source: World Food Council, *The Global State of Hunger and Malnutrition*. 1992 Report (New York, 1992), table 2, p. 8.

a    Under the age of 5 years.

per cent of children under five years were underweight. About 15 per cent showed signs of wasting, and 46 per cent showed signs of stunting. The poor were more disadvantaged.

In the Sudan, stunting, wasting and low birthweight are rife among children and infants. Sixty-three per cent of two-to-five-year-old children are stunted. In 1987, 13 per cent of the young children in northern Sudan were wasted, and the incidence of low birthweight babies was 15 per cent. In Peru, in the mid-1980s, almost 40 per cent of all children under five years of age were stunted. In Brazil, 31 per cent of the children under five years of age suffer from malnutrition. In El Salvador, malnutrition was a major concern. An estimated 44 per cent of the children under five were underweight and nearly a fifth stunted.

## C.  MICRONUTRIENT DEFICIENCIES AND NUTRITIONALLY RELATED DISEASES

Vitamin-A deficiency and the disorders associated with it — xerophthalmia and nutritional blindness — are endemic in large parts of Africa, Asia, Latin America and the Caribbean (see table 6.2). Worldwide, at least 190 million pre-school children are at risk

*Table 6.2*

Populations at risk of and affected by micronutrient
malnutrition, 1991 *(millions)*

| | Iodine deficiency | | Vitamin A deficiency (xerophthalmia) | | Iron deficiency or anaemia |
|---|---|---|---|---|---|
| | At risk | Affected | At risk | Affected | |
| Africa | 150 | 39 | 18 | 1.3 | 206 |
| Americas | 55 | 30 | 2 | 0.1 | 94 |
| South-East Asia | 280 | 100 | 138 | 10.0 | 616 |
| Europe | 82 | 14 | — | — | 27 |
| Eastern Mediterranean | 33 | 12 | 13 | 1.0 | 149 |
| Western Pacific | 405 | 30 | 19 | 1.4 | 1 058 |
| World | 1 005 | 225 | 190 | 13.8 | 2 150 |

Source: World Health Organization (WHO), *National Strategies for Overcoming
Micronutrient Malnutrition* (EB 89/27), table 1.

of vitamin-A deficiency; 14 million of them experience some degree
of xerophthalmia; each year, about 700,000 new cases of severe
vitamin-A deficiency (measured as eye damage) occur, with
approximately 350,000 victims going blind; 60 per cent of them die
shortly after losing their sight.[7] With school-age children and
women of child-bearing age, the estimate swells to about 800 million. A majority of vitamin-A deficient populations are in 37 countries, 18 of them in Africa.[8]

Iodine deficiency has a harmful effect on the growth and
development of children and can cause goitre. It is the most common form of preventable mental retardation. In severe cases it
causes cretinism, deaf-mutism and squint. Iodine deficiency is usually found in mountainous regions and flood-prone areas where the
soil lacks iodine and also in regions where little seafood is eaten.
Globally, about 1,000 million people are at risk of iodine deficiency; about 225 million of them have goitre, and nearly 6 million
suffer from overt cretinism. The problem is most serious in Asia,
with South and East Asia being particularly affected.[9]

Iron deficiency, or anemia, is a common nutritionally related
disease affecting at least 800 million people worldwide.

Measures have been taken at both the national and international levels to combat micronutrient deficiency diseases. These measures include dietary diversification, food fortification and supplementation and public health measures. People have been advised to increase their intake of local foods containing vitamin-A, iodine and iron — for example, green leafy vegetables, orange-coloured vegetables and fruits, pulses and seafood.[10] To reduce vitamin-A deficiency, vitamin-A capsules have been distributed to the public. Promising results were reported in many countries, including Brazil, India, Indonesia and the United Republic of Tanzania.

Iodine deficiency is being controlled by iodizing salt and by the injection of iodized oil. Good results have been realized in many countries, including China, Ecuador, Indonesia, Nepal and Zaire.

Many developing countries began to treat anaemia during pregnancy as part of prenatal care. Haemoglobin assessment and the provision of iron and folate tablets to all pregnant women have become standard procedures whenever prenatal care is provided at maternal and child health clinics.

## D. REGIONAL TRENDS IN FOOD PRODUCTION

One of the reasons why the vast majority of undernourished people in developing countries are so is because their domestic agricultural sector fails to produce sufficient food for their needs, and because variations are not adequately covered by supplies from outside. The relative failure of the developing countries to provide sufficient food for their populations can be judged from their food self-sufficiency ratios.

Of course, self-sufficiency at the level of the individual country need not be a goal of national policy for all countries. Possibilities of trade almost always exist. There is no reason why a country that has a comparative advantage in production of non-food items should not import food in exchange for the former. However, not many countries are in such a position in the early stages of their development. Moreover, the poor rural dwellers are usually those who are

the worst nourished within a country. Their poverty and undernourishment are often a result of not being able to produce enough food
to supply directly their own needs for nourishment and, if necessary,
to exchange for cash to purchase those other food requirements that
would assure them a balanced and nutritious diet. If increases in
their food production were an effective use of their resources, this
would go a long way to solving nutrition problems.

In the past 30 years the developed market economies have
moved from near self-sufficiency in major food groups to having a
substantial surplus (see table 6.3). The economies in transition and
the developing countries saw their self-sufficiency ratios fall[11] and
their share of world imports of food increase. In every developing
region there was a decline in self-sufficiency, except Asia where the
self-sufficiency ratio, however, stayed below 100.

*Table 6.3*
Shares in world food exports, food imports and food self-sufficiency
ratios in the developed economies, the economies in transition and
developing countries, 1961-1964 and 1983-1986[a]

|  | Developed market economies | Economies in transition | Developing countries |
|---|---|---|---|
| Share of world exports |  |  |  |
| 1961-1964 | 56 | 9 | 35 |
| 1983-1986 | 70 | 9 | 25 |
| Share of world imports |  |  |  |
| 1961-1964 | 58 | 16 | 27 |
| 1983-1986 | 40 | 20 | 41 |
| Self-sufficiency ratio |  |  |  |
| 1961-1964 | 99 | 99 | 103 |
| 1983-1986 | 113 | 94 | 98 |

Source: Rod Tyers and Kym Anderson, *Disarray in World Food Markets*
(Cambridge, Cambridge University Press, 1992), pp. 23-24.

a   The commodities covered were wheat, coarse grains, rice, ruminant and
    non-ruminant meat, dairy products and sugar.

Table 6.4 gives trends in agricultural output from 1980 to 1991
in total and per capita terms. (Trends in food production mirrored
trends in agricultural production.)

*Table 6.4*

Agricultural production and the agricultural labour force, 1980 and 1992

| | 1992[a] | 1992[b] | 1980[c] | 1992[d] | 1992/1980[e] | 1980[f] | 1992[g] | 1992/1980[h] |
|---|---|---|---|---|---|---|---|---|
| World | 125.0 | 101.4 | 50.8 | 45.7 | -10.0 | 993.1 | 1 117.2 | 11.1 |
| Developed market economies | 110.4 | 102.2 | 7.1 | 4.9 | -31.2 | 25.5 | 19.3 | 45.3 |
| North America | 114.1 | 102.3 | 3.6 | 2.2 | -39.5 | 4.4 | 3.1 | 63.2 |
| Europe | 107.4 | 103.2 | 7.7 | 6.0 | -22.5 | 12.3 | 10.2 | 30.0 |
| Australia and New Zealand | 117.1 | 99.5 | 7.6 | 5.3 | -30.1 | .6 | 0.5 | 35.2 |
| Other developed economies[i] | 100.3 | 89.7 | 11.8 | 7.0 | -40.8 | 8.1 | 5.5 | 46.8 |
| Former Soviet Union | 102.7 | 93.0 | 20.0 | 11.9 | -40.7 | 27.2 | 17.2 | 62.0 |
| Eastern Europe[j] | 88.6 | 85.0 | 30.2 | 15.8 | -47.7 | 14.3 | 7.8 | 62.1 |
| Developing countries | 145.2 | 112.9 | 65.7 | 58.3 | -11.3 | 923.0 | 1 070.7 | 25.2 |
| Africa | 133.0 | 92.0 | 73.6 | 67.2 | -8.7 | 118.8 | 145.9 | 8.3 |
| Latin America | 127.7 | 99.4 | 31.8 | 25.1 | -21.2 | 39.3 | 41.5 | 21.1 |
| Near East Asia | 137.7 | 98.8 | 48.7 | 38.2 | -21.5 | 32.4 | 35.7 | 24.9 |
| Far East Asia | 155.0 | 124.0 | 69.6 | 62.3 | -10.5 | 731.1 | 846.1 | 34.0 |
| China | 164.4 | 139.6 | 74.2 | 66.0 | -11.2 | 406.1 | 461.8 | 44.6 |
| India | 151.3 | 117.2 | 69.7 | 65.8 | -5.6 | 185.0 | 220.8 | 26.8 |
| Other developing countries | 114.0 | 88.3 | 63.1 | 53.0 | -16.0 | 1.4 | 1.5 | 6.4 |

Source: UN/DESIPA, based on FAO data.

Notes:

a   Index of total agricultural production (1979-1981 = 100).

b   Index of agricultural production per capita (1979-1981 = 100).

c   Percentage of the economically active population in agriculture, 1980.

d   Percentage of the economically active population in agriculture, 1992.

e   Percentage change in the share of agricultural workers in the economically active population.

f   Numbers of those economically active in agriculture, 1980 (millions).

g   Numbers of those economically active in agriculture, 1992 (millions).

h   Change in productivity per economically active agricultural worker between 1980 and 1992 (percentage).

i   Including South Africa.

j   Bulgaria, the Czech Republic, Hungary, Poland, Romania and Slovakia.

In the developed market economies, the total agricultural production was on average 10 per cent higher in 1992 than in 1979-1981.

In the developing countries, production expanded more rapidly than in the developed countries — by an average of 45 per cent. The increase was particularly strong in the Far East where China and India increased their output by over 60 per cent and 50 per cent respectively. African production increased by 33 per cent, considerably more than did production in Latin America. African production was adversely affected by drought in 1992: production was 37 per cent higher in 1991 than in 1979-1981.

An indicator for trends in the ability of the agricultural sector to produce sufficient food for the population is the trend in production per head of the population. As shown in table 6.4, per capita food production in the developing countries as a whole increased by some 13 per cent between 1979-1981 and 1992, but with large differences between the regions.

In the Near East, output per head of the population declined. The figures for Latin America show stagnation in per capita production for the period. Although its total production rose less than in the other identified regions, including Africa, this was almost compensated for by lower population growth.

The contrast between Africa and the Far East is striking. In Africa, agricultural production per head of the population was 8 per cent lower in 1992 (and 2 per cent lower in 1991) than in 1979-1981, whereas in the Far East it was 24 per cent higher — and 40 per cent higher in China. Low population growth and expanded agricultural production brought about a marked improvement in food supply.

## 1. Agricultural potential of different regions

Asia's agricultural success was dependent upon the use of irrigation and fertilizers on high-yielding crop varieties. It was not, then, necessarily a model for all other countries to follow. Some countries in Africa and Latin America were more akin to North America and Australia in having a relative abundance of land. With reliance on rains, this land could be expected to produce agricultural products without the use of as much fertilizer as Asian countries.

Moreover, Africa and Latin America also produced different crops from Asia. In 1991, fully 44 per cent of the total Asian tonnage of cereals, root crops and pulses consisted of rice. In that year, only 5 and 11 per cent, respectively, of the African and Latin American tonnages were rice. Furthermore, 58 and 32 per cent of the tonnage of their crops were root crops, whereas the Asian average was 22 per cent.[12]

Although Africa's yields for all crops might be lower than in other regions, because of the lack of infrastructure, irrigation and fertilizers, it might be expected they would do well with some crops. For cereals as a whole, African yields per hectare were only 40 per cent of the world average. For millet and sorghum, however, Africa's yields surpassed the world average and Africa devoted relatively more of its acreage to the production of these crops than did the rest of the world. Local farmers did, then, produce what they tended to be best at producing.

Overall comparisons among the developing regions show that Latin America and Africa have certain advantages. A continued increase in production can be expected, even as the relative size of the agricultural sector in employment continues to shrink. While their use of irrigation and fertilizer is expected to be lower than that of Asian countries, given their relatively greater abundance in land and geographic characteristics, they have nevertheless increased their areas under irrigation and their use of fertilizer. Further advances can be expected consistent with environmental protection.

Latin America and Africa still have not made the same advances as China and India towards reducing their food imports. These two countries reduced their food imports as a percentage of merchandise imports from 36 and 22 per cent respectively in 1974/75 to 2 and 5 per cent respectively in 1987/88. However, for sub-Saharan Africa the comparable figures show an increase from 14.5 to 18.8 per cent, and for Latin America a small reduction from

13.1 to 12 per cent. For the least developed countries as a group the percentage increased from 13.8 to 20.7 per cent.[13]

## 2. *Distortions against agriculture within developing countries*

In general, all efforts should be directed to helping the farmer decide how to use his or her existing resources most effectively, and removing obstacles is the way to do so. One of the major steps that national governments have been encouraged to take, particularly by international lending institutions, is to remove the price bias against agriculture. Previous studies have shown how a bias against agriculture has harmed domestic production by discouraging exports and encouraging imports.[14]

In countries with considerable agricultural potential, it was felt that this sector could be exploited to foster the overall development of the country. Prices paid to farmers would be low in order to keep the real wages of industrial workers from getting high and agricultural exports taxed to pay for imports of industrial machinery. The assumption behind much of this thinking was that farmers would keep delivering output to the market irrespective of the rewards they received. The bias against agriculture was reflected not only in prices but also in a lack of priority accorded to the needs of the agriculture sector, including the funding of extension services, rural infrastructure and agricultural research.

The argument that agriculture should be taxed in the early stages of development to finance the newly emerging industrial sector or to protect urban consumers has been increasingly questioned. The grounds for questioning it is that since the poor and hungry are both producers and consumers of agricultural products in poor countries, a policy that tries to assist them as consumers at the expense of encouraging them as producers could be counterproductive. It has been argued that in some parts of Africa where net food sellers are typically smallholders in the rural sector and net food buyers are mainly urban sector dwellers, who enjoy higher incomes, higher food prices could actually help the poor.[15]

The argument against bias is, in the end, based upon efficiency and the beneficial effects of free markets. If prices encourage producers to devote their resources to where they have the comparative advantage, they will concentrate on those products that they can produce efficiently. Bias against agriculture discourages farmers from raising their own production and incomes, and thereby the nutritional status of the country. It also lowers the export potential of the country in agriculture. Agricultural exports can be an important factor in export diversification.[16]

It is not higher food prices that are required in developing countries. Indeed, the real price of food can be expected to continue to decline. Rather, prices should reflect the real opportunity costs and allow farmers to compete "on a level playing field" with other producers and direct their resources to where they will obtain the greatest return. However, this argument in turn demands that prices should reflect opportunity costs, and, in the case of agriculture, the degree of intervention in international food markets has meant that prices are often a poor signal.

## E.  INTERNATIONAL FOOD MARKETS

The major players in international food markets are the developed market economies that have turned from being net importers to net exporters of foodstuffs. Their producer subsidy equivalents are invariably positive, ranging, in 1991, according to OECD estimates, from 4 per cent in New Zealand and 15 per cent in Australia, through 30 per cent for the United States, 45 per cent for Canada and 49 per cent for the EU, to 65 to 80 per cent for Japan and the EFTA countries.[17]

The high levels of support in some developed countries in themselves act to deter imports from other producers, as their domestic production is higher than it would otherwise be. Moreover, domestic consumption is in many cases depressed — and domestic production encouraged — by high domestic prices in those countries that choose to raise domestic prices above world levels by restrictions on imports.[18]

More and more it is realized that protectionist policies in the industrialized countries do not just impose an income transfer from their own domestic consumers to their domestic producers, but also from producers to consumers in other countries. Static analysis shows that producers in developing countries are hurt by the food policies of the industrialized market economies and that consumers benefit from the relatively low price of food imports. However, when the consequences of the industrialized countries' policies on the agricultural growth of the developing countries are taken into account, the benefits of trade liberalization can be large. If the distortions in the industrialized economies were removed, developed countries would be only 85 per cent self-sufficient in 2000. The developing countries would be 102 per cent self-sufficient while their net foreign exchange earnings from food trade would be $39 billion greater in the year. If the developing countries were to remove their own distorting policies, benefits accumulating to them would be even more significant.[19] Their self-sufficiency would reach 119 per cent, and their earnings from food would be $81 billion greater. If agricultural productivity were to grow with price incentives, instead of being assumed to be exogenous, developing countries' self-sufficiency would reach 108 per cent if the industrialized countries' policies were alone changed, and 125 per cent if their own policies were also changed.

## F.  POLICY RESPONSES TO THE FAMINE PROBLEM

Increased supply of food will not necessarily eliminate the hunger problem. Indeed, if current global food supplies would be distributed strictly according to the nutritional needs of the various regions of the world, theoretically they would have been sufficient to prevent chronic undernourishment. There is no global shortage of food.

The world has created a world food system in which "almost anyone in the world, if he or she has the means to do so, can have access to the world's supply of food if his or her Government permits such access".[20] Rather than the mere availability of food, it is the ability of individuals and households to acquire food through production, trade or purchase that mainly determines who is hungry and who is not.

People are chronically hungry and malnourished if the land they cultivate is too small or the yields too little, or because the incomes they earn are insufficient. Failures to command food can result from the loss of employment, crop or livestock; a reduction in demand for the commodity produced; reduction in real wages; or a deterioration in the terms of trade facing the individual. These factors have been called "pull" failures, as opposed to "response" failures, which occur when the market does not respond to the demand for food. Response failures can happen during a drought or other natural disaster, monopoly hoarding, inadequate transportation capacity, poor infrastructure or the insecurity and disruptions created by civil conflagrations.[21] The groups most affected by either failure usually include smallholders who lose their food or cash crops, farmers who lose or sell their livestock under duress, agricultural wage earners who lose their jobs and displaced persons.

In situations of famine prevention and extreme hunger relief, Governments in developing countries — usually with the support of the international community — have adopted a variety of measures ranging from cash relief and free food distribution to food- or cash-for-work programmes. The advantages of cash assistance have included the demand it has provided for sustained local food production, trade and transport. Temporary food assistance, on the other hand, has been necessary in cases of local response failures to the demand for food. Programmes of food-for-work or cash-for-work, e.g., employment guarantee schemes, have had the additional advantage of improving the productive capacity of the economy. In the case of Zambia's programme for the prevention of malnutrition, for instance, emphasis was given near the end of the 1992 drought to land preparation and planting.

Other forms of governmental intervention have included governmental maintenance of public food stocks; the addition of food supplies to commercial markets; and efforts to control cereal prices, support livestock prices, ration food supplies, create fair price shops, increase people's access to water, expand health care programmes, set up soup kitchens in urban uncontrolled settlements, and take measures to discourage excessive hoarding, speculation and other price-destabilization actions. Combinations of measures have often proven effective; for example, drought responses in the 1980s in Botswana and Cape Verde included public works providing cash relief on a large scale and direct food and cash transfers to vulnerable groups, especially children and pregnant and lactating women. Although those countries utilized food aid, they were not overly dependent on it, and in fact donated food supplies typically arrived after national action had already been taken.

Relief camps have been adopted in many countries as a last measure. While representing an efficient and cost-effective way of feeding a large number of people, they have disrupted normal social and economic activities, made rehabilitation and recovery more difficult, and in some cases triggered the outbreak of diseases. During 1992, for instance, cholera in Zambia and Mozambique first broke out in refugee camps and then spread to the general population, causing more than a thousand deaths in Zambia and more than 500 in Mozambique. Similar outbreaks of scurvy and pellagra have been reported in some countries.

Potential famines from natural disasters have been prevented with increasing success over the years because of prompt action by national governments and the international community. But the same has been less true in cases where war has worsened the effects of drought-induced production declines, as in Angola, Chad, Ethiopia, Mozambique, the Sudan and Uganda in the last 15 years. Of course the use of food as an instrument of war is probably as old as warfare. In civil wars in particular, little distinction is normally made between armed opponents (often guerillas) and their civilian supporters. Efforts to detroy the refuge, staging areas and support structure of opponents have included attacks aimed at disrupting the ability of civilians and armed opponents from producing or acquiring food.

While starvation has not been an objective of war, it has nonetheless been a consequence. Indeed, civil wars have negatively affected food production, distribution and relief often as a result of looting, requisitioning or destroying local food crops or the delivery of food relief; raiding or killing livestock; uprooting, killing or impressing young men into the military; displacing and converting much of the population into refugees; or disrupting grazing patterns and the capacity of people to implement their coping strategies when struck by drought. It is usually difficult, however, to determine the exact weight of wars versus natural disasters in creating conditions of famine. For example, in countries such as Ethiopia and the Sudan, where long-lasting wars have coincided with long periods of below-average rainfall and periodic droughts, the vulnerability of households grew as a result of both forms of external shock. On the other hand, Somalia is a recent case of a country where famine was almost exclusively a consequence of civil strife.

The international community has helped prevent or alleviate famines through timely and massive support. The communications industry, television in particular, has played an important role in appealing to humanitarian impulses in the developed countries by dramatizing the plight of hungry or starving persons, women and children especially.

Global food aid activities increased dramatically in the early 1990s. Sub-Saharan Africa received substantial deliveries to meet the needs of refugees, displaced people and drought victims. In all, the total deliveries of aid to the low-income, food-deficit countries and to the least developed countries in 1991 increased over the levels of the two previous years.

Although food aid is an immediate response to avoid famine, the longer-term solution to the problems of hunger and famine lies in attacking their root causes: poverty, highly unequal distribution of income and unemployment. Increasing agricultural productivity through improved rural infrastructure, agricultural research and extension and the elimination of distortions in agricultural markets are a part of the solution.

## Notes

[1] "Update on the nutrition situation", SCN News, no. 4 (late 1989), p. 4.

[2] See "The global state of hunger and malnutrition". Report of the World Food Council at its eighteenth ministerial session, Nairobi, Kenya, 23-26 June 1992 (WFC/1992/12), pp. 5-6.

[3] Ibid., p. 6.

[4] "Hunger and malnutrition in the world: situation and outlook". 1991 report of the World Food Council at its seventeenth ministrial session, Helsingør, Denmark, 5-8 June 1991 (WFC/1991/2).

[5] Bread for the World Institute on Hunger and Development, Hunger 1990: A Report on the State of World Hunger, (Washington, D. C., 1990), p. 20.

[6] "Update on the nutrition situation", loc. cit., p. 9.

[7] "The global state of hunger and malnutrition" . . ., p. 9.

[8] WHO, "National strategies for overcoming micronutrient malnutrition" (EB89/27, 27 December 1991), p. 4.

[9] "The global state of hunger and malnutrition" . . ., p. 10.

[10] See, for example, "Nutritional strategies for overcoming micronutrient malnutrition" (EB89/27), WHO, pp. 5-22; and FAO, "Towards better nutrition for all: preparing for the International Conference on Nutrition" (COAG/91, 7), paras. 51-69.

[11] Similar results of declining self-sufficiency were obtained by the International Fund for Agricultural Development (IFAD) calculations on the food staples (cereals, roots and tubers and pulses) self-sufficiency ratio. Between 1965-1967 and 1986-1988, this fell from 98 per cent to 95 per cent in the case of the 114 developing countries examined and from 100 to 95 per cent in the case of the least developed countries. In Latin America and the Caribbean, it fell from 112 to 93 per cent. All the other regions had ratios of under 100 in 1965-1967, and in every region except Asia there was a decline (Idriss Jazairy, Mohinddin Alamgir and Theresa Panuccio, The State of Rural World Poverty (New York, published for the International Fund for Agricultural Development by New York University Press, 1992), p. 33).

[12] All figures are from FAO, Production Yearbook.

[13] All figures are from Jazairy and others, op. cit., pp. 382-383.

[14] See, in particular, World Bank, World Development Report 1986 (Oxford, Oxford University Press, 1986).

[15] S. M. Ravi Kanbur, "Global food balances and individual hunger: three themes in an entitlement-based approach", in Jean Dreze and Amartya Sen, The Political Economy of Hunger, vol. 1 (Oxford, Claredon Press, 1991), p. 71.

[16] Chile can be taken as an example of a country that removed the distortions against agriculture and saw agricultural exports rise and its export base diversified. In 1970, 7.4 per cent of its export receipts were from agriculture: food (4.5 per cent) and agricultural raw materials (2.9 per cent). In 1989, the corresponding figures were 40.2 per cent, with 28.6 per cent from food and 11.6 per cent from agricultural raw materials. All figures from UNCTAD, Handbook of International Trade and Development Statistics (United Nations publication, Sales No. E/F.92.II.D.6).

[17] OECD, Agricultural Policies, Markets and Trade: Monitoring and Outlook 1992 (Paris, 1992), pp. 130-131.

[18] Farmers' incomes have in some countries been protected by "deficiency payments" (paying farmers the difference between domestic costs and lower import prices). In these cases, although domestic production is higher than it would be otherwise and, therefore, demand for food imports lower, the importation of foodstuffs need not be excluded by tariff or non-tariff measures. Moreover, domestic prices will be similar to world prices. The United Kingdom employed such a deficiency-payment system before it entered EU.

[19] For example, Rod Tyres and Kym Anderson estimated that in 1990 these policies had benefited consumers and taxpayers in developing economies to the extent of $15.3 billion annually and had harmed producer welfare to the amount of $26.5 billion, in United States dollars of 1985, in *Disarray in World Food Markets* (Cambridge, Cambridge University Press, 1992), p. 209.

[20] D. Gale Johnson, *World Agriculture in Disarray*, second edition (London, Macmillan, 1991).

[21] For an extensive analysis, see Jean Dreze and Amartya Sen, eds., *The Political Economy of Hunger*, 3 volumes, Clarendon Press, Oxford, 1990 and 1991.

# 7

# Health

SEVERAL major public health concerns have emerged during the past few years. Cholera had been endemic in Asia and Africa. It began to spread in parts of Latin America, pointing to the deterioration of sanitary conditions there in the 1980s. Malaria reemerged in parts of Africa and Asia as a widening threat to public health. The AIDS pandemic raged across much of Africa and threatened to do so in parts of Asia and Latin America after its initial spread in Europe and North America. Tuberculosis was an affliction common among those living in poverty and overcrowded conditions and was curable with antibiotic drugs. It has resurfaced with renewed ferocity in urban centres in the developed countries. Assaults on the environment, poisoning the air and water and releasing pathogenic substances into the atmosphere, most prominently in the former Soviet Union and the rural areas of central European countries, have made formerly salubrious habitations injurious to good health and life.

Remarkable advances have been made in medical technology, but at the same time the delivery of medical services has run into major problems in most parts of the world. In the developing countries, a shortage of imports has restricted the supplies of drugs and equipment. Pressures to cut government expenditure have reduced supplies, personnel and facilities. In the economies in transition, the breakdown of the old system of health care, without the formation of an adequate replacement, and the drop in economic activity and incomes have compounded the problems of providing health services. In the developed countries there are unresolved problems of inordinate increases in costs of health care and of organizing these services to ensure their equitable and efficient delivery.

## A.  HEALTH CONDITIONS

### 1. *Life expectancy and mortality*

The average life expectancy at birth for the world in the period 1985-1990 was 63.9 years, a gain of 3.5 years over 1975-1980 (see table 7.1).[1] In the less developed regions, life expectancy was 61.4 years, compared to 74.0 years in the more developed regions. Gains in longevity occurred in all groups of countries, the gain being

*Table 7.1*

Life expectancy at birth, 1975-1990 *(in years)*

| Regions and areas | 1975-1980 | 1980-1985 | 1985-1990 |
|---|---|---|---|
| World | 60.4 | 62.1 | 63.9 |
| More developed regions | 72.0 | 72.8 | 74.0 |
| Less developed regions | 57.4 | 59.4 | 61.4 |
| Africa | 47.9 | 49.6 | 52.0 |
| Eastern Africa | 47.1 | 47.9 | 50.6 |
| Middle Africa | 45.6 | 47.6 | 49.9 |
| Northern Africa | 53.9 | 56.6 | 59.1 |
| Southern Africa | 55.2 | 57.3 | 59.7 |
| Western Africa | 44.7 | 46.7 | 48.8 |
| Asia | 58.3 | 60.5 | 62.7 |
| Eastern Asia | 67.0 | 68.9 | 70.4 |
| South-eastern Asia | 54.1 | 57.9 | 60.9 |
| Southern Asia | 51.9 | 54.3 | 56.8 |
| Western Asia | 60.6 | 62.5 | 66.7 |
| Latin America | 63.3 | 65.2 | 66.7 |
| Caribbean | 66.2 | 67.7 | 69.0 |
| Central America | 63.4 | 65.6 | 67.6 |
| South America | 63.0 | 64.8 | 66.2 |
| Europe | 72.6 | 73.5 | 74.4 |
| Eastern Europe | 70.7 | 70.8 | 71.4 |
| Northern Europe | 73.3 | 74.5 | 75.5 |
| Southern Europe | 72.8 | 74.0 | 75.0 |
| Western Europe | 73.3 | 74.5 | 75.5 |
| Northern America | 73.3 | 74.7 | 75.6 |
| Soviet Union (former) | 67.9 | 67.9 | 70.0 |
| Oceania | 68.2 | 70.1 | 71.3 |

Source: *World Population Prospects 1990* (United Nations publication, Sales No. E.91.XIII.4).

smaller the higher the figure in the initial year. The difference between the developed and the developing regions has narrowed from 14.6 years in 1975-1980 to 12.6 years in 1985-1990. Yet the range of life expectancy for individual developed and developing countries is wide, going from 78.3 years in Japan and 77.1 years in Sweden and Switzerland to 41 years in Sierra Leone and 41.5 years in Afghanistan and Guinea-Bissau.[2]

Life expectancy in Africa is 10 years lower than in Asia and 15 years lower than in Latin America. In Northern and Southern Africa, the average life expectancy is about 60 years, while in Eastern, middle and Western Africa it is close to 50 years. In Asia, the range of averages for the few regions identified is from 56.8 years for Southern Asia to 70.4 years for Eastern Asia. The largest gains occurred in South-East Asia and Western Asia, reflecting remarkable progress in reducing mortality in China. Latin America was the developing region with the highest life expectancy, with a fairly small variance among the different regions.

Females continue to have a higher average life expectancy than males. The difference is greater in the developed countries, where females live on average 7.1 years longer than males; in developing countries, the difference is 2.7 years.

Maternal mortality is another important indicator of health status. It is estimated that more than half a million women die each year from causes related to pregnancy and childbirth, 99 per cent of them in the developing countries. Women in sub-Saharan Africa are 75 times more likely to die from causes related to pregnancy and childbirth than women in Western Europe.[3] Rates of up to 1,000 or more deaths of the mother per 100,000 live births have been reported in several rural areas of Africa and rates exceeding 500 have been reported in African cities. Most at risk are girls under age 15 who are 10 to 15 times more likely to die in childbirth than women in their twenties. Death resulting from unsafe abortions account for a significant proportion of maternal deaths. Because women in many developing countries tend to have many pregnancies, the cumulative lifetime risk of disease in pregnancy may reach 1 in 20.

Whereas in the developed countries there is virtually universal medical attention at childbirth, in the developing countries only 52 per cent of births are attended by trained personnel, and fewer take place in health-care institutions.[4] The highest proportion of births assisted by a trained health worker in the developing countries is in East Asia, where coverage levels are uniformly high. In South Asia, by contrast, they tend to be drastically lower — 10 per cent. In Africa, the level of maternity health coverage is low. In some countries, no more than 2 per cent of births are attended by health-care workers.

## 2. *Infant and child mortality*

Infant mortality rates, defined as the number of children in one thousand live births who die in the first year of life, decreased during the past decade more sharply in the developing countries than as a whole in the least-developed countries. The gap in infant mortality rates between developed and developing countries narrowed during the decade of the 1980s. The pace of change and the magnitude of improvement have varied considerably among countries. Yet, an infant born in a developing country was, on average, five times more likely to die during the first year of life than one born in a developed country (see table 7.2)

Africa has the highest infant mortality rates in the world, despite a decline from 126 per thousand in 1975-1980 to 103 in 1985-1990. Egypt had a remarkable achievement: infant mortality declined from 115 per thousand live births in 1980-1985 to 65 in 1985-1990.

In Latin America and the Caribbean region, infant mortality rates ranged from 11 per thousand live births in Barbados during 1985-1990 to 110 in Bolivia. Improvements were more marked in the Central American subregion than in the Caribbean or South American subregions.

Infant mortality rates varied enormously among the countries in Asia, ranging from 5 per thousand live births in Japan to 172 in Afghanistan during 1985-1990. Remarkable gains were made in Hong Kong, Singapore, Sri Lanka and Thailand.

*Table 7.2*

Infant mortality rates, by regions 1975-1990 *(per thousand live births)*

| Region and country or area | 1975-1980 | 1980-1985 | 1985-1990 |
|---|---|---|---|
| World total | 86 | 79 | 70 |
| More developed regions | 19 | 16 | 15 |
| Less developed regions | 97 | 89 | 78 |
| Africa | 126 | 116 | 103 |
| Eastern Africa | 131 | 126 | 114 |
| Middle Africa | 118 | 108 | 98 |
| Northern Africa | 121 | 105 | 79 |
| Southern Africa | 98 | 87 | 77 |
| Western Africa | 132 | 121 | 111 |
| Latin America | 70 | 61 | 54 |
| Caribbean | 65 | 58 | 52 |
| Central America | 65 | 55 | 47 |
| South America | 73 | 64 | 57 |
| Northern America | 14 | 11 | 10 |
| Asia | 91 | 83 | 72 |
| Eastern Asia | 39 | 37 | 31 |
| South-eastern Asia | 89 | 75 | 63 |
| Southern Asia | 127 | 113 | 102 |
| Western Asia | 101 | 88 | 71 |
| Europe | 19 | 15 | 13 |
| Eastern Europe | 23 | 19 | 17 |
| Northern Europe | 12 | 10 | 8 |
| Southern Europe | 23 | 18 | 15 |
| Western Europe | 13 | 10 | 9 |
| Oceania | 35 | 30 | 26 |
| Soviet Union (former) | 28 | 26 | 24 |

Source: *World Population Prospects 1990* (United Nations publication, Sales No. E.91.XIII.4), table 45.

In the more developed regions significant reductions were made despite already low levels of infant mortality. The lowest infant mortality rates were in Japan, namely, 5 per thousand, followed by rates below 7 in Finland, Sweden and Switzerland.

Infant mortality rates were much higher in the former Soviet Union and other centrally planned economies than in the developed market economies. During 1985-1990 the highest levels were in the former Yugoslavia and the former Soviet Union at 24 and 25 per thousand respectively.

A similar pattern of deaths is seen in children under age 5. Table 7.3 shows that for the world as a whole, the probability of dying before age 5 declined from 131 to 105 per thousand between 1975-1980 and 1985-1990 The under-five mortality rate continued to decline although economic conditions deteriorated in most of

*Table 7.3*

Under 5 mortality rates, 1975-1990 *(per thousand live births)*

| Region and country or area | 1975-1980 | 1980-1985 | 1985-1990 |
|---|---|---|---|
| World total | 131 | 118 | 105 |
| More developed regions | 24 | 19 | 17 |
| Less developed regions | 149 | 134 | 119 |
| Africa | 203 | 182 | 163 |
| Eastern Africa | 214 | 204 | 188 |
| Middle Africa | 212 | 195 | 178 |
| Northern Africa | 183 | 152 | 129 |
| Southern Africa | 136 | 119 | 103 |
| Western Africa | 225 | 206 | 188 |
| Latin America | 99 | 88 | 78 |
| Caribbean | 100 | 91 | 82 |
| Central America | 96 | 84 | 73 |
| Temperate South America | 49 | 38 | 34 |
| Tropical South America | 109 | 97 | 87 |
| Northern America | 17 | 13 | 11 |
| Asia | 139 | 124 | 108 |
| East Asia | 54 | 50 | 41 |
| South-eastern Asia | 129 | 111 | 96 |
| Southern Asia | 203 | 177 | 160 |
| Western Asia | 142 | 115 | 95 |
| Europe | 22 | 17 | 15 |
| Eastern Europe | 27 | 23 | 20 |
| Northern Europe | 15 | 11 | 10 |
| Southern Europe | 26 | 20 | 17 |
| Western Europe | 15 | 12 | 10 |
| Oceania | 47 | 40 | 33 |
| Soviet Union (former) | 37 | 31 | 27 |

Source: Mortality of children under age 5; World Estimates and Projections, 1950-2025 (United Nations publication, Sales No. E.88.XIII.4) table A.1.

Africa and Latin America. Among the more developed countries, there was a general convergence in mortality rates. The difference between the countries with the highest and the lowest mortality rates became smaller than in the previous decade. Among the less developed countries, there continued to be large differences between both levels and trends between countries.

The causes of the enormous disparities and the factors that reduce them are by now well understood. Poverty and consequent malnutrition of both mother and foetus are the predominant cause. Frequent pregnancies compound these deficiencies. Infections of all kinds, which opportunistically attack enfeebled bodies, are a second factor. The infectious diseases include respiratory diseases such as pneumonia and diarrhoea, pertussis and measles. With successful programmes of vaccination, acute respiratory infections had become the largest single cause of mortality among children in the developing countries. Between 30 and 50 per cent of all visits by children to treatment facilities and 30 to 40 per cent of their hospitalization is because of acute respiratory infections. Ignorance of proper sanitation and inadequacy of health facilities form a third factor. About 60 per cent of all children die from diarrhoea or pneumonia.[5] Children under five years of age in the developing countries suffer two to three episodes of diarrhoea each year.

In the former Soviet Union, respiratory infections and parasitic diseases account for nearly half of all infant deaths, compared to less than 10 per cent in the United States. These problems are more acute in the Central Asian republics. While infectious diseases among children in Central and Eastern Europe have decreased (with the exception of the former Soviet Union), there was a marked increase in the number of environmentally induced diseases, especially respiratory diseases, cancers and congenital malformations. Czechoslovakia, Poland and certain parts of the former Soviet Union are those most exposed to environmental health hazards. Almost 25 per cent of the children in the ecologically ruined areas of the former Soviet Union were born with genetic abnormalities. Bulgaria, Hungary and Yugoslavia were also exposed to considerable problems related to environmental pollution.

Although poverty is a major factor in poor health, public sector intervention has secured major successes in reducing infant and child mortality. In Chile, China, Costa Rica, Cuba, Malaysia, Mauritius, Panama and Sri Lanka, infant mortality rates were well below those in other countries at the same income per capita level, highlighting the success of these interventions. Measures to provide adequate nutrition, the education of females, public health policies to eradicate common infectious diseases and better access to health-care facilities have all played a part in these major improvements. Activities of the United Nations Children's Fund (UNICEF) and the World Health Organization (WHO) in promoting oral rehydration therapy (ORT) and the immunization of children against common infections have played another important part. ORT is now used by one family in three in the developing countries and the spread of the technique can save a large number of young lives.

## 3. *Morbidity patterns*

In 1985-1990 in the developing countries, infections and parasitic diseases continued to be by far the leading cause of mortality, accounting for almost one half of all deaths, compared to 1.4 per cent in the developed countries.[6] More than 2 billion people, almost half of the world's population, remained exposed to malaria in about 100 countries. Clinical cases were about 107 million per year and mortality 1 to 2 million per year. About three quarters of those deaths are estimated to occur among children under five years of age. Excluding Africa, where reporting was irregular, although trends varied, a general upward trend in the number of malaria cases has been reported in the Americas and some Asian countries.

Another widespread parasitic disease is schistosomiasis, endemic in 76 countries. Some 200 million people are infected with the disease.

In 1990 an estimated 1.7 billion people, or one third of the world's population, were infected with tuberculosis and more than

20 million people suffered from the disease. Every year, 8 million new cases are diagnosed. There is a threatening resurgence of tuberculosis in large cities in the developed countries, including Los Angeles and New York, because of conditions of poverty and the destruction of immune systems as a result of infection with HIV. However, more than 95 per cent of tuberculosis cases occur in the developing countries.[7]

The pattern of morbidity in the developed countries is fairly well established. Of the 11 million deaths that occur annually in these countries, roughly 2.4 million are due to ischemic heart diseases, 2.3 million to cancer, 1.5 million to stroke, 0.9 million to respiratory diseases and 0.8 million to violent causes, including 170,000 as a result of motor vehicle accidents, and at least 180,000 through suicide. Viewed from the standpoint of competing risks from various causes, roughly one in three people will eventually die from heart disease. The chances of dying from cancer are about one in five, from a stroke about one in seven and from respiratory disease or of dying a violent death, about 5 per cent in each case.[8]

Approximately one quarter of all deaths in the world each year are due to cardiovascular diseases. In the developed countries, cardiovascular diseases, particularly coronary diseases and stroke, are the leading cause of mortality and account for 40 to 50 per cent of all deaths. In the developing countries, they are the second leading cause of death (16 per cent), after infections and parasitic diseases (43 per cent). However, among adults, cardiovascular diseases are estimated to claim almost as many lives in the developing countries (6 million) each year as all infectious and parasitic diseases combined.

Cancer is one of the three main causes of death in both developed and developing countries. Each year about 7 million new cases occur, half of them in the developing countries. About 70 per cent of cancers are attributable to lifestyle and environment. The most common neoplasm for both sexes is cancer of the stomach. Incidents are high in Europe, East Asia and South America.

The number of lung cancer cases has been growing, and now

has achieved second place for both sexes. The vast majority of lung cancer mortality can be attributed to cigarette smoking. In several countries, including Australia, Canada and the United States, the rate of increase of lung cancer among males has slowed considerably, suggesting that the overall level of mortality may soon stabilize or even begin to decline. Among women, the incidence of lung cancer rates is rising rapidly. The possibility of death from cancer among women in the developed countries is now more than 200 per cent higher than in the early 1950s. Lung cancer is progressively replacing breast cancer as the leading cancer site for women in some countries, the United States in particular. In Japan, the number of women who die from lung cancer exceeds the number of those who die from breast cancer by more than 50 per cent.[9]

About 300 million people in the world suffer from mental or neurological disorders. Epilepsy affects 8 million people in the developed countries and over 35 million in the rest of the world. The number of mentally retarded persons is between 90 million and 130 million. The number with chronic schizophrenia and those disabled with dementia (typically occurring among the elderly) is increasing. Schizophrenia and other psychoses affect 55 million and some 120 million suffer from affective disorders. Dementias affect 5 to 8 per cent of the population aged over 65, or about 30 million people.[10] There has also been an increase in mental disturbances.

Suicide is a major cause of death in many countries. Mortality from suicide is now 35 to 40 per cent higher than in the 1950s. In the developed countries, almost 100,000 persons below the age of 65 commit suicide each year. By far the highest suicide rates are in Hungary. The lowest rates are reported in Spain, the United Kingdom and Italy.

Accidents and injuries are estimated to account for about 6 per cent of deaths in the developing countries. In the developed countries, the proportion is 7 per cent but is much higher for males (9.6 per cent of deaths) than females (4.3 per cent). The principal causes of disability and death from injuries are associated with motor vehicle accidents, falls, drownings, burns and poisoning.

Traffic accidents are the leading cause of death among young adults (15 to 34 years) and account for a substantial proportion of premature mortality in the developed countries. Deaths from motor vehicle accidents per 100,000 of population have remained relatively constant during the past five years. Among males the highest death rate from traffic accidents in the developed countries occurs in Portugal, followed by Luxembourg and New Zealand. The lowest rates of death from traffic accidents are found in the United Kingdom, Sweden and the Netherlands.

### 4. *AIDS*

The spread of the AIDS epidemic in both developing and developed countries has become a health problem of alarming proportions. By mid-1992, half a million cases of AIDS have been reported in 164 countries. Because of less than complete diagnosis and reporting and delays in reporting, the actual cumulative total number of adult AIDS cases was estimated to be 1.5 million. By 1991, an estimated 12 to 13 million people, including 1 million children, had been infected with HIV.[11] It is projected that about 40 million will be infected by the year 2000.[12] Of these, about 1 million a year are expected to die of AIDS.

One in three of the total number of AIDS cases are children. They were born to mothers infected with AIDS and die before five years of age. Other children become orphans after the death of the mother or both parents. Most of these childen are in Africa. In sub-Saharan Africa, alone, some 10 million childen are likely to be orphaned in this manner.

About 50 per cent of those infected with HIV were in Africa, 40 per cent in the Americas and the balance elsewhere. Since HIV infection started in Asia substantially later than in Africa, the annual number of HIV infections in Asia is expected to increase later in the 1990s. Out of 1 million deaths from AIDS in the year 2000, half will be in Africa, a quarter in Asia and the balance elsewhere. Much less is known about the extent of infection and the incidence of the disease in the former Soviet Union and Eastern Europe.

From being primarily an infection among homosexual men and intravenous drug users, HIV has come to attack men and women in equal proportions. In both Africa and Latin America and the Caribbean, the proportion of women infected with HIV and afflicted with AIDS is much higher than in North America and Europe. In 1991, among those infected with HIV in North America, 60 per cent were homosexual men and 18 per cent were intravenous drug users. In Europe, the corresponding figures were 46 and 30 per cent. In contrast, in the Caribbean region in 1988, the proportion of those infected from heterosexual contact was 65 per cent. The incidence of AIDS among men was three times that for women, contrasting with 10 times that for women in North America. In 1992, nearly half of the population infected with HIV in the world were women. At the present time, in contrast with the early 1980s, both the infection and the eventual development of AIDS victimizes a large proportion of women.

The main sources of infection with HIV include transfusion of contaminated blood and transplanting contaminated body parts, use of contaminated syringes, mostly by narcotic drug users, neonatal infection and homosexual and heterosexual contact. More than 75 per cent of cumulative HIV infections in adults up to 1992 were through heterosexual contact. In the first six months of 1992, 90 per cent of the increase in AIDS cases were those who had been infected through heterosexual contact.[13] Infection from sexual contact, increasingly heterosexual contact, and the infection of the foetus by infected mothers are the most frequent and rising risks at the present time.

AIDS has serious socio-economic ramifications, imposing a burden on the population of the developing countries and their already inadequate health-care systems. The impact of the epidemic on population growth will be noticeable. In Africa, where HIV prevalence rates have reached 10 per cent and greater, deaths due to AIDS among children have already negated gains made by child survival programmes in reducing mortality.

The direct costs of treatment are high, ranging from 78 per

cent to 932 per cent of per capita gross national product (GNP) for the annual treatment of a patient in Zaire and from 36 per cent to 218 per cent of per capita GNP for a patient in the United Republic of Tanzania. For many countries the health and social support infrastructures available are inadequate to cope with the clinical burden of HIV-related diseases. Larger percentages of total government health-care expenditure in Africa was being used on AIDS patients. In some African countries, over half of the admissons to hospitals are AIDS cases.[14] The patients will require long hospital stays and expensive drugs; they will occupy hospital places that other patients with curable ailments will be denied.

No vaccine to prevent HIV infection and no cure for AIDS exists. As a consequence, only behavioural changes can protect people from infection and eventually AIDS. Avoiding sexual contact with several partners will reduce the risk of infection. Using protective devices such as condoms during sexual intercourse is another means. Avoiding unsterilized instruments such as needles, syringes or other skin-piercing instruments is another requirement. Hospitals need to take special care to protect blood, blood products and donated organs from being the means of infecting a person with HIV.

While most preventive measures require some resources, education is the most powerful instrument for bringing the nature of the disease and measures of preventing it to the public. It is especially important to educate women, who may, in some cultures, lack authority to prevent an infected partner from transmitting the disease to her. Early diagnosis is an essential element in advising people to modify behaviour. Some developing countries lack the equipment to screen blood. The widespread scarcity of resources in hospitals is a principal reason for reusing skin-piercing instruments. The habit of intravenously injecting drugs needs to be cured to eliminate that method of being infected with HIV. HIV cannot be casually transmitted, but those who engage in risky behaviour expose themselves to a higher probability of being infected. As science and technology still have no means of preventing infection, nor is there a cure once afflicted, eliminating risks of infection is the only means now available to ward off infection.

## B.  ISSUES IN HEALTH POLICY

1. *Immunization*

The most dramatic public health success in the developing countries during the past decade has been the immunization of children against diphtheria, pertussis, tetanus, measles, poliomyelitis and tuberculosis. When the World Health Organization (WHO) launched the Expanded Programme on Immunization in 1974, fewer than 5 per cent of children in the developing countries were immunized. Three years later the target of universal child immunization (UCI) by 1990 was adopted; it aimed at immunizing 80 per cent of one-year-olds in the developing countries. By 1981, about 20 per cent of the world's children had been immunized. In 1990, the goal of 80 per cent immunization coverage of young children was reached.

The remarkable progress of universal child immunization is in part the result of improvement in vaccines and the equipment used to transport and store them. Heat-stable vaccines, reliable cold chains and continuing research and training by a growing number of health workers trained in the management and organization of immunization programmes have contributed to the success of the UCI programme. The massive immunization programmes brought many side-benefits that should improve the overall health of children. Public health facilities in rural areas have allowed clinics to offer numerous other services, such as education about oral rehydration therapy. The improved health facilities have also allowed health workers to increase the distribution of vitamin A to reduce mortality and prevent blindness, of iodine to curtail goitre and mental retardation and of simple antibiotics to treat pneumonia. However, approximately 3 million children still die each year from vaccine-preventable diseases.

In the former Soviet Union, the incidence of communicable diseases that could be prevented by immunization has been particularly high. For the past decade the incidence of diphtheria, pertussis and polio has been increasing. Morbidity from pertussis doubled after 1985. The annual incidence of diphtheria more than doubled between 1980 and 1990. The number of reported polio cases in 1990 was 312, four times higher than in the previous year.[15]

The world now stands poised to achieve the goals for the year 2000 adopted by the World Summit for Children in 1990. Major goals for child health include global eradication of poliomyelitis by the year 2000; elimination of neonatal tetanus by 1995; reduction by 95 per cent of measles deaths and by 90 per cent of measles cases; maintenance of a high level of immunization coverage; reduction by 50 per cent in deaths due to diarrhoea in children under age 5; and reduction by one third in deaths due to acute respiratory infections in children under age 5.

2. *Access and equity*

WHO adopted as a primary objective the achievement of equity in the availability of health care. One key was to make the essential elements of health care available to all. Access to primary health care in most developed countries is almost universal. In most developing countries, maternal and child health services coverage has increased. In countries reporting to WHO, which contain about two thirds of the world's pregnant women, 60 per cent of them receive care from trained personnel during both pregnancy and delivery. In the least developed countries, these figures are down to 33 and 20 per cent, respectively.[16]

Disparities in access to health-care services depend on one's income, gender and region of residence. In most developing countries, such factors have great weight in determining access to health services. The rural population tends to be discriminated against compared to the politically more powerful and economically more prosperous urban groups. In one third of the developing countries, rural people are only half as likely to be covered by health services as those in urban areas. Inequality in the coverage of the social infrastructure also exists.

In Brazil, almost 80 per cent of the national health budget

goes to hospital care in urban areas, mainly in the south of the country, while rates of illness and infant mortality in the north-east are among the highest in the world. The Niger devotes 50 per cent of the government health budget to hospital services in urban areas, 40 per cent to provincial facilities in main towns, and only 10 per cent to rural areas, where 80 per cent of the population live.[17]

The main hindrance to providing health-care personnel to rural areas is that their earnings potential is far greater in urban areas. Some countries have taken specific steps to achieve a more equitable distribution of personnel between urban and rural areas. These steps include mandatory services in rural areas for all graduating health professionals, improvements in living and working conditions in difficult areas and financial incentives and brighter career opportunities. Only a few countries have made much progress with these policies.

Within the family, gender inequality in access to health care is also a concern. Infant girls are discriminated against in favour of males in nutrition and access to care. Studies in Bangladesh found that boys under 5 years of age were given 16 per cent more food than girls. In India, too, boys were given far more fatty and milky food than girls. Not surprisingly, girls were four times as likely as boys to suffer from acute malnutrition. Girls were more than 40 times less likely to be taken to hospital.

Differential feeding, nurturing and care of female children lead to excess female mortality in childhood, and in some cases lower female life expectancy. In many developing countries, more girls than boys die between the ages of one and four years, in sharp contrast to the developed countries, where deaths of boys are more than 20 per cent higher than those of girls in the relevant age group. The differences in the developing countries indicate the extent of bias against girls in childhood in access to nutrition, health care and medical attention.

## C. FINANCING

The market for health-care services is peculiar. An individual consumer's expenditure on health care must depend heavily on the advice and recommendations of an intermediary — a physician or a surgeon — who normally stands to benefit from that expenditure. And major spending on health care is episodic and an insurable risk, so that in many countries, health expenditure is financed out of insurance premiums paid by or on behalf of the consumer. These insurance schemes may be government or private-sector owned. In some other countries, health-care costs are for the most part paid out of tax revenue. Consumers pay a part of the costs as user fees. In a large number of countries, hospitals and related institutions are the property of the Government and are run by them. In most countries one finds a combination of these arrangements.

In many countries the rising cost of health care has stimulated new solutions to avert fiscal crisis. Policies and programmes include reducing unnecessary health services and cutting back on excessive consumption of pharmaceuticals, drawing up a list of generic drugs equivalent to more expensive products, promoting competition among providers and introducing alternative financing schemes.

In several developed countries, restraints have been imposed on payments to hospitals and physicians. The diagnosis-related group payment system in the United States and the prospectively set global budgets in France are examples of price-restraint policies embodying incentives reform. The evidence from the United States indicates substantial reductions in the length of stay in hospital as a result of these innovations.

In the developing countries, user fees are a means of cost-sharing. Even a small charge tends to make clients avoid superfluous services. If the charges remain moderate, a majority of the population may find them affordable. Revenue from user charges allows the extension of some services. Revenue from user charges as a percentage of total government expenditure on health services in the early 1980s ranged from 2 per cent in Pakistan to 17 per cent in Colombia. The average for developing countries was 7 per cent.[18]

Differentiated user fees are used to improve targeting in favour of disadvantaged households. In the Republic of Korea, under the medical assistance scheme, the poor get free medical care. Those with an income of about $50 per month and subsistence farmers pay 20 per cent of in-patient fees, except in Seoul where they pay 50 per cent. The scheme enables them to receive primary health care at private clinics designated by the Ministry of Health and Social Affairs or from health centres and community health practitioners. About half of the medical facilities nationwide are designated for this purpose. The scheme benefits 3.3 million people, about 8 per cent of the total population.[19]

To reduce costs, many countries have promoted the use of generic rather than brand-name drugs and established community pharmacies. Sri Lanka saved a considerable sum by centralizing the purchase of pharmaceutical products through one State company. Several countries that have their own domestic pharmaceutical industry, including Argentina, Brazil, India and Mexico, have made similiar significant savings.

In the developing countries, health insurance programmes cover only a small proportion of low-income households. Only 15 per cent of the people in the developing countries, not including China, participate in any form of risk coverage for health care. Several countries in Latin America have shown marked improvement in widening insurance coverage. Brazil and Mexico are examples of countries with improved systems.

China has provided low-cost health services, using several approaches to financing. These include both direct and indirect government spending, insurance plans, and spending by collectives and by the private consumer. Government has always paid a significant share of health-care costs. The Government pays staff salaries in health bureaus, public hospitals and other health institutions. The labour pool and dependants covered by the various insurance arrangements appear to be about 20 per cent of China's population. Another 10 to 15 per cent may have communal insurance coverage. There are still about 800 million uninsured Chinese, whose access to health care depends on their ability to pay.[20] For all practical purposes, all rural, primary health services are now provided on a fee-for-service basis. Rural doctors charge a small consultation fee and earn the bulk of their income from profits on medicines they dispense.

One of the most significant changes in health-care financing in recent years in Latin America has been the creation of private health insurance schemes. A private health insurance scheme was launched in Chile in 1981. Workers were allowed to transfer their health insurance from the government-operated system to these institutions. Insurance institutions have working agreements with physicians, medical centres, laboratories and hospitals for the care of their subscribers at set fees. Users can freely choose their provider. Between 1981 and 1985 the number of institutions grew from 2 to 15. The number of those insured rose from 26,000 to 147,000.

In several OECD countries, health insurance schemes are provided by the Government. In Sweden a high proportion of the cost of health care is paid for by taxes raised at the county level, supplemented by funds from general social insurance schemes. In Canada there is a national, universal health insurance scheme supervised by the federal Government and financed by both federal and provincial governments. Health-care services are almost entirely provided by private entrepreneurs. In Germany social welfare insurance is compulsory and absorbs about 13 per cent of the wages.

A major development recently in private insurance of health care in the developed countries is the trend towards "managed care", provided under health maintenance organizations (HMOs) and preferred provider organizations (PPOs). These new arrangements have the potential to reduce spending through the effective provision of health care. Several cost-containment measures are included in the arrangements, such as lower rates of payment and shared financial risks. Expenditure can be reduced through incentives to provide preventive care (HMOs), reduced rates reimbursement for individual services in exchange for guarantees as to volume (PPOs), the substitution of less expensive home care for institutional care (nursing homes for hospitals) and out-patient for in-patient care (free-standing clinics of various types, home health care, or the prevention of illness).

In many developing countries, missionaries and other non-profit providers, independent physicians, pharmacists and traditional healers are all active and important in the health sector. Direct payments to these groups account for up to one half of all spending on health in many developing countries. The expansion of non-governmental health services tends to reduce the financial burden on the Government and broadens the consumer's options. In the provision of simple curative care, the private sector providers are often more efficient than the Government and provide better service at lower cost. Partnership between the public and the private sectors is common in countries where non-governmental organizations have provided an important share of health-care services. In Rwanda, where missionaries provide 40 per cent of the health-care services, the Government reimburses them for 86 per cent of their staff salaries. The Governments of Zambia and Zimbabwe also cover a substantial part of mission spending on health care.[21] Contracting to non-governmental providers is also common in several countries, Indonesia and the Philippines, for example.

Countries in Central and Eastern Europe have initiated a restructuring of their health-care services, while coping with serious shortages of essential drugs, basic medical equipment and disillusionment among health workers. They are exploring ways to raise pay, morale, quality and equity in their health sector by transferring financial responsibility to third-party (insurance) payers and to consumers. They also propose to increase competition among health-care providers. One of the options, proposed in Poland, focuses on "managed competition" among health-care providers such as family doctors and self-governing hospitals.

## D. CONCLUSIONS

Considerable progress in the health status of the world's population is evidenced by declining infant mortality rates, rising life expectancy and some improvements in maternal and under-five mortality. Advances have been made to improve access to at least the essential elements of primary health care and to make available basic curative health services, including care of women during pregnancy and childbirth. A major achievement has been the vaccination of 80 per cent of the world's children against common childhood infections.

Much of the progress observed is clearly attributed to strong government intervention. Better designed and targeted programmes have contributed to steady progress. A major contributor to these successes was the focus on affordable low-cost child survival techniques such as immunization and the use of oral rehydration therapy. The immunization of 80 per cent of the world's children has been the most significant public health success in the past decade.

Perhaps the major achievements of the past decade have been to establish more clearly than ever before the main parameters of an effective health policy. Good health policy begins with adequate nutrition, safe drinking water, sanitary sewage disposal and the education of females. Immunization against common infectious diseases can be attained at costs that are affordable even in poor countries. The universal provision of primary health-care facilities improves health conditions at low cost. Generic drugs and a basic list of drugs have been shown to be inexpensive and adequate.

These achievements notwithstanding, the health of the mass of people in developing countries remains poor. Many of the public health problems associated with communicable diseases are still major challenges. There are enormous disparities in access to health-care facilities because of a lack of infrastructure, a severe scarcity of resources and misguided policy. In some developed countries, faulty organizational forms restrict the availability of health care. In many of these countries, soaring costs of health care have not yet been contained.

While university hospitals in urban centres are essential for training health-care personnel, every effort must be made to spread health-care facilities to rural areas. The education of females is an essential precondition for the removal of intra-family inequities in access to medical care. Lack of access to health-care services in developed countries because of inability to pay has been shown to be correctable by the reorganization of the provision of those services.

The rising cost of health care and the means of financing it are major concerns. Measures to improve public health that can make remarkable contributions to raising the condition of health in most countries, especially the developing countries, do not require the outlay of large resources. Public health regulations, education about sources of infection and the best means of destroying or avoiding them, the vaccination of children and the introduction of simple and inexpensive procedures such as oral rehydration therapy (ORT) will help reduce morbidity and mortality. Changing risky behaviour patterns remains the only way of warding off HIV infection and eventually AIDS. Efforts to focus on healthy lifestyles is a key aspect of health services.

International cooperation to improve health conditions must continue unabated. It is an essential element in strategies to eradicate poverty in developing countries. The work of WHO and UNICEF has helped to define priorities among objectives of public expenditure, introduced cost-effective procedures and stressed the importance of education and community participation in improving health conditions. The emphasis on primary health care in the developing countries owes much to them, More now needs to be done in the transfer of expertise to teach, to design syllabuses and to conduct research.

## Notes

[1] Some of the statistical data on mortality are projections provided by the Population Division of Economic and Social Development of the United Nations Secretariat. They have, in general, withstood eventual verification in the past.

[2] *World Population Prospects 1990* (United Nations publication, Sales No. E.92.XIII.4), p. 27.

[3] WHO, *Implementation of the Global Strategy for Health for All by the Year 2000, Second evaluation;* and *Eighth Report on the World Health Situation,* forty-fifth World Health Assembly (A45/3), 6 March 1992, p. 102.

[4] WHO, *World Health Statistics Annual,* (1991), p. 11.

[5] UNICEF, *The State of the World's Children, 1991* (Oxford and New York, Oxford University Press, 1991), p. 12.

[6] WHO, *World Health Statistics Quarterly*, vol. 43, no. 2 (1990), p. 102.

[7] WHO, *Global Estimates for Health Situation Assessment and Projections* (1990), p. 32.

[8] WHO, *World Health Statistics Annual* (1989), p. 17.

[9] WHO, *World Health Statistics Quarterly*, vol. 43, no. 2 (1990), p. 110.

[10] WHO, *Implementation of the Global Strategy for Health for All by the Year 2000, Second Evaluation, and Eighth Report on the World Health Situation,* p. 114.

[11] Note by the Secretary General on the prevention and control of acquired immune deficiency syndrome (AIDS) (A/47/289-E/1992/68).

[12] The Global AIDS Policy Coalition based at Harvard University, Cambridge, Massachusetts, estimated that the relevant figure might be 110 million.

[13] Report of the Secretary General on the prevention and control of HIV/AIDS and programmes addressed to the mitigation of its negative socio-economic consequences (E/1991/67).

[14] World Bank, *World Development Report 1991* (Oxford and New York, Oxford University Press, 1991), p. 63.

[15] United States Agency for International Development and United States Department of State, "Health care needs in the Commonwealth of Independent States" ...

[16] WHO, *Global Strategy for Health for All by the Year 2000,* second report on monitoring progress in implementing strategies for health for all, forty-second World Health Assembly (A42/4), 10 March 1989, p. 239.

[17] "Financing health services in developing countries: an agenda for reform", a World Bank policy study (1987), p. 17.

[18] World Bank, Charles C. Griffin, *User Charges for Health Care in Principle and Practice* (Washington, D.C., 1988), p. 21.

[19] WHO, *Economic Support for National Health for All Strategies* (A/40/Technical discussions/2) (1987), p. 68.

[20] World Bank, "Long-term issues and options in the health transition", *China*, vol. 1 (1990), p. 108.

[21] World Bank, *World Development Report 1991* . . ., p. 68.

# 8

# Education and literacy

EDUCATION has been beneficial to social integration and economic development, mainly as a result of its effects on various dimensions of human development. It has helped reduce poverty by increasing the value and efficiency of the labour of the poor. Moreover, education has had an important influence on health, especially in the case of mothers and the health and nutrition of their households. Similarily, there is a close relationship between educational development and changes in demographic trends, in particular the decline of mortality and fertility rates, marriage patterns and changes in the structure, size and composition of families.

In developing countries, for example, women with more than four years of primary education are estimated to have 30 per cent fewer children than women with no education, and their children have mortality rates only half as high.[1] Primary education has also led to changes in the aspirations and strategies of each social stratum concerning education itself: children of educated parents are more likely to enrol in school and complete more years of school than children of uneducated parents. In addition, education is centrally important to good citizenship, social integration, respect for human rights and the democratization processes currently under way in many developing countries. Finally, as economies worldwide are transformed by technological advances and new production methods that depend on a well-trained and intellectually flexible labour force, education becomes ever more significant to societies and their political, economic and scientific institutions.

Educational policy received sustained attention during the 1980s. Governments in both developed and developing countries, non-governmental organizations, parents' associations, international organizations and international financial institutions attempted to reorient education policy in response to several pressures. However, more than 40 years after the adoption of the UNESCO Charter, recognizing everyone's "right to education", more than 100 million children, in 1990, including at least 60 million girls, were without access to primary schooling; more than 960 million adults, two thirds of them women, were illiterate; more than 100 million children and countless adults failed to complete basic education; and millions more satisfied attendance requirements but did not acquire knowledge and skills. If enrolment ratios remain at current levels, by the year 2000 there will be more than 160 million children worldwide without access to primary schools.[2]

## A. ENROLMENT IN SCHOOL — THE DEVELOPING COUNTRIES

During the past several decades, developing countries have registered a rapid rise in the average educational level of the population, especially in parts of Asia and much of Latin America. This educational expansion has been all the more remarkable in view of the fact that the school-age population was growing at around 3 per cent a year on average in the countries concerned. Other factors that educational systems have had to contend with in developing countries have been the massive inflow of rural migrants to cities, increased female enrolments, and the social demands for additional years of education in the face of changes in the structure of employment opportunities.

Public expenditure on education in the developing countries stayed relatively stable at 3.9 per cent of GNP during the period 1980-1990. When allowance is made for population growth, however, the real resources allocated to education dropped. In 1990, public spending on education per person in the developing countries was $US30, compared to $US750 in the developed countries (see table 8.1). Much tighter budgets in the developing countries resulted in a distinct break in educational progress.

*Table 8.1*
Public expenditure on education, 1970, 1980 and 1990

| Region | Public expenditure on education as a percentage of gross national product | | | Public expenditure on education, per person *(in United States dollars, at current prices)* | | |
|---|---|---|---|---|---|---|
| | 1970 | 1980 | 1990 | 1970 | 1980 | 1990 |
| Developing countries | 3.3 | 3.9 | 3.9 | 7.0 | 30.0 | 38.0 |
| Africa (excluding Arab States) | 3.7 | 5.2 | 4.9 | 7.0 | 33.0 | 17.0 |
| Asia (excluding Arab States) | 3.5 | 4.6 | 4.1 | 10.0 | 38.0 | 70.0 |
| Arab States | 5.0 | 4.5 | 5.8 | 15.0 | 112.0 | 114.0 |
| Latin America and Caribbean | 3.3 | 4.1 | 4.0 | 20.0 | 94.0 | 99.0 |
| Developed countries | 5.7 | 5.4 | 5.2 | 136.0 | 426.0 | 750.0 |
| World | 5.4 | 5.1 | 5.0 | 57.0 | 133.0 | 202.0 |

Source: UNESCO, *Statistical Yearbook, 1982 and 1992* (Paris), tables 2.12 and 2.9.

The distribution of resources among the different levels of education, and to vocational education as well, became a question of much significance. Many developing countries with net primary enrolment ratios of less than 90 per cent allocated 60 per cent or more of public expenditure on education to primary education. In several developing countries, including Guinea and Nepal, the proportion of current public spending allocated to tertiary education exceeded 25 per cent. In 23 out of 26 developed countries, the comparable allocation was less than 20 per cent. In a large number of developed countries, the allocation to vocational technical education was less than 5 per cent.

1. *The primary level*

By 1990, most developing countries had a provision for compulsory education lasting 5 to 12 years. This provision reflects their desire to extend education widely and equitably. However, the goals were achieved in only a few developing countries. In most of these countries, especially in Africa, enrolment at the primary level continued to be low. The net enrolment ratio (the proportion of children in the age group enrolled in primary school) for the age group 6-11 in the developing countries was 78 per cent in 1990: 59 per cent in Africa, 76 per cent in the Arab States, 81 per cent in Asia and 88 per cent in Latin America. and the Caribbean. In the OECD countries and the economies in transition, the primary level net enrolment ratio was 92 per cent in 1990.

Globally, the increase in enrolment fell from 5.4 per cent per annum during the period 1970-1980 to 1.3 per cent per annum from 1980-1990 (see table 8.2) The deceleration was not due to a saturation in net enrolment. Out of the 37 developing countries for which there were data, only 12 countries had a net enrolment ratio of 90 per cent or over. Even where the enrolment ratio was 90 per cent or over, enrolment grew faster in the Islamic Republic of Iran, Mauritius, Singapore and Tunisia in the 1980s than in the 1970s. In contrast, no developing country had a net enrolment ratio less than 40 per cent in which growth in enrolment accelerated. In fact, in sub-Saharan Africa and the Arab States, 20 to 25 per cent of children of school age did not have access to primary schooling.

Not all pupils enrolled in primary schools reached grade four, the minimum necessary for the acquisition of literacy. Those who did not, swelled the ranks of the illiterate.

Retention rates varied in the developing regions.[3] Even in East Asia, about one sixth of the age cohort at the end of the 1980s did not stay in school long enough to complete grade four. In Latin America and the Caribbean, 36 per cent of the relevant age cohort did not complete grade four; in South-East Asia the figure was 41 per cent and in sub-Saharan Africa, 45 per cent. In sub-Saharan Africa alone, the proportion of children enrolled in primary school who did not complete grade four increased during the last decade.

Developing countries generally have made much progress in expanding schooling during the past several decades, but these trends conceal some shortcomings. In the poorest countries, espe-

*Table 8.2*

Average annual increase in enrolment, 1970-1980 and 1980-1990, enrolment ratio and female enrolment *(percentage)*

| World and regions | Average annual increase in enrolment | | Enrolment ratio (both sexes) | | Female enrolment | |
|---|---|---|---|---|---|---|
| | 1970-80 | 1980-90 | 1980 | 1990 | 1980 | 1990 |
| I. *All 3 levels* | | | | | | |
| Developing countries | 8.6 | 1.7 | 45.6 | 48.6 | 42 | 44 |
| Africa (excluding Arab States) | 6.7 | 2.3 | 39.6 | 42.1 | 42 | 44 |
| Asia (excluding Arab States) | 9.1 | 1.3 | 45.5 | 47.7 | 42 | 43 |
| Arab States | 6.2 | 4.1 | 45.5 | 53.9 | 39 | 42 |
| Latin America/Caribbean | 5.0 | 2.0 | 58.8 | 64.0 | 49 | 49 |
| Developed countries | -0.3 | 0.3 | 67.2 | 72.2 | 49 | 49 |
| World | 5.4 | 1.3 | 49.9 | 52.7 | 44 | 45 |
| II. *Primary* | | | | | | |
| Developing countries | 8.1 | 1.1 | 69.6 | 77.8 | 44 | 45 |
| Africa (excluding Arab States) | 6.1 | 1.9 | 58.5 | 59.8 | 44 | 41 |
| Asia (excluding Arab States) | 8.8 | 0.7 | 70.5 | 80.8 | 43 | 45 |
| Arab States | 5.0 | 3.3 | 68.1 | 76.4 | 41 | 43 |
| Latin America/Caribbean | 4.7 | 1.6 | 82.4 | 87.6 | 49 | 49 |
| Developed countries | -2.8 | 0.1 | 92.2 | 91.5 | 49 | 49 |
| World | 4.8 | 0.9 | 73.5 | 80.1 | 45 | 46 |
| III. *Secondary* | | | | | | |
| Developing countries | 10.3 | 2.7 | 43.0 | 48.2 | 39 | 42 |
| Africa (excluding Arab States) | 11.5 | 4.3 | 42.9 | 45.7 | 34 | 41 |
| Asia (excluding Arab States) | 9.9 | 2.3 | 41.8 | 46.3 | 39 | 41 |
| Arab States | 9.1 | 5.9 | 42.9 | 53.7 | 37 | 41 |
| Latin America/Caribbean | 5.0 | 3.6 | 62.6 | 71.6 | 50 | 52 |
| Developed countries | 2.7 | -0.1 | 81.0 | 88.3 | 50 | 50 |
| World | 6.9 | 1.8 | 50.6 | 55.1 | 43 | 44 |
| IV. *Tertiary* | | | | | | |
| Developing countries | 9.4 | 5.6 | 15.6 | 16.4 | 34 | 37 |
| Africa (excluding Arab States) | 6.9 | 7.5 | 6.4 | 10.0 | 18 | 25 |
| Asia (excluding Arab States) | 6.9 | 5.6 | 15.8 | 15.7 | 31 | 35 |
| Arab States | 13.2 | 5.2 | 16.6 | 22.0 | 31 | 36 |
| Latin America/Caribbean | 11.2 | 4.4 | 23.6 | 27.1 | 43 | 47 |
| Developed countries | 3.3 | 1.9 | 30.8 | 37.9 | 48 | 50 |
| World | 5.2 | 3.4 | 16.1 | 17.5 | 42 | 45 |

Source: UNESCO, *Statistical Yearbook 1967* (Paris), tables 2.1 and 2.3 and *Statistical Yearbook 1992*, tables 2.2 and 2.3.

cially in Africa, many children never go to school. Enrolments are particularly low in isolated rural areas, for lower socio-economic groups and sometimes for girls. Of the more than 100 million school-age children out of school in developing countries, the vast majority come from one or more of the traditionally disadvantaged groups in society: rural, female and poor.[4] Major obstacles to their participation include factors such as high costs of school attendance, lack of nearby schools in some areas, too few spaces in schools, limited parental demand in the local environment for education, household and farm chores that compete for time in the child's schedule, and discriminatory treatment in school, in particular with respect to language of instruction and gender. Of those who go to school, fewer than 60 per cent of first graders in the poorest countries complete primary school.[5] The principal school-related determinants of dropping out are poor learning and repetition, with repetition rates in low-income countries as much as five times higher than those in middle-income developing countries.[6] Moreover, of those children who complete primary school, many fail to acquire basic literacy and numeracy skills.

## 2. The tertiary level

Enrolment at the tertiary level in the developing countries in 1990 was 16.4 per cent of the age group compared to 37.9 per cent in the developed countries. In sub-Saharan Africa, the ratio was 10 per cent, in Asia 16 per cent, and in the Arab States and Latin America and the Caribbean, more than 20 per cent (see table 8.2) The aggregates mask large disparities among countries. In most African countries, in some Asian and Pacific countries and in a few Central American countries, the gross enrolment ratio at the tertiary level was below 5 per cent.[7]

In many developing countries the proportion of public funds allocated to vocational and technical education and training in 1988 was 5 per cent or less.[8] In contrast, 25 per cent or more of current public expenditure was devoted to tertiary education in some developing countries, including Guinea and Nepal. Of the developing countries listed in table 8.3, 23 allocated less than 20 per cent of current public expenditure to tertiary education.

## B. LITERACY AND ADULT EDUCATION

Literacy is still a major problem despite gains in school enrolment worldwide in the past 30 years.[9] There were 948 million adults aged 15 years and over in the world who were illiterate in 1990, of whom 97 per cent were in the developing countries (see table 8.4). Illiteracy among females was higher than among males (see figure 8.1). It was also higher among rural residents than among urban residents. While the relative magnitudes of the illiterate population fell in all regions of the world, the absolute figures rose in sub-Saharan Africa, South Asia and the Arab States; they tapered off in East Asia and Latin America and the Caribbean. If present trends continue to the year 2000, there will be close to one billion illiterate adults in the world, 98 per cent of them in the developing countries.

Even when literacy campaigns have been carried out successfully and the illiterate have acquired literacy, there are problems of literacy consolidation, retention and use.

Various volunteers, including primary-school teachers, literate farmers, village leaders and literacy graduates themselves, were used in both the literacy campaigns and the post-literacy campaigns meant to prevent the new literates from relapsing into illiteracy. The success of the campaigns was due in no small part to the activities of these volunteer teachers, whose hallmark was dedication, commitment to the campaigns' goals and objectives and political awareness.

In the developing countries where literacy campaigns were successful, for instance, Brazil, China, Cuba, Nicaragua and the United Republic of Tanzania, permanent, post-literacy adult programmes were set up to continue the process of lifelong learning.

New institutions were also established. The means used to prevent backsliding included village newspapers, community libraries and reading centres, special pages in newspapers for new literates,

*Table 8.3*

Distribution of developing countries or areas by duration of compulsory education, 1990

| Years of compulsory education | | | |
|---|---|---|---|
| 5 | 6 | 7 | 8 |
| Madagascar | Benin | Lesotho | Angola |
| Colombia | Burkina Faso | Mali | Chad |
| Bangladesh | Burundi | Morocco | Malawi |
| Iran, Islamic | Cameroon | Mozambique | Niger |
| Rep. of | Cape Verde | Tanzania, U.R. of | Rwanda |
| Macau | Central African Rep. | Zambia | Somalia |
| Myanmar | Côte d'Ivoire | Argentina | Western Sahara |
| Nepal | Djibouti | | Zimbabwe |
| Vietnam | Ethiopia | | Belize |
| | Guinea | | Dominican Rep. |
| | Guinea-Bissau | | Bolivia |
| | Nigeria | | Brazil |
| | Senegal | | Chile |
| | Togo | | Guyana |
| | Zaire | | Afghanistan |
| | Cuba | | Democratic Yemen |
| | Guatemala | | Kuwait |
| | Haiti | | Lao People's D.R. |
| | Honduras | | Mongolia |
| | Jamaica | | |
| | Mexico | | |
| | Nicaragua | | |
| | Panama | | |
| | Trinidad and Tobago | | |
| | Ecuador | | |
| | Paraguay | | |
| | Peru | | |
| | Suriname | | |
| | Uruguay | | |
| | Cambodia | | |
| | Indonesia | | |
| | Iraq | | |
| | Korea Rep. of | | |
| | Philippines | | |
| | Syrian Arab Rep. | | |
| | Thailand | | |
| | United Arab Emirates | | |
| | Yemen | | |
| | Tonga | | |

*(continued)*

*Table 8.3 (continued)*

| Years of compulsory education | | | |
|---|---|---|---|
| 9 | 10 | 11 | 12 |
| Algeria | Congo | Antigua and | Bermuda |
| Comoros | Gabon | Barbuda | St. Kitts and |
| Egypt | Ghana | Barbados | Nevis |
| Liberia | Bahamas | Grenada | |
| Libyan Arab J. | Dominica | | |
| Namibia | Bahamas | | |
| Seychelles | Venezuela | | |
| Costa Rica | Korea, | | |
| El Salvador | Dem. P.R. of. | | |
| Brunei Darussalam | Sri Lanka | | |
| China | Nauru | | |
| Jordan | | | |
| Malaysia | | | |
| Kiribati | | | |
| Tuvalu | | | |

Source: United Nations/DESD, based on UNESCO, *Statistical Yearbook*, 1990 (Paris), table 3.1.

*Figure 8.1*
Illiteracy rates by sex, 1990 *(percentage)*

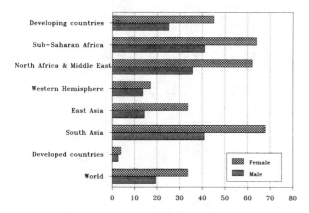

Source: UNESCO, Compendium of Statistics on Illiteracy, 1990 edition, No. 31 (Paris, 1990).

*Table 8.4*

Estimated illiterate population aged 15 years and over, 1970, 1985, 1990 and 2000[a]

| | Number (In millions) | | | | Ratio of illiterate to population 15 years and over (Percentage) | | | | | | | | | |
| | | | | | Both sexes | | | | Male | | | Female | | |
| | 1970 | 1985 | 1990 | 2000 | 1970 | 1985 | 1990 | 2000 | 1970 | 1990 | 2000 | 1970 | 1990 | 2000 |
|---|---|---|---|---|---|---|---|---|---|---|---|---|---|---|
| Developing countries | 842.3 | 907.2 | 916.6 | 919.7 | 54.7 | 39.3 | 34.9 | 28.1 | 42.2 | 25.1 | 19.7 | 67.4 | 45.0 | 36.8 |
| Sub-Saharan Africa[b] | 115.0 | 133.9 | 138.8 | 146.8 | 77.4 | 59.2 | 52.7 | 40.3 | 67.5 | 41.0 | 29.8 | 86.8 | 63.9 | 50.4 |
| Arab States[b] | 49.7 | 58.6 | 61.1 | 65.6 | 73.5 | 54.5 | 48.7 | 38.0 | 60.5 | 35.7 | 26.9 | 86.3 | 62.0 | 49.4 |
| Latin America/Caribbean | 43.0 | 44.6 | 43.9 | 41.7 | 26.2 | 17.7 | 15.3 | 11.5 | 22.5 | 13.6 | 10.3 | 29.9 | 17.0 | 12.7 |
| East Asia | 324.1 | 295.3 | 278.8 | 236.5 | 46.8 | 28.5 | 23.8 | 17.2 | 32.7 | 14.3 | 10.0 | 61.3 | 33.6 | 24.6 |
| South Asia | 302.3 | 374.8 | 398.1 | 437.1 | 68.7 | 57.8 | 53.9 | 45.9 | 55.2 | 40.9 | 33.8 | 83.1 | 67.8 | 58.8 |
| Least-developed countries[c] | 104.8 | 138.4 | 148.2 | 170.1 | 77.5 | 65.2 | 60.4 | 51.0 | 68.1 | 48.6 | 39.2 | 87.0 | 72.1 | 62.7 |
| Developed countries | 47.8 | 42.3 | 31.5 | 15.7 | 6.2 | 4.6 | 3.3 | 1.5 | 5.0 | 2.6 | 1.0 | 7.3 | 3.9 | 2.0 |
| World | 890.1 | 949.5 | 948.1 | 935.4 | 35.8 | 29.4 | 26.5 | 21.8 | 30.4 | 19.4 | 15.4 | 46.5 | 33.6 | 28.2 |

Source: UNESCO, *Compendium of Statistics on Illiteracy*, 1990 edition, No. 31 (Paris, 1990), tables 1 and 2.

a   Projected.

b   Some Sub-Saharan African countries are included in Arab States, as well.

c   The 42 least developed countries are included in their respective regions, as well.

wall posters and booklets on subjects such as agriculture and health, radio and television programmes and facilities for further education and training. For example, enthusiastic students and others in Nicaragua were kept as teachers for post-literacy and adult education activities. The United Republic of Tanzania established rural newspapers and libraries as part of its post-literacy measures.[10]

Adult literacy programmes remained important features of education policy in most countries. They were used for purposes well beyond those of providing literacy, and radio and television were most useful. In countries where literacy rates are low, post-literacy campaigns provide technical skills training.

In countries such as Afghanistan, Bangladesh, India and Viet Nam, literacy campaigns were used to support community development. Some of these countries have campaigns specifically for illiterate women and girls.

In the Philippines, the Institute for Science and Mathematics Education Development of the University of the Philippines used adult education to initiate many community-based projects, contributing to improved living standards. For example, at San Salvador, a fishing village in the southern province, in addition to literacy classes and the building of a reading centre, seminars and workshops were conducted for adults on methods of increasing their income-earning capacity and improving their diets and surroundings.

In Africa, Botswana, Lesotho and Zambia combined the teaching of basic reading, writing and arithmetic with some agriculture-related skills in their adult literacy campaigns.

In some Central American countries, programmes to help out-of-school youths took the form of integrated rural reform since they entailed improvements in literacy, health and productivity and in rural life generally.

In China,[11] adult education has always been given priority by the Government and people since the founding of the People's Republic of China in 1949. Its objectives have been to improve the level of education of the people, to reduce inequality by giving opportunities to those who have not benefited from education, to popularize science and technology and to train qualified manpower. Adult education is the concern not only of the Government but also of labour unions, factories, mines and other enterprises. Townships, villages and other economic units mobilize peasants to build and equip schools and choose from among them those who can teach.

About 20 per cent of the population 15 years and older in the developed countries are functionally illiterate.[12] Governments, labour unions, business and industry joined hands to start literacy programmes. In Canada, adult literacy programmes are conducted as institutional programmes by colleges, workplace programmes (taking programmes to the people) and community-based programmes; the latter have much leeway in experimenting and innovating in delivering their services. In British Columbia, adult education encompasses adult literacy, career development and trade programmes. Knowledge and skills are imparted to out-of-school youth and adults through curriculum guides, resource books and student learning materials to give them a second chance to acquire skills and become productive citizens.[13]

The use of computers in some of the workplaces allowed the participants to learn at their own pace and also provided flexibility among learning, work and other duties.

In several developed countries, non-formal, post-compulsory-level education and training programmes were conducted to equip adults — the unemployed, women and disadvantaged groups — with marketable skills. In some countries, for example, Germany and Switzerland, most young people enter apprenticeships with a view to having both on-the-job training and part-time education. In the United States, comprehensive, all-embracing adult literacy programmes teach out-of-school youths and adults not only basic literacy skills but also occupational skills and competencies to enable them to hold jobs and lead more productive and satisfying lives.

## C. WOMEN'S ACCESS TO EDUCATION, ESPECIALLY IN SCIENCE

Fewer females than males and fewer rural children than urban children in most developing countries had access to schools. Within technical and vocational education there is a preponderance of female enrolment in fields such as domestic science, commercial/ secretarial studies, health and craft skills, where compensation is usually lower than in fields where males predominate, for example, electronics, carpentry and automobile mechanics. Traditional and parental influence affect these choices.

At the tertiary level, female enrolment as a percentage of total enrolment increased in developing countries from 29 per cent in 1970 to 37 per cent in 1990. Gross enrolment ratios for females were persistently lower than for males in all African countries. In the developed countries, 50 per cent of the total enrolment was female in 1990.

Females studying mathematics and the sciences at the tertiary level continued to be low. Within these fields, female enrolments in the natural sciences, medicine and health-related fields are usually between one quarter and one half of the total enrolments worldwide. However, mathematics and engineering remained bastions of male domination.

In several countries, deliberate efforts were made to interest girls and women in science and technology courses at school and university and in careers in science and technology.[14]

In the developed countries, women still lag behind men in science and technology.[15] In the United Kingdom, the proportion of women professors in the sciences at universities in 1990 was 1.9 per cent in the biological sciences, 1.3 per cent in the physical sciences, 0.8 per cent in mathematics, and 0.7 per cent in engineering. The proportion of female teaching staff at universities decreased as one went up the academic ladder from lectureship to professorship. For example, in computer sciences, they made up 13.5 per cent of the lecturers, 6.8 per cent of readers and zero per cent of professors. Similar patterns repeat themselves in France and Germany. In Japan, 8 per cent of all scientists and engineers in 1991 were women.

Women face discriminatory practices in careers in science and technology in both universities and industry. Dozens of female mathematicians reported having encountered a climate of hostility on their way to professional success.[16]

Women also have the double burden of being a female scientist and a wife and mother in a society that expects women, but not men, to put family ahead of career. Women scientists also had difficulty in their initial years finding senior scientists who could guide their research to career success. Women in industry earned less than men. In 1991, women chemists earned, on average, 88 per cent of what their male counterparts earned, even when allowance was made for age, experience and academic degrees. Women in science in universities earned less than men at every stage of their scientific careers, and the disparity increased at the highest levels of experience.[17]

## D.  REFORMS AND INNOVATIONS

Responding to the need to bring learning in schools closer to work experience and to integrate science and technology into the curriculum, significant changes in curricula at all levels were made in most countries.

The irrelevance of school curricula and programmes to economic life, particularly in rural areas and urban slums, in the developing countries was emphasized. The curriculum was often more suitable for students who would eventually go to university, whereas most pupils would have primary education as their only formal education and would likely follow agricultural pursuits. Moreover, a significant proportion of them would drop out even before completing primary education.

In the reformed curricula, greater emphasis was placed on mathematics, science and technology. At the primary level, the revised curricula incorporated as much science and mathematics as the pupils would need in practical, real-life situations. The reformed science curricula were integrated and interdisciplinary in approach. They emphasized skills that would be used to solve problems related to water resources, sanitation, health and nutrition, and food preservation, to organize productive activities such as cooperatives for farmers or fishermen, and to improve simple technology for making such things as charcoal and fish nets. The reformed curricula linked science with the practical problems and basic technical skills needed for productive work where the pupils lived.

In the Caribbean, pride of place was given to food and nutrition education in the reformed curricula. Food and nutrition concepts and their relationship to science, social studies and physical education were emphasized. A handbook based on this integrated approach was prepared for use by primary-school teachers throughout the English-speaking Caribbean.

At the secondary level the development of practical skills was stressed in revising curricula. The Thai Community Secondary School Project, the Malaysian Living Skills course and the Papua New Guinea School Community's Extension Project had such objectives in view. The Barangay high schools in the Philippines and vocational high schools in China involved the school directly in the production process, in making technical and ethical decisions about alternative technologies and in implementing new ideas and methods to solve human and environmental problems.[18]

The curriculum reforms encountered impediments. In some developing countries, parents in rural areas objected to the rural bias in primary-school curricula. They feared that the new curricula would confine their children to rural life and limit their chances of entry into the next level of schooling and into the modern sector, where wages and salaries are higher. Although in most developing countries there were rapid increases in enrolment in vocational and technical institutions, the provision of essential inputs, for example, workshops and materials, did not increase simultaneously. For instance, in Algeria, Egypt and Morocco, the rapid increase in enrolment in vocational and technical institutions during the 1980s was not accompanied by a commensurate increase in equipment, instructional materials, well-trained instructors and efficient management.[19] Budgetary constraints made it difficult for them to provide these necessary inputs, contributing to a deterioration in the quality of training. Stagnation or recession in economies adversely affected the demand for skilled labour, causing unemployment among the graduates of vocational and technical schools in these three North African countries.

In the developed countries, curriculum changes tried to ensure that pathways for development were not overly restrictive, preparing students for entry only into higher education or leading to a dead end that did not allow even lateral movement into another track.[20] Towards the end of the 1980s, Governments in France, Japan and the United Kingdom set up committees to establish guidelines for the reform of school curricula.

Some countries tried to make technology an integral part of general education for all children. In France, a new programme of technology education, which included electronics, informatics, mechanics and nutrition, replaced manual and technical subjects in secondary schools. In the United Kingdom, technology was accorded a prominent place in the 10-year programme of technical and vocational education for all 14- to 18-year-olds. In Scotland, a trial programme was conducted in the mid-1980s, in primary schools, in the hope that a technology problem-solving attitude would contribute to the children's general education and would stand them in good stead in later life.[21]

Some developed countries tried to diffuse science and technology knowledge among students by forging school-industry links. These links related classroom study to the world of work and employment. They gave the students opportunities for training in a real workplace and increased their knowledge and practical experience.

In the United States, cooperative education programmes for secondary-school and college students combined classroom instruction with work experience and on-the-job training related to students' career goals. These programmes were beneficial to both the participating students and the enterprises. They improved workforce preparation, facilitating youths' transition from school to work and employers gained access to a pre-screened pool of employees.[22]

In Finland,[23] visits to plants by secondary-school students in physics and chemistry to get hands-on experience, through student-centred work, has proved to be successful. After initial trials, the Government extended the programme to the entire educational system and links between schools and industry have been strengthened. These visits received the enthusiastic support of Government, industry, teachers and students alike. Industry was happy about good public relations and good exposure for the quality of its products. The teachers thought the visits were worthwhile. From the students' perspective, practical work that showed them the relationship between school physics and chemistry and industrial processes was exhilarating as the practical value of their studies and experiments at school were confirmed. Some of the students found summer jobs at the plants they visited and a few even decided to make a career in those fields.

## E.  EDUCATIONAL INPUTS

Constraints on the availability of resources imposed by the general economic downturn and problems of public finance, in particular, limited opportunities to improve the quality of education. In primary schools, in 1988, the pupil/teacher ratio was more than 31 to 1 in about 60 developing countries. In contrast, in 27 developed countries, the comparable ratio was 20 to 1. Most developing countries with a ratio higher than 31 to 1 were in Africa, Asia and the Arab States (see table 8.5)

Teachers were not only overburdened but also often inadequately trained, low-paid and low in morale. In most developing countries, primary teachers had only about nine years of general education and were generally the least able of their classmates. Deficiencies in the trainees' general education necessitated extra costs on remedial programmes. Poor working conditions, including low salaries, resulted in high rates of turnover and absenteeism as some teachers (and civil servants in general) engaged in other activities to earn extra income. In many developing countries, average

*Table 8.5*

Pupil-teacher ratio at the primary level, 1970, 1980 and 1988

| Region | | Number of countries with pupil/teacher ratio of | | | | | |
|---|---|---|---|---|---|---|---|
| | | 20 and under | 21-30 | 31-40 | 41-50 | 51-60 | over 60 |
| Developing countries | 1970 | 11 | 53 | 48 | 28 | 7 | 5 |
| | 1980 | 27 | 52 | 44 | 19 | 8 | 5 |
| | 1988 | 28 | 60 | 41 | 12 | 7 | 7 |
| Africa | 1970 | 1 | 4 | 15 | 17 | 3 | 5 |
| (excluding Arab States) | 1980 | 2 | 6 | 13 | 12 | 5 | 5 |
| | 1988 | 2 | 7 | 19 | 3 | 5 | 7 |
| Asia | 1970 | 2 | 12 | 6 | 6 | 1 | - |
| (excluding Arab States) | 1980 | 2 | 11 | 10 | 3 | 3 | - |
| | 1988 | 3 | 11 | 9 | 4 | 2 | - |
| Arab States | 1970 | 2 | 8 | 8 | 2 | 1 | - |
| | 1980 | 6 | 5 | 9 | 1 | - | - |
| | 1988 | 6 | 11 | 1 | 3 | - | - |
| Latin America and Caribbean | 1970 | 4 | 17 | 17 | 4 | 2 | - |
| | 1980 | 10 | 20 | 11 | 3 | - | - |
| | 1988 | 9 | 22 | 11 | 2 | - | - |
| Developed countries | 1970 | 12 | 24 | 3 | 1 | - | - |
| | 1980 | 23 | 15 | - | - | - | - |
| | 1988 | 27 | 11 | - | - | - | - |
| World | 1970 | 23 | 77 | 51 | 29 | 7 | 5 |
| | 1980 | 50 | 67 | 44 | 19 | 8 | 5 |
| | 1988 | 55 | 71 | 41 | 12 | 7 | 7 |

Source: UNESCO, *Statistical Yearbook*, 1982, table 2.7 A and 1990, table 2.7.

teacher salaries decreased over the past two decades. The fall has been estimated at 30 per cent in West African countries and 20 per cent in East African countries between 1970 and 1990.[24] In many instances, teachers were paid later than when due. Students themselves were hungry and malnourished, making it extremely difficult to get the best of educational opportunities.

## F.  BOOKS, NEWSPAPERS, RADIO AND TELEVISION

During the two decades ending in 1990, there was a phenomenal expansion worldwide in the supply of newspapers, books and films and both radio and television receivers. Globally, the number of book titles published increased from an estimated 521,000 in 1970 to 834,500 in 1988. The circulation of daily newspapers increased from 395 million in 1973 to 575 million in 1988. However, newspaper circulation per 1,000 inhabitants declined from 129 to 113. Annual cinema attendance rose from 13.3 billion in 1970 to 14.2 billion in 1987. The number of radio broadcasting receivers more than doubled, from 735 million in 1970 to 1.9 billion in 1988. The total number of television receivers rose from 290 million in 1970 to 756 million in 1988.

The wider availability of books and newspapers and radio and television receivers made the task of combating illiteracy easier around the globe. They were used in the developed countries as well as in the developing countries to impart knowledge in both formal and non-formal education programmes.

1. *Use of communication media in education*

The rapid changes in science and technology and their wide spread broadened the role of communication media in education. Newspapers, films, radio, television, computers, satellites and other sophisticated delivery systems, videos and accompanying printed materials were used to produce and distribute teaching materials.

In India,[25] a satellite television system was used, on an experimental basis, in six states to provide education in health, family planning and agriculture. Specially made community television sets were placed in a school or community hall. Daily in-school programmes for children aged 5 to 12 years were broadcast to schools in the morning. They consisted of entertainment and information intended to enrich the children's school experience and science instruction. An evaluation of the satellite broadcast experiment showed that pupils in classrooms that made use of the broadcasts had gained in comparison with non-participating pupils.

In the United Republic of Tanzania the Government used the radio to provide education to illiterate adults, to stimulate national development, to improve health knowledge in rural areas and to promote increased agricultural production and improved nutrition. The radio programmes were deemed to have achieved most of their objectives.

## G.  CONCLUSIONS

The expansion of primary education and the diversification of secondary and tertiary education remain the most important objective of education policy in most countries. Providing females with increased access to education is especially important. Fast technological changes and the compelling necessity to raise productivity underlie the need for diversification. Greater emphasis on science and mathematics at all levels and closer ties between formal education and workplaces form other aspects of the process of diversification.

A scarcity of resources in the developing countries, especially in Africa and Latin America and the Caribbean, slowed down progress in education. The diversion of public-sector spending to debt-servicing, military and other purposes reduced resources for education, as well as other social services. However, there was much room for shifting resources among levels of education to give higher priority to primary education.

Efficiency in the management of educational institutions was of much concern in the developed countries. In several countries, measures were taken to make educational institutions compete for resources from students, so that those less efficient would have clear incentives to improve the quality of their services. These policies have run up against two major problems. The first is the desire on the part of workers in education, mostly teachers, to avoid the uncertainty that is a concomitant of competition. The second is the problem of equity, where knowledgeable teachers and parents would teach more able students well, while neglecting other institutions and students.

Educational reforms attracted considerable attention in both developed and developing countries. This process is likely to continue well into the 1990s.

### Notes

[1] See S. Cochrane, "The effects of education on fertility and mortality", Education and Training Department Discussion Paper 26, World Bank, Washington, D.C., 1986.
[2] Inter-Agency Commission for the World Conference on Education for All, *World Declaration on Education for All and Framework for Action to Meet Basic Learning Needs* (New York, April 1990), preamble, p. 1.

[3] See Suren Gajraj and F. Tandart, "Education for all and the literacy benchmark", in International Institute for Educational Planning (IIEP), *Newsletter*, vol. X, no. 2 (April-June 1992), pp. 9-10.

[4] See World Bank, *Primary Education: A World Bank Policy Paper*, Washington, D.C., 1990, p. 5.

[5] See M. Lockwood and D. Jamison, *Improving Primary Education in Developing Countries*, Oxford University Press, New York, 1991.

[6] See World Bank, op. cit., table A-1.

[7] See UNESCO, *Statistical Yearbook*, 1990 (Paris, 1990), tables 3.2 and 3.11.

[8] Ibid; table 4.3.

[9] An illiterate person is one "who cannot with understanding both read and write a short, simple statement on his/her everyday life". UNESCO, *Compendium of Statistics on Illiteracy*, 1990 edition, no. 31 (Paris, 1990), p. 2.

[10] For details, see John C. Cairns, "Lessons from past literacy campaigns: a critical assessment", *Prospects: Quarterly Review of Education*, vol. XIX, no.4 (Paris, UNESCO, 1989), p. 555.

[11] See Yu Bo and Xu Hong Yan, *Adult Higher Education, A Case Study on the Workers' Colleges in the People's Republic of Çhina* (Paris, UNESCO, International Institute for Educational Planning, 1988).

[12] Audrey M. Thomas, "The social and economic costs of illiteracy", *Prospects: Quarterly Review of Education*, vol. XIX, no. 4 (Paris, UNESCO, 1989), pp. 47-58.

[13] See *Exemplary Adult Education Programs and Innovative Practices in Canada*, Province of British Columbia, Ministry of Advanced Education and Job Training and Ministry Responsible for Science and Technology (Victoria, B.C., Canada, 1989).

[14] For details of the approach in Sweden, see Ingrid Grantsam, "Girls and women in science and technology education", in D. Layton, ed. *Innovations in Science and Technology Education*, vol. II (Paris, UNESCO, 1988) pp. 47-58.

[15] The data are from "Data points. Where women get their Ph.D.s.", *Science*, vol. 255, no. 5050 (Washington, D.C., American Association for the Advancement of Science, 13 March 1992), p. 1376.

[16] Paul Selvin, "Profile of a field: mathematics. Heroism is still the norm", *Science* . . ., p. 1382.

[17] See note 15.

[18] Colin Power, "New methods for training and retraining science and technology teachers", in D. Layton, op. cit., p. 292.

[19] J. Salmi, "Vocational education in Algeria, Egypt and Morocco", *Prospects: Quarterly Review of Education*, vol. XX, no. 1 (Paris, UNESCO, 1990), p. 98.

[20] See Organisation for Economic Cooperation and Development, *Education and the Economy in a Changing Society* (Paris, 1989), p. 97.

[21] George Mills, "An introduction to technology in the early years of schooling", in D. Layton, op. cit., p. 42.

[22] United States General Accounting Office, *Transition from School to Work: Linking Education and Worksite Training*, Report to Congressional Requesters (Washington, D.C., August 1991), (GAO/HRD-91-105), p. 3.

[23] For details, see H. Kuitunen and V. Meisalo, "Science and technology education and industry", in D. Layton, op. cit., pp. 141-154.

[24] World Bank, *Primary Education*, World Bank Policy Paper (Washington, D.C., 1990), p. 24.

[25] Data on India, Nicaragua, the United Republic of Tanzania and the Dominican Republic are based on Emily G. McAnany and John K. Mayo, "Communication media in education for low-income countries: Implications for planning", *Fundamentals of Educational Planning*, no. 29 (Paris, UNESCO, IIEP, 1980), 20-52.

# 9

# Housing and sanitation

HOUSING is an investment which generates a flow of basic-need requirements that are consumed daily. It provides shelter and privacy from the outside world, and access to potable water, sanitation and electricity. In addition to the consumption benefits provided to occupants, the ancillary facilities of housing, namely drinking water and sanitation, have important public good effects in reducing the risk of infectious diseases transmission in densely populated urban areas.

Shelter is also important to households in economic terms. After food, it accounts for the largest share of consumers' budgets in most countries. Among many households, moreover, the decision whether to own or rent can have a major impact on saving and consumption behaviour. In fact, home equity is usually the largest single investment that families ever make. Housing is also often an essential base of economic activities among the self-employed in urban and rural areas.

In view of the advantages of good housing, it is unfortunate that in recent years housing conditions in most countries have deteriorated. High real interest rates have discouraged the construction of houses. Governments with budgetary restrictions have been more restrained than earlier in investments in the housing sector. Demand for housing has become weaker as real income growth slowed. The deterioration in housing conditions has been particularly evident in the heavily indebted developing countries, with high inflation and compressed import capacity keeping out the import of building materials. It has also emerged as a critical social issue in the economies in transition. Investment in housing has slowed in the developed market-economy countries more as a result of demographic trends than of economic stagnation, where housing the poor has emerged as a significant problem.

## A. DEVELOPING COUNTRIES

The shortage of housing has been a major social concern in the developing countries experiencing rapid urbanization. Rapid urbanization has caused urban land and housing prices to rise dramatically. Uncontrolled settlements have grown and overcrowding has reached serious proportions. Drinking-water supplies, sanitation and other critical public services have been tested beyond their limits. The pressure on cities has also contributed to environmental degradation.[1]

The urban housing stock data normally available are limited to the stock of standard authorized dwelling units built on land with clear title that comply with building codes and have indoor piped water and sanitation. However, much of the urban population lives in substandard housing. Generally, one in every four newly formed households has access to standard authorized housing. The construction of standard dwelling units per capita varies among countries at comparable levels of development and per capita income. Yet the correlation with income is strong.

On average, nine new households were formed for each new standard dwelling built in the middle-income developing countries. Because households are larger in the developing countries than in the developed countries, there are more people per habitable room in the former than in the latter: 1.9 persons in the developing countries compared with 0.9 in the developed countries. Three out of four households in Kumasi, Ghana, one out of two in Calcutta and one out of three in Mexico City live in one-room accommodations.[2] In the worst of cases, tenement densities have reached the point where one-room dwellings have been split up into units in which several households live simultaneously or alternate with one another in day-and-night shifts.[3]

Poverty contributes to overcrowding in the informal housing stock but so do public sector policies of prohibiting unauthorized construction and rent-control legislation that has discouraged new construction.[4] Substantial declines in government investment in housing further reduced the supply of affordable housing in many countries.

Growth in the informal housing stock has been most pronounced in the principal cities of the developing countries, where it makes up between one third and four fifths of the total urban housing stock. Much of this housing is not durably built, lacks asbestos cement or similar roofing, brick or cement block walls and wood or cement floors. Building materials frequently have to be replaced, posing major problems and inconveniences to the inhabitants.

Because of rising land and construction costs and difficult access to housing credit, a marked shift to rental housing has occurred in recent years. The ratio of renting to ownership has grown in most of Latin America and Africa, while trends are ambiguous in Asia.[5]

The principal barrier to owner-occupancy for low-income groups has been the remoteness of peripheral undeveloped land from urban centres and the rising costs of commuting to work and school. Rented accommodation also provides better amenities, including piped water, electricity and sanitation. Although created initially by self-help owners/builders, well-located consolidated settlements have developed into extensive rental systems. Owner-occupant landlords resemble their tenants in income and education but are generally older and have had the good fortune of immigrating earlier when urban land was cheaper and more readily available.[6] As housing prices have risen more rapidly than personal income, recent immigrants have little prospect of becoming homeowners.

In most instances, urban housing in the developing countries is worse than need be because housing markets have functioned poorly. Unrealistically high standards for subdivision, infrastructure and construction have made it impossible to build low-income housing in most cities. Mortage lending, often at subsidized interest rates to finance the construction of expensive high-standard dwellings has financed not more than 10 to 20 per cent of annual housing investment. Most housing has had to be financed out of household saving and current income and built in stages as funds became available.[7] Government regulations have also restricted the allocation of inputs, such as serviced land and building materials, raising costs of construction to those who are not entitled to these allocations.[8]

Housing in rural areas is not as pressing a problem as it is in rapidly growing cities. Land is plentiful and the construction of low-cost housing affordable. Pit latrines meet basic sanitation requirements. Rural housing has improved where remittances from emigrant workers have been substantial. With the exception of access to potable water, the housing problems of rural areas and slow-growing towns, despite their often substandard quality and overcrowded conditions, are generally not as pressing as those of households in large cities.

## 1. *Sanitation*

The shortage of infrastructure for providing services has made the price of developed land 10 to 15 times that of undeveloped land.[9] Simply providing piped water has been found to nearly double the value of otherwise comparable dwellings.[10] Annual public sector investments in water and sanitation have averaged about 1.5 per cent of GDP, or about 5 per cent of total public expenditure in the developing countries.[11] Despite general cutbacks in public investment in Latin America during the 1980s, house connections to the urban water supply system rose from 71 per cent in 1980 to 80 per cent at the end of 1990. Dwellings serviced with sewage connections rose from 42 per cent to 50 per cent (see table 9.1).[12]

Much of the expanded coverage in Africa and parts of Latin America consisted of minimum-standard shared-use services, such as public water taps and communal latrines, in low-income urban and rural settlements. The continued expansion of coverage in the 1980s was made possible in part by high levels of official development assistance (ODA) to finance physical infrastructure. Of about $31 billion invested on sanitation in Latin America, approximately

*Table 9.1*

Percentage of population with access to safe water supplies and sanitation facilities

| | | Urban water supply | | Urban sanitation facilities | | Rural water supplies | Rural sanitation facilities |
|---|---|---|---|---|---|---|---|
| | | House connection | Stand-post | Sewer connection | Other | | |
| Africa | 1970 | 33 | 33 | 8 | 39 | 13 | 23 |
| | 1980 | 29 | 31 | 11 | 43 | 22 | 20 |
| | 1985 | 33 | 33 | 12 | 59 | 25 | 25 |
| | 1990 | 49 | 20 | 32 | 41 | 32 | 22 |
| Latin America | 1970 | 61 | 15 | 36 | 40 | 24 | 24 |
| | 1980 | 71 | 7 | 42 | 14 | 42 | 20 |
| | 1985 | 71 | 13 | 41 | 39 | 47 | 27 |
| | 1990 | 80 | 11 | 50 | 33 | 52 | 36 |

Source: WHO, "The International Drinking Water Supply and Sanitation Decade"; end of the Decade review (as of December 1990) WHO/CWS/92.12, table A.3.2.

half was financed from external sources. In Africa, out of $US 13.2 billion, nearly three quarters came from external assistance.[13]

Public water taps are prized in low-income urban settlements since in their absence households must pay up to 15 times the official tariff when buying water from vendors, or must resort to the use of polluted water from shallow wells. However, problems of long waiting lines are frequent, as are broken or malfunctioning water taps, interruptions in service and the risk of waste water seeping into temporarily empty pipes through cracks, thereby sparking epidemics of water-borne diseases.[14]

As for communal sanitation, suitable solutions for high-density areas have often proved ellusive. The use of public toilets has revealed problems of upkeep, cleanliness and public acceptance, the latter partly a consequence of the first two and partly owing to personal discomfiture. Electricity is more commonly available with legal and illegal home connections. As for rural homes, relatively few are connected to water pipes, sewers or electricity lines, except in major villages and towns.

A major problem in water supply in the developing countries is that of financing and cost recovery. While half the population is still deprived of adequate water supplies, half of all water supplied was unaccounted for or remained unpaid for. New investments were constantly required, while operating incomes were low. Tariffs were set so low that revenue did not even cover administrative costs, not to mention depreciation. As a result, water systems were not properly maintained and the pace of extending them to new settlements fell behind needs. In recent years, as part of the sectoral stabilization and adjustment measures, tariffs have been increased to economic levels. Higher tariffs on households with piped water have helped cross-subsidize the costs of servicing low-income settlements with neighbourhood standpipes.

## B.  DEVELOPED MARKET-ECONOMY COUNTRIES

Physical indicators of housing conditions in the developed market-economy countries show a generally satisfactory situation in quantitative and qualitative terms. On the whole, a rough parity exists between household and standard dwelling numbers. Aggregate statistics, however, mask differences in social access to adequate housing. Although in many developed market-economy countries virtually the entire population is adequately housed, in countries where social inequality is more pronounced the rich are often "overhoused" in relation to need and the vulnerable poor end up homeless. Since the mid-1970s, moreover, new housing requirements have emerged as the patterns of housing demand shifted toward smaller households and, in some cases, more central locations.

Housing conditions in the market-economy countries have improved markedly over the years. With housing construction outpacing population growth, the scarcity of dwellings that existed at the end of the Second World War was eliminated by the mid-1970s. Household crowding declined significantly. Since the mid-1970s, however, improvements in housing conditions in many countries faltered as incomes failed to keep up with housing prices and various distortions emerged in the housing markets.[15]

The mismatch between supply and demand owing to problems

of affordability, tenure and location of the housing stock is pointed
up by estimates that there are half a million dwellings, including
250,000 public housing units in the United Kingdom and 10.3 million dwellings in the United States that stand unoccupied, while 1.2
million households stand on waiting lists for public housing in the
United Kingdom and 1 million families have their names on waiting lists for public housing in the United States. An additional 12
million are deemed to be in need of assistance to pay rent.[16] The
problem is especially acute with low-income households, unskilled
labour and the chronically unemployed. Rent-controlled housing is
often occupied by those in higher-income groups. Some of the
older housing stock has been rehabilitated and modernized and
rented at high prices.[17] There is an acute shortage of inexpensive
rental accommodation, driving up the cost of housing in the unreg-
ulated sector.

Homelessness has grown rapidly in some countries during the
past decade as a result of insufficient new public housing construction, long-term unemployment, the growth of drug abuse and, in
the case of Italy and the United States, the de-institutionalization
of many mentally ill persons from hospitals without adequate out-
patient follow-up treatment. In the United States, low-income
rental units have disappeared at the rate of half a million a year,
there has been little new construction of public housing and government housing allowances have failed to keep pace with rising
rents.[18] Reliable data on homelessness are lacking in all countries,
with estimates in the United States ranging from 250,000 to 3 million,[19] complicating the analysis of homelessness. Generally, countries with adequate public housing and comprehensive social assistance programmes have had few if any problems of homelessness.

Public policies to deal with housing needs have included various mixes of subsidies and the construction of dwellings. In the
1980s, housing capital expenditure and operating subsidies ranged
from 0.1 per cent to 8.2 per cent of central government outlays,
with a mode close to 4 per cent.[20] The composition of those outlays,
however, shifted over the years from the construction of dwellings

to transfer payments to support poorer households. The reasons for this change include the large stock of public housing in a number of countries,[21] high real interest rates and a growing disillusionment in some countries about the effectivenness of public housing in solving the residential needs of low-income groups. Instead, the focus of public intervention has been to regulate rents, protect the rights of tenants, provide rent subsidies for poor tenants in non-rent-controlled premises and assist private lessors by means of tax incentives and public subsidies for new construction.[22] Public sector subsidies, as a result, are increasingly made up of rent support transfer payments to poorer households and of various forms of support to lower-income housing landlords.[23]

Rent supplements have gained recognition for the advantages they provide over other housing policy approaches: they are more effectively targeted at needy people than rent controls or tax relief, less costly per beneficiary than public housing construction and more flexible with regard to site, mobility and shifting household needs than other policy approaches. The impetus for the adoption of rent supplements in Germany came from the need to ease the financial strain on lower-income families after rent decontrol.[24] Rent-control regulations continue to be controversial in many countries because they deter new construction, discourage maintenance and repair of the housing stock, induce owners to keep vacant premises off the rental market,[25] discourage labour mobility from economically depressed areas to cities where employment prospects are brighter[26] and impede the filtering down of older housing from well-off occupants of rent-controlled premises to poorer newcomers in need of shelter.[27]

Subsidies to home-owners resulting from deducting the cost of mortgage interest payments from taxable income rose in the early 1980s when interest rates and inflation and housing costs all rose. At their peak, these implicit subsidies came to approximately 50 per cent of the total fiscal subsidy in the housing sector in France, Germany and the United Kingdom.[28] They encouraged overconsumption of housing by the wealthy and benefited existing home-owners and sellers at the expense of first-time buyers by bidding up housing prices more than would have occurred in their absence. Recently they have declined in some countries. Tax codes have placed caps on mortgage interest relief, restricted tax concessions to first-time purchasers during the first several years of the loan or lowered the effective tax brackets at which households may claim deductions.[29] While recent reforms have helped reduce the dead-weight losses resulting from the favourable tax treatment of home-ownership, they have not in all cases made the incidence of mort-gage interest subsidies less regressive.[30]

Home-ownership includes the prospect of the value of the housing unit rising and the risk of it falling. In countries where housing prices outpaced inflation, home-owners obtained substan-tial windfall gains when selling their homes. Moreover, given the surge in housing prices in Japan, the United Kingdom, the United States and a number of other countries during the 1980s, home-owners borrowed at record levels, in relation to income.[31] Since 1990, however, house prices have fallen by 16 per cent on average in real terms. Home-owners worrying about their shrinking wealth and ability to repay what they borrowed contributed to prolonging the economic slow-down.[32] In view of the forecasts of the formation of fewer households, real housing prices are expected to stagnate or decline in developed market-economy countries during the 1990s.[33] The correction downward in house prices has been a boon to first-time home-buyers and home-owners wishing to trade up to better housing and tenants.

Future housing requirements are likely to vary from country to country. In countries where a severe shortage of good quality hous-ing still exists, as in some large cities of the Mediterranean region and Japan, new construction will probably continue to account for the bulk of housing investment. In others with low population growth and an adequate supply of standard housing, investment in the main-tenance and modernization of the existing housing stock will likely continue growing at a higher rate than new construction. The demand for rental accommodation will probably increase not only because of stagnating incomes but also as a consequence of demographic and economic changes: fewer children per household, high rates of divorce, occupationally mobile single persons who prefer to rent, prospects of lower price appreciation and the preference of a growing number of elderly persons to consume their capital during retirement rather than tie it up in housing. A return to home-ownership trends, however, cannot be precluded in countries where "baby boomers" are reaching the peak age in their life and work cycles, when households are most likely to be owner-occupants.[34]

As with housing production, investments in new or larger capacity sewers and water mains declined after the 1970s. Except in Japan, where the expansion of urban infrastructure is an urgent priority, public spending on infrastructure in the developed market-economy countries has been directed mainly at improving or repairing urban water and sewage systems.[35] Environmental concerns, such as the contamination of potable water supplies by surface water run-off and the effluent from waste-water treatment processes, are likely in future years to contribute to a growing sense of urgency to repair existing water and sewage systems.[36]

## C. ECONOMIES IN TRANSITION

Under socialism and central planning, countries adopted the principle that housing was a social right: the State had the duty to supply it to all who needed it. The centrally planned economy countries on average invested up to 5 to 6 per cent of net material product in housing construction in response to rapid urbanization and industrialization and the need to replace substandard housing and the stock destroyed during the Second World War. As a consequence, by the mid-1980s, more than 85 per cent of the population of the former Soviet Union lived in accommodations built after the Second World War, as did about two thirds of the population of Hungary and more than half in the former Czechoslovakia.[37]

The provision of ancillary infrastructure also improved during the post-war period. Eighty-nine per cent of the urban housing stock of the former Soviet Union was equipped with fixed lavatories and central heating by 1985.[38] However, residential accommodation remained in short supply, as reflected in long waiting lists for housing, overcrowding (see table 9.2) and the difficulties of relocating because of social preferences relating to life-cycle needs and labour market changes.[39] The average floor space per resident in these economies is less than half the average in developed market-economy countries. Further evidence of the scarcity of adequate housing in the Russian Federation was the delay in repatriating troops stationed in other member countries of the Warsaw Pact.

*Table 9.2*
Housing conditions in Eastern Europe and the former Soviet Union, 1980-1990

| Country | Ratio of new dwellings built to total marriages and divorces | Floor space per person (sq. m.) | Dwellings completed per 1,000 inhabitants | | Total housing stock per 1,000 inhabitants | Share of housing in household expenditure mid-1980s including utilities |
|---|---|---|---|---|---|---|
| | 1985 | 1985 | 1980 | 1990 | 1985 | |
| Bulgaria | 0.80 | 19 | 8.4 | 2.9 | 353 | 12.1 |
| Czechoslovakia | 0.66 | 26 | 8.8 | 4.7 | 367 | .. |
| Hungary | 0.71 | 19 | 8.3 | 4.2 | 361 | 8.7 |
| Poland | 0.60 | 15 | 6.1 | 4.0 | 287 | 4.4 |
| Romania | 0.54 | .. | 8.9 | 2.1 | .. | .. |
| Soviet Union | 0.55 | 15 | 7.5 | 7.4 | .. | 2.5 |

Sources: *Annual Bulletin of Housing and Building Statistics for Europe* (United Nations publication, Sales No. E/F/R.91.II.E.11), 1991; Statistichesky ezhegodnik stran-chlenov SEV 1986, Moscow; and Renaud, B., *Housing Reform in Socialist Economies*, World Bank Discussion Paper No. 125, June 1991, table 3.

Past approaches to housing provision have been further criticized for their low productivity and government subsidies on the order of 3 to 5 per cent of net material product, not including subsidies from enterprises and local governments.[40] Because of low-quality production and poor finishes, moreover, much of the housing stock is currently entering a phase in which maintenance costs are high and some housing stock may have to be completely replaced.[41]

Recent trends in housing construction show a considerable decline in Eastern Europe, with no signs of recovery in the near term. A decline in the output of building materials has also occurred. Owing to economic contraction and shortages of building materials, the housing sector has become a residual concern in most countries.[42] The former centrally planned economy countries broadly agree that the inefficiencies, distortions and inequities of past housing systems must be reformed.[43] Rents and utility charges have been raised in Bulgaria, Hungary and the Russian Federation. Public sector apartments have been offered to sitting tenants at nominal prices. Similiar measures are under active consideration in Poland and Romania.[44] Despite low prices, however, most offers have been rejected because of poor quality and maintenance. The large and well-located apartments rented to, and currently owned by, former high-level officials have been bought up.[45]

The challenges to new housing construction in this period of transition are formidable. An entirely new institutional structure has to emerge. Viable housing finance systems are difficult to put in place because current household incomes are far too low in relation to housing prices.[46] High inflation and economic uncertainty make loan maturities too short and interest rates too high. Retail prices of building material are two to three times higher than wholesale prices.[47] It will be some time before a working housing market emerges.

## D. CONCLUSIONS

The housing situation varies considerably among the developing countries, the developed market economies and the economies in transition. However, all countries have common problems: distortions that raise prices and reduce access to housing, rigidities in access to housing that hinder labour mobility, and insufficient housing facilities to meet the needs of the urban poor. While in some instances the provision of more public housing would help meet the demand, a more cost-effective approach would be to remove perverse housing incentives and introduce or expand measures that would strengthen the market for housing inputs supply and offer households greater choice.

The emphasis needs to be on urban housing markets in the developing market economies. Reforms in financial intermediation and increased land tenure security would encourage people to undertake construction. The provision of infrastructure, relaxation of the legal and regulatory framework affecting housing and land ownership, reducing barriers to entry and greater competition in the construction and building materials industry would reduce costs. Specific measures that Governments could take would include reducing uncertainty in interpreting and applying regulations, removing bureaucratic bottlenecks that impede, delay and increase transaction costs, modifying building codes for lower-income communities, providing standard levels of infrastructure facilities to all communities located on land where ownership is not seriously contested, supplying land titles and ex post facto legal recognition to solidly built dwellings in consolidated settlements in acceptable urban locations, and waiving the application of rent-control laws to small-scale owner-occupied premises and phasing out such regulations in all rental premises. Research on local inexpensive building materials that comply with minimum performance standards would also help substantially.

In the developed market-economy countries, the imbalances of "overconsumption" of housing by the rich and the homelessness of the poor can be reduced by shifting public subsidies away from upper-income home-owners to rent supplements for low-income households. Tax exemption of interest payments should aim to help reduce payments by first-time buyers during the first few years of their mortgages. Rent controls should be phased out to reduce distortions in the rental market and activate the filtering down of older rental stock to low-income groups and to increase labour mobility.

In the economies in transition, chronic housing shortages and overcrowding and the process of transition create special problems. Renewed activity in the housing sector is likely to wait for market mechanisms to emerge. A part of the reforms will activate the market for existing dwelling units.[48] Further institutional changes will need to be made for clarifying property rights between renters and owners, providing transitional subsidies before shifting to a system of targeted housing allowances for disadvantaged households, introducing mortgage financing for housing, increasing competition in the housing construction industry and making urban planning more efficient in site selection, space utilization and infrastructure provision.

## Notes

[1] See, for example, R. Stren and R. White, eds., *African Cities in Crisis: Managing Rapid Urban Growth* (Boulder, Colorado, Westview Press, 1989).

[2] See Housing and Economic Adjustment (United Nations publications, Sales No. E.88.IV.1), p. 5.

[3] See J. Breman, "Calcutta and the urban order in Asia", *Development and Change*, vol. 14, no. 2 (April 1983), pp. 157-158.

[4] See S. Malpezzi, G. Tipple and K. Willis, *Costs and Benefits of Rent Control: A Case Study in Kumasi, Ghana*, World Bank Discussion Paper No. 74 (Washington, D.C., 1990).

[5] See for example, K. Sunil and F. van den Eerenbeemt, "Renting — its place in the housing market of developing countries", *Bulletin for the Institute for Housing Studies BIE* (Rotterdam, 1988); World Bank, "Rental housing: a rediscovered priority", *The Urban Edge*, vol. 8, no. 2 (1984), pp. 1-5; A. Lemar, "The role of rental housing in developing countries: a need for balance", World Bank Report No. UDD-104 (Washington, D.C., 1987); and M. Edwards, "Rental housing and the urban poor: Africa and Latin America compared", in P. Amis and P. Lloyd, eds., *Housing Africa's Urban Poor* (Manchester, Manchester University Press, 1990), pp. 253-272. For Latin America, see A. Gilbert, "Renting and the transition to owner occupancy in Latin American cities", *Habitat International*, vol. 15, no 1/2 (1991), pp. 87-99. For Africa, see T. Akin Aina, "Petty landlords and poor tenants in a low-income settlement in metropolitan Lagos, Nigeria", in P. Amis and P. Lloyd, eds., *Housing Africa's Urban Poor . . .*, pp. 87-101; P. Amis, "Squatters or tenants: the commercialization of unauthorized housing in Nairobi", *World Development*, vol. 12, no. 1 (1984), pp. 87-96; and C. Grootaert and J. Dubois, "Tenancy choice and the demand for rental housing in the cities of the Ivory Coast", *Journal of Urban Economics*, vol. 24 (1988), pp. 44-63. For Asia, see M. Hoffman and others, "Rental housing in urban Indonesia", Habitat International, vol. 15, no. 1/2 (1991), pp. 181-206.

[6] See M. Edwards, op. cit., pp. 256-257.

[7] See B. Renaud, *The Role of Housing Finance in Development: Issues and Policies* (Washington, D.C., World Bank, July 1989).

[8] This argument emerges from analysing the results of a stock-user matrix applied to a hypothetical city in a developing country. See P. Strassmann, *Housing and Building Technology in Developing Countries* (East Lansing, Michigan State University Press, 1978), chap. 7.

[9] See "Housing: enabling markets to work", World Bank Policy Paper (Washington, D.C., May 1992), p. 14.

[10] See P. Strassmann, "The timing of urban infrastructure and housing improvements by owner-occupants", *World Development*, vol. 12, no. 7 (July 1984), pp. 743-754.

[11] See *Living conditions in developing countries in the mid-1980s: Supplement to the 1985 Report on the World Social Situation* (United Nations publication, Sales no. E.85.IV.3), p. 47.

[12]See WHO, "The International Drinking Water Supply and Sanitation Decade: end of the decade review (as of December 1990)" (Geneva, August 1992) (WHO/CWS/92.12).

[13]Ibid., pp. 30-32 and 47-49.

[14]See B. Koeppel, "Water: save now or pay later", *The Urban Edge*, vol. 15, no. 3 (April 1991), pp. 1-6.

[15]In the United States, during the 20 years from 1970 to 1990, the median price of a starter home for a typical married couple between 25 and 29 years of age rose by 21 per cent in constant dollars, while the income of this typical couple declined by 7 per cent, from $28,500 to $26,700, in constant dollars. During the same time-span, incomes of couples 10 or more years older than this age group stayed even or rose and the older group took advantage of their improving finances to increase their share of home-ownership. Accordingly, the proportion of all households headed by people aged 25 to 34 years who own their home has dropped, from 51 per cent in 1973 to 44 per cent in 1990, while the proportion of people 45 to 64 years rose from 76 to 78 per cent between 1973 and 1990. The tabulations are largely based on the 1973, 1976 and 1980 editions of the *American Housing Survey* and the 1983, 1987 and 1990 editions of the *Current Population Survey* of the Harvard/MIT Joint Center for Housing Studies.

[16]See *Housing and Economic Adjustment . . .*, pp. 40-41.

[17]See OECD, *Maintenance and Modernization of Urban Housing* (Paris, 1986), p. 45.

[18]See *Housing and Economic Adjustment . . .*, pp. 40-41.

[19]See S. Redburn and T. Russ, *Responding to America's Homeless: Public Policy Alternatives* (New York, Praeger, 1986), p. 102.

[20]See OECD, *The Control and Management of Government Expenditure* (Paris, 1987).

[21]As of the mid-1980s, the share of public housing in the total housing stock was 38 per cent in Sweden, 31 per cent in the Netherlands, 30 per cent in the United Kingdom, 17 per cent in Denmark, 17 per cent in France, 7 per cent in Germany, 5 per cent in Italy, 2 per cent in Spain and 2 per cent in the United States. See B. Renaud, *Housing Reform in Socialist Economies*, World Bank Discussion Paper No. 125 (June 1991), p. 38.

[22]See *Rent Policy in ECE Countries* (United Nations publication, Sales No. E.90.II.E.29).

[23]See *Housing and Economic Adjustment . . .*, p. 42.

[24]See, for instance, S. Mayo, "Sources of inefficiency in subsidized housing programs: a comparison of U.S. and German experiences", *Journal of Urban Economics*, vol. 20 (1986), p. 236.

[25]In London, Paris and Rome, for example, thousands of privately owned flats stand empty owing to rent laws that make it nearly impossible to remove current tenants. See "Time to let go", *The Economist*, 17-24 January 1987, p. 53.

[26]See *Housing and Economic Adjustment . . .*, p. 42.

[27]In a survey of 50 cities in the United States, there was evidence of significant correlation between increases in homelessness and the existence of rent controls. See W. Tucker, "Where do the homeless come from?", *National Review*, 25 September 1987.

[28]See OECD, *Tax Expenditure: A Review of the Issues and Country Experiences* (Paris, 1984), p. 81.

[29]See *Housing and Economic Adjustment . . .*, p. 46.

[30]In the United States, under the Tax Reform Act of 1986, several million middle-income home-owners were denied the deduction of interest on home mortgage debt from income assessed to tax. High-income households, in contrast, continued itemizing their deductions, with the result that in 1988 more than half of the implicit subsidy associated with mortgage interest deductions accrued to the 8 per cent of tax-payers with the highest incomes. See J. Porteba, "Taxation and housing: old questions, new answers", NBER Working Paper No. 3963 (January 1992).

[31]In Japan, the United Kingdom and the United States, house prices during the 1980s increased by 300, 75 and 30 per cent, respectively, and household debts in those countries were in the range of 96 to 117 per cent of disposable income in 1991, as opposed to 60 to 82 per cent in 1980. See "Economic focus: in the valley of the shadow of debt", *The Economist*, 7-13 November 1992, p. 97.

[32]Ibid.

[33]In the United States, they are projected to fall by 10 to 15 per cent during the period 1988-2007. See P. Hendershott, "Are real prices likely to decline by 47 per cent", NBER Working Paper No. 3880 (October 1991).

[34]See, for example, M. Boleat, "Home ownership and renting: international comparisons", *Housing Finance International*, vol. 1, no. 4 (May 1987), p. 7.

[35]See OECD, *Urban Infrastructure: Finance and Management* (Paris, 1991), p. 14.

[36]See OECD, *Environmental Policies for Cities in the 1990s* (Paris, 1990).

[37]See *Housing and Economic Adjustment* . . ., pp. 28-29.

[38]See *Narodnovy Khoziaystvo SSR v 1985 Godu* (Moscow, 1986), p. 430.

[39]According to national sources, the waiting period for an apartment is likely to range from 15 to 30 years in Poland, 10 years or more in the former Soviet Union, 4 to 10 years in Hungary and about 5 years in the former Czechoslovakia. See *Housing and Economic Adjustment* . . ., p. 39. As for mobility, the rate of housing turnover was as low as 1 per cent in Poland and Romania in the late 1980s, as compared to 15 to 20 per cent in developed market-economy countries. See B. Renaud, op. cit., p. 13.

[40]See *Housing and Economic Adjustment* . . ., p. 39; and B. Renaud, *Housing Reform in Socialist Economies* . . ., p. 30.

[41]See B. Renaud, *Housing Reform in Socialist Economies* . . ., p. 26.

[42]The difficulties of the housing sector in competing for materials in short supply in centrally planned economies were apparent by the early 1980s. See *Relationship between Housing and the National Economy* (United Nations publication, Sales No. E.85.II.E.16).

[43]See B. Renaud, *Housing Reform in Socialist Economies* . . ., p. 30.

[44]See UNCHS (Habitat), "Report on the subregional seminar for Eastern European countries", Moscow, 3-7 September 1990.

[45]See. R. Buckley, "Hungary's reforms: where gradual is better", *The Urban Edge*, vol. 15, no. 1 (January/February 1991), p. 2; "Local government re-organization and housing policy in Budapest: a round-table discussion", *International Journal of Urban and Regional Research*, vol. 16, no. 3 (September 1992), p. 483. For a broad discussion of the access by high-level officials to choice large apartments, luxury cars, vacation travel abroad, government health clinics with modern imported equipment and other privileges, see J. Winiecki, *Resistance to Change in the Soviet Economic System: A Property Rights Approach* (London, Routledge, 1991).

[46]House price to income ratio (the ratio of the average trading price of a housing unit to the average cash incomes of households in a given city) is estimated to range between 10 and 20 in Poland, 8 and 13 in Hungary and 7 and 10 in the former Soviet Union, as opposed to a median of 3.9 in the developed market-economy countries and 5.5 in the developing countries. See *Housing: Enabling Markets to Work*, World Bank Policy Paper (May 1992), table 2.1.

[47]See "Russia's value gap", *The Economist*, 24-30 October 1992, p. 75.

[48]The primary purpose of privatization of the existing housing stock is to place the stock in the hands of owners who will utilize the existing stock of housing more efficiently and rationally than the State, thereby reducing inter-market spillovers and stimulating better maintenance and improvements in the stock. See J. Kornai, *The Road to a Free Economy*, (New York, W. W. Norton, 1990), p. 82.

# 10

## Social security

SOCIAL security programmes aim to protect citizens from severe deprivation and to eliminate vulnerability by transferring incomes from some groups in society to others.[1]

The gains to society from social provisions and the broader programmes of welfare have been immense. They have reduced the extent and severity of poverty, helped redistribute income more evenly, promoted investment in human capital and reduced economic uncertainty.[2] In most developing countries, care of and support for the aged, the sick, the unemployed, the poor and children are a family responsibility.[3] Voluntary organizations play significant roles. In the centrally planned economies, those responsibilities were almost wholly borne by the State and State-owned enterprises, and by families to a lesser degree.[4] In developed market economy countries, families and relations, voluntary organizations and the State all play significant roles, the most prominent being played by the State.[5]

Social security policies have faced severe challenges in all countries over the past decade — most dramatically in the former centrally planned economies now in transition, less dramatically but none the less highly visible in developed market economy countries, and also in those developing countries whose economies have deteriorated.

In the former centrally planned economies, the transition to market economies will destroy the "iron bowl of rice" that reduced insecurity. Unemployment, both between jobs and cyclical, will require mechanisms to maintain incomes. New provisions will have to be made for pensions to the retired and to support children from poor families. The poor and the disabled will need support. In the absence of voluntary organizations and any worthwhile assets in private hands that could be liquidated in situations of hardship, the breakdown of State provision will mean severe hardship for many during the period of transition.

In developed market economies, persistently high unemployment, especially long-term unemployment, has eroded the assumptions that unemployment would be temporary and that the unemployed would not make permanent claims on funds. The ageing of populations and the rising costs of medical care have made for alarming increases in the transfers to the older generations. The growth of single-parent families, of the homeless and of those unable to earn a living has increased burdens on welfare budgets. The design of a policy of public assistance has been questioned, because the policies seem to create disincentives to work and raise deadweight costs to the economy.[6] Where programmes are financed through the government budget, there has been a pronounced reluctance to pay higher taxes.

In developing countries formal social security benefits are available only to a small section of the population, except in Latin America. As families become smaller and populations age, two income earners may have to support and care for four parents for long periods of time. Urbanization and the separation between the home and the workplace make earlier ways of looking after aged parents impracticable. Ageing increases the burden on the working generations to provide for the welfare of the old. The general squeeze on government finances reduces the capacity of Governments to provide social security. Fiscal constraints have prompted new efforts to target social security to prevent abuses and to ensure that benefits go to those who need them most. But successful targeting calls for administrative capacities that are scarce in developing countries.[7]

## A.  DEVELOPED MARKET-ECONOMY COUNTRIES

Public spending for social security has grown rapidly in the developed market economy countries (see table 10.1). Social security expenditure in 1960 was 3 to 12 per cent of GDP; it rose to 7 to 23 per cent by the late 1970s. Then growth slowed as Governments tried to restrain budget deficits and also curb tax burdens. None the less, social security payments remain a major item in public spending.

*Table 10.1*
Public expenditure on social security, developed market-economy countries, 1960-1990 *(percentage of GDP)*

|  | 1960 | 1970 | 1985 | 1990 |
|---|---|---|---|---|
| Austria | 10.8 | 13.9 | 20.6 | 19.8 |
| Belgium | 10.6 | 14.1 | .. | 24.8 |
| Canada | 4.7 | 8.7 | 15.1 | 12.8 |
| Finland | 4.8 | 7.6 | 13.2 | 12.1 |
| France | 9.2 | .. | 22.3 | 23.5 |
| Germany | 11.3 | 13.0 | 19.7 | 19.3 |
| Italy | 9.8 | 13.3 | 21.8 | 18.9 |
| Netherlands | 9.9 | 17.6 | 20.3 | 29.1 |
| Sweden | 6.8 | 14.1 | 20.4 | 21.2 |
| Switzerland | 5.7 | 7.8 | 13.8 | 13.9 |
| United States | 3.4 | 5.6 | 12.0 | 11.5 |

Sources: The Department of Economic and Social Development of the United Nations Secretariat, based on OECD, *The Future of Social Protection*, OECD Policy Studies No. 6 (Paris, 1988), table 3; ILO, *World Labour Report 1* (Geneva, 1984), table 6.3. H. Oxley and J. Martin, "Controlling government spending and deficits: Trends in the 1980s and prospects for the 1990s", *OECD Economic Studies*, no. (17 autumn 1991), table 2.

The proportion of expenditure on pensioners, health and unemployment benefits vary, although the bulk is for pensions and health care. In total public spending on social services, an average of 35 per cent is allocated to pensions and 7 per cent to unemployment compensation.[8] In some countries, the number of persons who benefit at any one time from these transfers can be as high as one third of the total population.[9] Together with social welfare programmes, the transfers contribute to a marked reduction in poverty.[10] By helping maintain aggregate demand, unemployment compensation has played a role in reducing the amplitude and duration of downturns in the business cycle.

Concern about social security arrangements is growing for a number of reasons. One is the expected continuation of slow economic growth in these economies. Others are population ageing, the maturation of pension schemes and concern over abuses and disincentive effects. Fear exists that current methods of funding are inadequate to meet emerging needs. To date, however, efforts to alter the sources of funding and the payments to beneficiaries have been small. The lingering question is whether universal benefits for all makes sense, or whether benefits should not be targeted to those most in need. Concern is expressed that in their current form, the social security systems of most developed countries are inadequate to cope with ageing, changes in family composition, high long-term unemployment and evolution of more flexible working patterns for men and women.

## 1. *Public pension provisions*

The objective of public pension schemes is to ensure a minimum standard of living in retirement. Minimum entitlement levels for elderly persons ensure a reasonably satisfactory standard of living for every pensioner, irrespective of his or her prior earnings. While a few retirees depend solely on public pension benefits in their old age, most live on employer-provided benefits topped up with public pensions. When added together, employer plans and public sector provisions provide retirement benefits that generally range from 40 to 60 per cent of earnings during employment.[11] In many developed countries, workers retire several years before they receive a public pension and live adequately on pensions provided by their employers.[12] This is *prima facie* evidence that for a sizeable proportion of the retiring population, public pensions are a supplement; they could live reasonably well without them.

Virtually all public pension schemes in the developed market economy countries are pay-as-you-go schemes where the current working generation pays for the current generation of retirees.[13] Workers' and employers' social security contributions have been rising over the years and are projected to rise even more steeply in a number of countries in the years ahead (see table 10.2) This increase has been due in part to the fall in the ratio of workers over

*Table 10.2*
Projected social security contribution rates to cover public pensions
in developed market economy countries, 1990-2050 *(percentage of
pay)*

| Country | 1990 | 2000 | 2010 | 2020 | 2030 | 2040 | 2050 |
|---|---|---|---|---|---|---|---|
| Japan | 4.5 | 7.7 | 12.9 | 18.8 | 19.8 | 22.9 | 23.0 |
| Germany | 13.5 | 16.4 | 18.6 | 22.4 | 29.2 | 28.9 | 28.9 |
| United States | 12.1 | 11.9 | 12.0 | 12.2 | 12.3 | 16.8 | 16.4 |

Source: R. Hagemann and G. Nicoletti, "Population ageing: economic effects and
some policy implications", *OECD Economic Studies*, no. 12 (spring 1989), table 7.

retired people. In 1980 there were roughly five persons of working
age for every retiree in the major developed market economy countries; in 2025, there are expected to be only three persons of working age for each retiree.[14]

Pensions are not only the major form of social security but,
after unemployment compensation, the fastest growing element of
social security systems. Public spending on pensions has grown on
average twice as fast as GDP since 1960. The increases were due in
approximately equal parts to growth in the number of people over
65; coverage to include women, the self-employed and other previously excluded working groups; and increases in the real level of
pensions per beneficiary. With the share of pensioners in the population expected to rise from about 13 per cent in 1985 to probably
over 20 per cent by 2040, developed countries will have to transfer
more resources to the retired population. A small proportion of the
increase will be offset by a decrease in the child dependency ratio,
as spending on child-rearing and education declines. Higher payroll
tax rates in the private sector will raise costs of production.

Modifications in public pension financing have been modest to
date.[15] They have consisted mainly of reducing entitlements, tightening eligibility conditions and raising the retirement age. The 1983
Social Security Amendment Act of the United States, for example,
reduced early retirement benefits, subjected half of the pensions of
people with high incomes to taxation and raised the retirement age

from 65 to 67 years, effective after the year 2000. In Germany the basis of pension determination was changed in 1986 from gross to net earnings. In Japan several pension schemes and pension provisions for spouses were unified under the 1985 Pension Reform Act to eliminate the possibility of individuals or households receiving excessive pensions through eligibility under multiple pension schemes.

The scope for radical transformation or reforms of public pension schemes is limited and has been so perceived by policy makers. The option to finance pensions out of general revenue has been resisted in most countries. Proposals for a pronounced shift towards private-sector pension schemes have been met with concern over equity. Substantial reductions in pension benefits have not been seriously considered owing to the acquired rights of current retirees and persons soon to retire and the political strength of growing numbers of well-organized pensioners.

Several factors have joined to produce a crisis in these institutional arrangements. In contrast to the 1950s and the 1960s, the decade of the 1980s was not one of sustained economic growth. Ageing adds to the demand for social security by increasing the number of people entitled to health care.[16] Measures to contain health care costs would help to reduce the burden.

## 2. *Unemployment compensation*

Unemployment compensation programmes guarantee an income to unemployed persons with a previous record of employment. The recipients are expected to return to work within a relatively short time. Most commonly, a uniform basic benefit is supplemented by another amount that varies with the worker's past income. Unemployment benefits are usually paid for a year or less. In France and Germany, the period is longer for older workers; in Canada, it varies with the length of previous employment.

While spending on unemployment compensation is relatively small compared to public pensions and public health care, the effect of unemployment on the government budget is substantial when revenue losses are also taken into account. Revenue losses include income taxes and social security contributions the unemployed would otherwise have paid.[17] Some countries have also been concerned that overly generous benefits raise a moral hazard problem and sometimes result in abuses.

Since the early 1970s, expenditure on unemployment compensation has risen in the developed market economy countries as a result of both higher unemployment levels and increases in benefits. Benefits increased mainly because more high-income employees lost their jobs and were paid higher earnings-related benefits. On the other hand, unemployment coverage since the early 1980s has fallen as a result of new labour-market conditions. Youth unemployment and long-term unemployment have risen in many countries, but many youths lack a previous employment record and cannot claim unemployment compensation, and many long-term unemployed have exhausted their claims to benefits. Married women also represent a rising proportion of the unemployed and are often inadequately covered by unemployment insurance because of incomplete or part-time employment records.

3. *Family allowances*

The purpose of family benefits is primarily income maintenance. Typically, assistance is provided to families with dependent children, either directly as government expenditure or indirectly as tax concessions. Germany and the United Kingdom rely on government expenditure; Canada and France offer a combination of direct grants and tax concessions; the United States provides supplementary welfare benefits to poor families which increase with the number of children, as well as tax concessions. Because of the heavy reliance in many countries on tax concessions, the effective cost of family benefits is larger than appears from an analysis of direct spending alone.

Mainly because of the drop in the number of children, family benefits have been on the decline.[18] The trend has been modified by the need to support a growing number of lone-parent, mostly low-income families. Lone-parent families now make up 10 to 15 per cent of all families with children.[19] Divorce rates have risen dramatically, and rates of re-marriage have declined. Births out of wedlock have also increased in incidence. As late as 1960, only 7 per cent of all children lived with single mothers. The proportion is now more than 20 per cent. In the United States more than half the children born today will spend some time in a mother-only family, and half of all similar families are likely to be poor.[20]

These changes have eroded the income security that nuclear family structures have traditionally provided. While public perceptions and opinions vary about parental responsibility and childbirth out of wedlock, the consensus is that children should not be left unprotected. The challenge with respect to lone-parent families has been finding means to make absconding parents, often fathers, pay for child support and to enable the lone parent to find adequately remunerative work. Programmes to provide child care for working mothers perform an important function here.


## B.  DEVELOPING COUNTRIES

Providing social security in low-income countries is in practice a very different proposition from doing so in richer countries. Natural disasters there often throw people into destitution, both because the absence of infrastructure raises the destructiveness of disasters and because resources to fall back on tend to be slim. Consequently, famine relief and disaster relief occupy a much more prominent place in social security programmes in developing countries than in developed countries.

Further, providing social assistance to the poor when they are 50 to 75 per cent of the population is not the same thing as providing for them when they are 10 or 15 per cent. For many in developing countries, severe deprivation is not a matter of an unfortunate fall from a previously more comfortable position but rather a chronic state arising from the absence of any assets to ensure an income. It is difficult to design the administration of a social security system where financial markets are rudimentary, employment is casual and the beneficiaries are illiterate.[21]

Social security schemes have grown impressively during the past two decades, but they cater mainly to people with secure jobs and steady incomes and exclude those whose needs for social security are the biggest.[22]

Among the regions, social security systems are most extensive and developed in Latin America. In several countries, they cover more than 50 per cent of the economically active population. In Argentina, Chile, Costa Rica and Uruguay, the ratio of social security expenditure to GDP exceeds 10 per cent, while in Central American countries, the corresponding ratio is about 2 per cent. They are much less extensive in coverage and less generous in Asia.[23] Sub-Saharan African countries have the most rudimentary systems. The percentage of the labour force, not including civil servants, covered by social security benefits in Africa ranged from 1 per cent in Chad, Gambia and Niger to 22 per cent in Egypt and 24 per cent in Tunisia.[24]

Social security pensions in most of the developing countries are limited to military personnel, civil servants and workers in large-scale enterprises. These are a privileged minority. This inequity is compounded in countries where proceeds from general revenue have to supplement payroll taxes in funding social security transfers. It is estimated that in Latin America the insured pay less than one third of the benefits they receive, with the rest coming from the population at large through government subsidies and employer contributions.[25]

The role of the State in social security varies from country to country, ranging from government participation in tripartite financing systems to the administration and financing of the entire social security system. Evasion or delay in the payment of contributions is in some countries quite common both of employers and Governments, disrupting the system profoundly.

In the initial stages of social security systems, social security funds accumulate surpluses. In some countries these surpluses may rise to half of GDP.[26] Often they are invested in low-yielding government bonds to cover budget deficits, but when soundly invested, as in the case of the Central Provident Fund in Singapore, these surpluses can help develop infrastructure, including low-income housing and ensure adequate returns.[27] A contrasting example is the collapse of Brazil's Banco National de Habitacao where in recent years the value of its mortgage loan contracts fell behind the general price level of rapid inflation.[28] The large initial reserves are depleted by negative real yields from investments and the rising spending. The National Retirement System, begun in 1904 in Argentina, is now deeply in debt because of recurring current account deficits, and it pays a wholly inadequate pension. Recourse has to be had to general revenue.

Social security funds for health care benefits are common in developing countries but are narrow in coverage. Where curative services are provided in hospitals that are administered and financed by social security institutions, it is not uncommon for the affiliated members to try to block collaborative arrangements with the health ministry to keep the level and quality of services provided through social security institutions at a higher level than in other institutions.[29]

In some countries in Africa and Latin America, social security benefits include family allowances. These schemes typically consist of aid to mothers and infants in the form of antenatal allowances, maternity allowances, medical expenses during pregnancy, family allowances as such and daily allowances paid to wage-earning women on maternity leave. However, because they are financed from employers' social insurance contributions, the benefits go to only a small number of families in the formal sector.

The fact that the mass of the population is excluded from social insurance schemes has induced Governments to move beyond conventional approaches and to attempt to provide social protection on a wider basis. Because of the low incomes of the excluded groups, the measures that have been introduced to protect self-employed and informal-sector workers have relied heavily on general revenue. The primary emphasis has been on universal health care and other means to ensure a minimum level of well-being. In Latin America, in particular, policies of restricting insured health care protection to relatively small, privileged groups have been replaced by health care systems that also embrace self-employed workers and marginalized social groups.

Health protection measures for the wider population are often indistinguishable from national primary health care programmes. For example, Brazil, Costa Rica and Uruguay have achieved virtually complete health care coverage through public assistance programmes, with social security participation consisting of budgetary support to the health sector via levies on affiliated employers. In Mexico and Ecuador, special health care programmes for the rural population have been funded out of general revenue and administered by social security institutions.[30]

A number of developing countries provide contributory old-age pensions to self-employed workers. Old-age, invalidity and death or survivorship benefits are available to the self-employed in Argentina, Chile, Costa Rica, Guatemala, Mexico and other Latin American countries. The population covered in most countries is not extensive.[31] Technical and administrative difficulties in identifying and enrolling target populations partly explain the narrow coverage.[32] Public-sector subsidies have been necessary for self-employed workers who do not have employers to make payroll tax contributions on their behalf.[33]

The social security systems of some countries also include a number of complementary, non-contributory social assistance schemes. Emergency employment programmes, for instance, have been mounted in urban areas as forms of economic stabilization and adjustment. In Chile in 1983, for example, employment in urban infrastructure construction was offered to 13 per cent of the labour force, bringing the unemployment rate down from 32 per cent to 19 per cent.[34] Other self-selection public employment schemes have provided a form of insurance against a risky agricultural environment by offering unskilled work to anyone who wants it at a wage rate that only the poor find attractive.[35] The social security systems of some countries also include distributing food to poor and vulnerable groups. In Jamaica, food stamps are targeted through public health systems to pregnant women and infants. The reduction or removal of food subsidies or other social assistance entitlements risks creating negative reactions among recipients denied the benefit.[36]

## C. ECONOMIES IN TRANSITION

Market-oriented reforms in Eastern Europe and the former Soviet Union have put severe strains on public programmes for social protection. Policy makers are confronted with several issues largely unknown in the recent past, including a sharp rise in unemployment, the loss of purchasing power due to sharp price increases and worsening poverty among vulnerable social groups.

The contraction of output and government revenue means that government spending must be restrained to reduce inflationary pressures. The mass of the population continues to expect that society will honour its welfare commitments. In a spirit of social solidarity, it could revitalize collaboration between the Government and civic organizations to extend a "safety net" to the growing number of vulnerable people. The contrasting wish is to reduce the size of Government and the notion that wealth creation is more important than redistribution, but it has also been argued that the creation of safety nets may be a condition for economic reforms.[37]

The ratio of government expenditure on social security to GDP has been traditionally high in economies in transition, comparable to that in OECD countries (see table 10.3). Although these welfare provisions have been criticized as formal and inadequate,[38] they were important in household incomes. In Hungary at the end of the 1980s, consumer subsidies were between 48 and 72 per cent of the personal income of the poorest 20 per cent of the population; for large families, the proportion ran as high as 82 per cent.[39] In 1991 the size of family allowances as a percentage of gross income varied between 5 and 6 per cent in Czechoslovakia, Hungary and Poland, and between 2 and 3 per cent in Bulgaria and the Russian Federation.[40]

*Table 10.3*

Ratio of expenditure on social security to GDP in European economies in transition, 1988-1991

|                      | 1988 | 1990 | 1991 |
|----------------------|------|------|------|
| Bulgaria             | 10.1 | 13.0 | 12.1 |
| Czechoslovakia       | 11.7 | 12.0 | 15.0 |
| Hungary              | 15.4 | 17.5 | 24.0 |
| Poland               | 11.2 | ..   | ..   |
| Romania              | 7.9  | 8.6  | 7.3  |
| OECD Europe (1989)   | ..   | 19.0 | ..   |

Source: Department of Economic and Social Development, United Nations Secretariat, based on Bank for International Settlements, *62nd Annual Report*, (Basel, 1992).

The share of pensions in household gross incomes varied significantly. According to some estimates, at the end of the 1980s, pensions as a percentage of average wages in State-sector jobs were about 68 per cent in Hungary and Yugoslavia, 48 per cent in Bulgaria, Czechoslovakia and Poland, and 37 per cent in the former Soviet Union.[41]

The pension systems have run into several problems. The ageing of the population and the growing number of beneficiaries under old age, disability and survivor benefit programmes have made it difficult to maintain the payments. The effective retirement age, typically 60 years for men and 55 for women, is lower in many Eastern European countries than in OECD countries. Social assistance was treated as a residual element of expenditure, of secondary importance. That practice resulted in numerous distortions and "holes" in the safety net, particularly for pensioners, disabled persons and other disadvantaged groups, who were brought to the brink of poverty. For example, in Czechoslovakia between 1965 and 1988, there was a decline in the real value of disability, family and pension benefits.[42] Many retired people were forced to take part-time jobs to supplement their income because pensions did not keep up with wages and consumer prices.

The lack of a detailed legal framework led to arbitrary interpretations in administering social assistance. When legal criteria for implementing the provisions of the law were absent, internal administrative instructions of each ministry took over. Thus, in Poland, broad provisions in the laws and their lack of precision left room for arbitrary decisions in providing social assistance.[43] Numerous instructions and regulations issued by government offices often contradicted the spirit, if not the letter, of the laws.

Understanding is growing that the value of social assistance is more substantial when this assistance is well-targeted. The differentiation of incomes will most probably continue, making the plight of the poorest and most vulnerable groups more sensitive. In most countries, efforts to make assistance more focused relied, along with cash transfers, on services in kind (provision of free or subsidized meals, special home delivery programmes and food coupons).

Consumer subsidies were an important part of social security programmes in these countries. Despite the best intentions of Governments, the bulk of these benefits went to non-vulnerable groups. In addition, subsidized prices gave the wrong signals for resource allocation.[44] The elimination of subsidies became one of the obvious priorities in stabilization programmes. The decline in government revenue made the reduction of subsidies even more compelling. Subsidies were discontinued for a wide range of consumer goods and social services, compensating the neediest groups with cash transfers. In 1990-1991 the share of subsidies as a percentage of GDP decreased in Bulgaria from 16.1 to 3.5 per cent, in Czechoslovakia from 14.0 to 4.2 per cent, and in Romania from 7.5 to 5.7 per cent. Clearly, to eliminate subsidies fast would be to endanger the physical survival of groups at high risk. It was decided to target the subsidies more precisely for vulnerable groups.

New models of social security and, in broader terms, social policy itself, have been at the centre of public debate. Political developments, including rising public anger over deteriorating living conditions, put the social impact of the reform programmes high on the agenda. Policy makers were forced to reassess the social implications of the transition. The nature of the new arrangements is clearer in the countries that started the process earlier, although everywhere there is an evident quest for new approaches.

In the short term, Governments started a number of immediate measures to mitigate the adverse social effects of their stabilization programmes, to shield the most vulnerable segments of the population and to reduce social tensions. Those steps included poverty relief measures to offset rising prices and the provision of a minimum unemployment benefit. Introduction of unemployment insurance was one of the first measures of social reform undertaken in practically all European economies in transition. Although introduced as transition measures, those policies are likely to be retained and to form a basis for new social security schemes.

Facing serious financial constraints, economies in transition find it hard to maintain living standards for the elderly. Because of continued inflation, it has been difficult to secure the value of pensions in real terms. Different schemes have been introduced to remedy the situation. In Hungary, for example, one of the options envisoned is a ceiling on pensions while at the same time indexing all pensions. In the Russian Federation, a national insurance pension fund has been sponsored by a private insurance company, two commercial banks and the ministries of social protection and labour. Its profits are expected to provide benefits to individual members and to become an important supplement to their government-provided pensions.[45]

To speed the integration of the disabled into the new market-oriented system, far-reaching laws were enacted in Poland in July 1991 to provide equal opportunities for disabled people at work. The law requires enterprises to create conditions of work that would enable those who had suffered from occupational diseases or accidents at work to continue working. Enterprises failing to create such conditions are required to pay out of their after-tax profits to the State Rehabilitation Fund for the Disabled a sum equal to 40 times the monthly national average wage of each worker. The Fund provides financial assistance and training to the disabled.[46]

In some cases the generosity of pensions has been one of the main reasons for the escalating costs of social security. Since 1990, for example, Poland has had a growing number of pensioners because of liberal disability allowances and early retirement lay-offs. The other factor contributing to higher costs has been an increase in pensions relative to average wages. At the same time there has been a decrease in revenue due to a lower level of employment.[47]

Local rather than central governments are better positioned to provide some types of assistance to families in need and to reach target groups.[48] The budgetary independence of local governments varies. In Romania and Bulgaria, the social spending of local governments continued to be funded primarily by the central government, which also retained supervisory functions. In Czechoslovakia and Poland, local authorities became financially independent, complementing centrally allotted funds with additional revenue from taxes on enterprises or individual residents.

Sharing social security payments between the central government and other entities, including the private sector, became an important feature of reform. The creation of alternative private pension plans was recognized as an extension of the freedom of choice and an increase in security for the retirees. In Hungary the pension fund was separated from the central budget in 1989. In Poland the Social Insurance Fund, providing benefits like pensions, family allowances and sickness and maternity benefits, and operating on a pay-as-you-go basis, is financed by contributions from enterprises with deficits covered by transfers from the central government budget.

The commitment of public enterprises to provide social security has been scaled back. The old practice limited benefits to the employees of those enterprises. Crèches and kindergartens are being transferred to local governments. At the same time, administration of health insurance and of certain welfare activities that used to be in the hands of trade unions was shifted back to national or local government institutions.

Demands for macroeconomic and price stability compete with the political necessity to maintain social security benefits. The creation of an effective and financially sustainable system of social security becomes an immediate priority. Without it, the process of change itself might run into unsustainable political opposition.[49]

## D.  TARGETING

Targeting social service spending towards the most deserving has stimulated strong interest, especially given the severe limits on government expenditure. However, several practical problems are associated with schemes to narrow entitlements to social security benefits.

The first is that schemes to benefit weaker groups of society may not be socially acceptable. A part of the economic price paid for the scheme to be politically acceptable may be to extend benefits beyond targeted groups. Free university education in many developing countries is made use of mostly by the higher-income classes; this is the price paid for providing lower-income groups with access to university education. Programmes for raising living standards of the poorest sections of the population have been most successful in economies where facilities have been provided universally.

Secondly, costs of administering targeted schemes are high. In the United Kingdom, universal schemes cost 3.5 per cent of total outlay to administer, contrasted with a range of 5 to 15 per cent in targeted schemes.[50] In developing countries the low competence in public administration and the widespread illiteracy among beneficiaries make the problems worse. The collection of information itself is costly. The selection process provides opportunities for corruption at many levels, especially where the weaker sections of the population come into contact with low-level officials in the administration.

Thirdly, however well designed, the process of selection will cut out some deserving persons, whereas that will not occur in a universal scheme.

Finally, there are questions of stigma and the surrender of private information to Goverments. For example, household registration books (*hukou bu*) in China and similar documents in other countries contain information not only necessary to target social services but also useful in controlling the movement of people.[51]

These problems point to the need for great care in designing and implementing policies to target benefits to particular groups.

## E. CONCLUSIONS

Ageing populations, slow economic growth, a more unequal distribution of income and changing family structures have all raised fundamental questions about the provision of social security in all countries. In the economies in transition, a search for new arrangements is under way. In developing countries the emergence of new poverty groups has heightened the need to extend social security. The new demands arise in a period of fiscal stringency brought about by a need to keep down government spending in order to restrain aggregate demand. The public is also reluctant to pay higher taxes. In the design of social security schemes, new flaws have been identified. Some provisions have become disincentives to work; others have been found to be inequitable and inefficient in delivery.

Social security provisions come from transfer payments. In developed countries the concern is that as marginal rates of transfer increase, the losses in economic efficiency are larger than the gains. Increased productivity per worker, delayed retirement or a larger proportion of young workers in the labour force, by encouraging net immigration, might reduce these losses. Lower unemployment would both reduce payments to the unemployed and increase contributions to social security funds. Legal remedies are being sought to compel absconding parents, often fathers, to pay for the maintenance of their children. Delivery systems have been decentralized to reduce inefficiency. Measures have been passed to target benefits better to reduce spending and to raise efficiency and equity.

In economies in transition, the weaving of "safety nets" is essential if radical institutional changes in the economy and society are to be politically acceptable. Since it takes time to put safety nets in place, the pace of economic transition has to be slow.

In developing countries, social security is provided mostly by family and voluntary agencies. Government services tend to benefit those in the higher income brackets. Much is done in times of emergency to provide food and shelter. Social security has some-times been successfully provided in countries with low levels of income by means of food subsidies, public health services and simi-lar benefits. However, social security in those societies depends pri-marily on economic development and the eradication of poverty.

## Notes

[1] The emphasis here is on what Dreze and Sen term "protective" social services, as distinct from "promotional" services. For the distinction, see Ahmad Ehtisham, and others, eds., *Social Security in Developing Countries* (Oxford, Clarendon Press: 1991), pp. 1-40.

[2] See Assar Lindbeck, "Consequences of the advanced welfare state", *The World Economy* (March 1988), pp. 19-37. Also see Gary Burtless, "The economist's lament: public assistance in America", *Journal of Economic Perspectives*, vol. 4, no. 1 (winter 1990), pp. 57-78, who argues that "evidence cannot resolve the underlying conflict between those who believe more should be done to help the working poor and their children and those who resent subsidizing illegitmacy, family desertion and consumption of leisure among able-bodied adults. Neither economists nor moral philosophers can suggest a formula that will resolve the conflict: no such formulas exist". Aslo see Ralph Dahrendorf, *The Modern Social Conflict: An Essay on Politics and Liberty* (London, Weidenfeld and Nicholson, 1988).

[3] For a discussion of some of these arrangements, see Jean-Philippe Platteau, "Tra-ditional systems of social security and hunger insurance: past achievements and modern challenges" in Ehtisham and others, eds., op. cit., pp. 112-170.

[4] For a general discussion of the social security issues in Eastern Europe, see A. McAuley, "The economic transition in Eastern Europe: employment, income dis-tribution, and the social security net", *Oxford Review of Economic Policy*, vol. 7, no. 4 (winter, 1991), pp. 93-105.

[5] For a general discussion of issues relevant to market-economy countries, see ILO, *Into the Twenty-First Century: The Development of Social Security* (Geneva, 1986); and R. Titmuss, "The social division of welfare", in *Essays on the Welfare State*, R. Titmuss, ed., (London, Allen and Unwin, 1958).

[6] See Lindbeck, op. cit., pp. 22-23.

[7] See Amartya Sen, " The political economy of targeting", prepared for the World Bank Conference on Public Expenditure and the Poor: Incidence and Targeting, 17-19 June 1992, Washington, D.C.

[8] OECD, *The Future of Social Protection*, OECD Social Policy Studies No. 6 (Paris, 1988), table 3.

[9] See OECD, *Social Expenditure, 1960-1990: Problems of Growth and Control*, OECD Social Policy Studies No. 1 (Paris, 1985).

[10] See, for example, W. Beckerman and S. Clark, *Poverty and Social Security in Britain since 1961* (Oxford, Oxford University Press, 1982); and S. Danziger and D. Wein-berg, eds., *Fighting Poverty: What Works and What Doesn't* (Cambridge, Harvard University Press, 1986).

[11] OECD, *Reforming Public Pensions*, OECD Social Policy Studies No. 5 (Paris, 1988), table 4.4.

[12] Ibid., tables 7.1 and 7.4.

[13] In real terms, all transfers are made from current income. In financial terms, some schemes may be fully or partially funded. In those instances, retirees are paid out of reserves built up through the contributions they make to a pension fund as well as their employers over the course of the retirees' working years, together with earnings from the investment of such funds.

[14] See P. Heller, R. Hemming and P. Kohnert, *Aging and Social Expenditure in the Major Industrial Countries, 1980-2025*, IMF Occasional Paper No. 47 (Washington, D.C., International Monetary Fund, 1986), table 20.

[15] For a brief account of changes in social security provisions in developed and developing countries during the past two decades, see J. P. Dumont, "The evolution of social security during the recession", *International Labour Review*, vol. 120, no. 1 (Jan.-Feb. 1987), pp. 1-19.

[16] In the United States, more than a quarter of total Medicare spending is on enrollees in the last year of their lives, even though such enrollees constitute 5 per cent of the enrolled population. See United States Council of Economic Advisors, "Health status and medical care", *Economic Report of the President* (Washington, D.C., Government Printing Office, 1985), pp. 129-186. For additional information on ageing and morbidity, see, for example, K. Manton, "Changing concepts of morbidity and mortality in the elderly population", *Milbank Memorial Fund Quarterly/Health and Society*, vol. 60 (1982), pp. 183-244; and D. Rice and J. Feldman, "Living longer in the United States: demographic changes and health needs of the elderly", *Milbank Memorial Fund Quarterly/ Health and Society*, vol. 61 (1983), pp. 362-396.

[17] See OECD, *The Challenge of Unemployment* (Paris, 1982), p. 19.

[18] OECD, *Ageing Populations: The Social Policy Implications*, (Paris, 1988).

[19] For a comprehensive review of lone-parent families, see OECD, *Lone-Parent Families: The Economic Challenge*, OECD Social Policy Studies No. 8 (Paris, 1990).

[20] This account is based on Judith M. Gueron, "Work and Welfare: lessons on employment programmes", *Journal of Economic Prospectives*, vol. 4, no. 1 (winter, 1990), pp. 79-98.

[21] Well-functioning capital markets allow individuals to borrow in difficult circumstances and to save for their retirement; insurance markets help protect individuals from the need to borrow as a result of difficult circumstances, while minimizing moral hazard and adverse selection instances; and labour markets and the process of wage determination are the main determinants of income for most individuals. In the case of social insurance, for instance, Lord Beveridge argued that State intervention was "justified in terms of the failure of private insurance markets to provide adequate cover for the relevant risks as a result of adverse selection and moral hazard problems. Where insurance companies cannot identify the riskiness of individual customers, and there are problems of adverse selection, the private market for insurance is unlikely to be perfectly competitive". See W. Beveridge, *Social Insurance and Allied Services*, Cmd. 6404 (London, HM Stationery Office, 1942), p. 286. In many developing countries, insurance markets are poorly developed. See R. Burgess and N. Stern, "Social security in developing countries: what, why, who and how", and A. Atkinson and J. Hills, "Social security in developed countries: are there lessons for developing countries?", in Ehtisham and others, op. cit., pp. 48-53 and p. 105.

[22] For an extended analysis, see J. Midgley, *Social Security, Inequality and the Third World* (Chichester, John Wiley, 1984).

[23] See Ha-Cheong Yeon, "Inter-generational security in Asian countries", *Asian Development Review*, vol. 8, no. 1 (1990), pp. 71-89.

[24] See J. V. Gruat, "Social security schemes in Africa: current trends and problems", *International Labour Review*, vol. 129, no. 4 (1990), table 2.

[25] See C. Mesa-Lago, "Social security and extreme poverty in Latin America", *Journal of Development Economics*, vol. 12, nos. 1/2 (February/April 1983), p. 101. For a general review of social security in Latin America, see also G. A. Mackenzie, "Social security issues in developing countries: the Latin American experience", *IMF Staff Papers*, vol. 35, no. 3 (September 1988), pp. 496-522.

[26] See ILO, *L'investissement des fonds de la sécurité sociale dans les pays en développement* (Geneva, 1987).

[27] See Lim Chong-Yah and Tay Boon-Nga, Shelter for the poor: housing policy in Singapore", *Asian Development Review*, vol. 8, no. 1 (1990).

[28] See Pinto-Lima, "The financing of housing in Brazil", *Housing Finance International* (November, 1990).

[29] For the case of Africa, see T. Nkanagu, "African experience in sickness insurance and health protection under social security", *International Social Security Review*, no. 2 (1985), pp. 119-140. For the case of Latin America, see L. Asis Eirute, "Trends, policies and strategies in medical care provision in Latin America", *International Social Security Review*, no. 4 (1988), pp. 409-432.

[30] See Beirute, loc. cit., pp. 422-424. For more information on health care security provided to the rural poor in Mexico, see Mexican Social Insurance Institute, "The National IMSS/Coplamar Programme of Social Solidarity through Community Co-operation: a programme of care for rural marginal groups in Mexico", *International Social Security Review*, no. 1 (1985), pp. 62-74. For details on social security in rural areas of Argentina, Bolivia, Brazil, Colombia, Costa Rica, Ecuador, Guatemala, Mexico and Venezuela, see Asociacion Internacional de la Seguridad Social, *La Proteccion Social Rural*, Grupo de Trabajo Regional Americano sobre la Proteccion Social de la Poblacion Rural (Buenos Aires), 1991).

[31] For details, see R. Tibaudin, "Social security for self-employed workers in Latin America", *International Social Security Review*, no. 4 (1985), pp. 396-417. As for Sri Lanka, see "Sri Lanka: institution of an agricultural social security scheme", *International Social Security Review*, no. 3 (1987), p. 302.

[32] See C. Mesa-Lago, *La Seguridad Social y el Sector Informal*, Investigaciones sobre Empleo No. 32, (Santiago, Regional Employment Programme for Latin America and the Caribbean, 1990).

[33] See, for example, M. Murray and D. Bueckman, "Social insurance in developing countries; are there net benefits to program participation", *Journal of Developing Areas*, vol. 26, no. 2 (January 1992), pp. 193-212.

[34] See J. Martinez, "Efectos sociales des la crisis economica: Chile 1980-1985" (LC/R.519, October 1986).

[35] See J. Dreze and A. Sen, *Hunger and Public Action* (Oxford, Clarendon Press, 1989), chap. 8.

[36] Violent reactions to reductions or removal of food subsidies, for example, were experienced in Egypt, Tunisia, Venezuela and Zambia, illustrating the political forces that can be unleashed by such measures. See H. Bienen and M. Gersovitz, "Consumer stability cuts, violence, and political stability", *Comparative Politics*, vol. 19, no. 1 (1986); and R. Hopkins, "Political considerations in subsidizing food", in *Consumer-Oriented Food Subsidies: Costs, Benefits and Policy Options for Developing Countries*, P. Pinstrup-Anderson, ed. (Baltimore, Johns Hopkins, 1988).

[37] See Daniel C. Hardy, "Soft budget constraints, firm commitments and the social safety nets", *IMF Staff Papers*, vol. 39, no. 2 (June 1992), pp. 310-329.

[38] Z. Ferge, "Social security systems in the new democracies of Central and Eastern Europe: past legacies and possible futures", in *Children and the Transition to the Market Economy*, G. A. Cornia and S. Sipos, eds. (London, Avebury, England, 1991); I. Tomes, "Social reform: a cornerstone in Czechoslovakia's new economic structure", *International Labour Review*, vol. 130, no. 2 (1991); and L. P. Yakushev, "New approaches to social security provision in the USSR", *International Labour Review*, vol. 130, no. 3 (1991).

[39] M. Zam, "Economic reforms and safety nets in Hungary: limits to protection", in Cornia and Sipos, eds., op. cit., p. 194.

[40] B. Milanovic, "Distributional incidence of cash and in-kind transfers in Eastern Europe and Russia", paper prepared for the World Bank Conference on Public Expenditures and the Poor: Incidence and Targeting, 17-19 June 1992, Washington, D.C., p. 15.

[41] Ibid; p. 12.

[42] Igor Tomes, "Social reform: a cornerstone in Czechoslovakia's new economic structure", *International Labour Review*, vol. 130, no. 2 (1991), p. 194.

[43] Government of Poland, *Raport o stanie panstwa rzadu J. K. Bieleckiego*, (Report on the state of the nation under the Government of J. K. Bieleckiego) (Warsaw, 1992), p. 83.

[44] A. McAuley, "The economic transition in Eastern Europe: employment, income distribution, and the social security net", *Oxford Review of Economic Policy*, vol. 7, no. 4 (1991), pp. 100-101.

[45] "Pensionery budut nischimi do teh por, poka zabotits'ay o nih budet tol'ko gosudarstvo" (Pensioners doomed to be paupers until the State remains the only provider), *Izvestiya*, 29 January 1992: "Starikim Rosii beretsya pomoch Strahovoy pensionny fond" (The Insurance Pension Fund will take care of Russia's elderly), *Izvestiya*, 18 May 1992.

[46] *Social and Labour Bulletin*, nos. 3-4 (Sept.-Dec. 1991), p. 338.

[47] OECD, *Poland 1992*, OECD Economic Surveys (Paris, 1992), pp. 75-76.

[48] See "Social policies in the transition to a market economy", report of a mission to the Russian Federation organized by the United Nations, January 1992 (Edinburgh, David Hume Institute, 1992).

[49] See E. V. K. Fitzgerald, "Economic reform and citizen entitlements in Eastern Europe: some social implications of structural adjustments in semi-industrial economies", Discussion Paper No. 27 (Geneva, UNRISD, June 1991).

[50] See G. A. Cornia and F. Stewart, "Two errors of targeting", paper presented at the World Bank Conference on Public Expenditures and the Poor: Incidence and Targeting, 17-19 June 1992, Washington, D.C.

[51] See Ahmad Ehtisham and Athar Hussain, "Social security in China: a historical perspective", in (ed) Ehtisham and others, eds., op. cit., pp. 247-301.

# 11

---

# Quality of life

"QUALITY of life" is a pluralistic conception of well-being that is closely linked to the notion of development and human progress. While at the common-sense level the term seems clear enough, it can mean different things to people with different standards of living and cultural viewpoints. Since there is no common mould to fit the term, quality of life is best measured by a combination of social and economic indicators and by subjective measures of a person's relative satisfaction with his or her conditions of life and well-being. As discussed in the present chapter, there exists in most countries an ambiguous relationship between economic, physical and economic betterment, on the one hand, and social progress and satisfaction with the quality of life on the other. As many of the indicators on living standards have already been presented in other chapters, the present chapter is concerned mainly with indicators that reflect growing prosperity, changes in life-style, individual perceptions of happiness, and the fraying of the social fabric. The objective dimensions of the quality of life are first examined, followed by an analysis of the social responses to material betterment, with particular attention to the situation in the developed market-economy countries.

## A. OBJECTIVE DIMENSIONS

Those elements of the quality of life that are readily measurable by economic and social indicators reflect some of the most important dimensions of human existence. Per capita gross national product (GNP) in particular is a proxy measure of human well-being and social progress at the national level: the higher the income, the higher society's potential capacity to provide improved health care, education and other services. However, per capita income measures have serious flaws when it is a question of assessing the quality of life. To capture social reality more comprehensively, those measures must be complemented by other indicators. Table 11.1 accordingly presents additional indicators — of life expectancy at birth, caloric intake, adult literacy and educational attainment.

Life expectancy at birth is important as an indicator of human welfare, as it sums up the combined effects of nutritional status, public health, the general physical environment, and the circumstances in which people are born, live and die. Literacy and educational attainments have a favourable impact on the quality of life by enlarging human choice and participation in material and social progress. Nutritional status data are also included in the table, in view of the importance to general well-being of adequate food and a proper diet.

The social indicators utilized in table 11.1 also reflect the distribution of social progress among population groups. An improvement in longevity, caloric consumption and literacy means that at least the proportion of people sharing such benefits has risen, even if the improvement does not explicitly identify how the benefits it reflects are distributed among specific segments of the population. With regard, for instance, to improvement in life expectancy and caloric consumption, it can be assumed — in view of the natural biophysical ceiling already (nearly) attained by their indicators among the well-to-do — that the greater benefit accrues to the poor.

As may be seen in table 11.1, improvements in social conditions and living standards are strongly and positively correlated with economic growth. These improvements have proceeded at rates that, historically speaking, are high compared with those of the industrialized countries at comparable stages in their development. However, the progress rates in table 11.1 show a tendency to decline and eventually level off as incomes increase. There are finite limits, for instance, to life expectancy and caloric intake that make it increasingly unlikely that their indicators will continue to reflect a rising trend, and in the case of caloric intake such a trend would be undesirable.[1]

*Table 11.1*

Trends in selected indicators of the quality of life

| Indicators | Low-income countries | Middle-income countries | High-income countries |
|---|---|---|---|
| | *1989 US dollars* | | |
| Per capita gross national product (GNP) | 80-500 | 581-5 999 | 6 000-29 880 |
| Life expectancy at birth[a] | | | |
| 1965 | 49 | 58 | 71 |
| 1989 | 62 | 66 | 76 |
| Daily per capita calorie intake[a] | | | |
| 1965 | 1 988 | 2 482 | 3 082 |
| 1988 | 2 331 | 2 834 | 3 398 |
| Average number of years of complete schooling per worker, around 1980[a] | 1.8 | 4.8 | 9.6 |
| | *Percentage* | | |
| Adult literacy[a] | | | |
| 1960 | 26 | 49 | 98 |
| 1985 | 56 | 75 | 99 |
| Average annual GNP growth rate, in real terms, 1965-89[a] | 2.9 | 2.3 | 2.4 |

Sources: Department of Economic and Social Development of the United Nations Secretariat, based on World Bank Development Report, various years; World Bank, Social Indicators of Development 1990 (Baltimore, Maryland, Johns Hopkins University Press, 1991); World Health Organization (WHO), World Health Statistics Annual, various years; and United Nations Educational, Scientific and Cultural Organization (UNESCO), Compendium of Statistics on Illiteracy, 1988.

a     Weighted averages of countries.

As literacy becomes more nearly universal in the developed countries, other social betterment objectives, including improved universal education, have assumed a higher priority in recent years. That is one reason why average number of years of completed schooling was included in table 11.1; the other reason was that each year of education beyond the literacy level could be presumed to have a favourable impact on the enlargement of people's capabilities, choices, participation and life opportunities in modern society.

Individual indicators provide useful measures of improvements that have occurred for various dimensions of well-being;

however, the design of composite indicators that provide an overall measure of the quality of life involves greater difficulty. All efforts to this end have met with thorny conceptual and theoretical problems of coherence and causality. In all cases, arbitrary assumptions have had to be made in selecting the weights for combining and aggregating the respective indicators within one quality-of-life index.[2] The underlying arbitrariness of quality-of-life indices reduces their credibility as objective measures for classifying and ranking countries according to welfare criteria.

Additional conceptual problems (besides the methodological ones of integrating, calibrating and summing composite indicators) have hindered efforts at developing indices of political freedom and civil rights.[3] That human freedom has an ultimate worth of profound importance to one's personal life and positive self-identity has long been noted in history.[4] The concept of human freedom, however, is too culture-specific to be captured in any general measure. There are complex questions of participation and control in many societies that are not necessarily exhausted by an approach to addressing those questions based on the presence or absence of a particular set of political arrangements.[5] Moreover, while there may be a positive correlation between increased freedom, as conventionally defined, and economic growth, the direction of movement from cause to effect is not clear.[6]

Good arguments can be made for relying on a single indicator, per capita income, rather than seeking to develop better quality-of-life indices. Indeed, country classifications and rankings obtained through the use of quality-of-life indices differ little from the results achieved with per capita GNP data alone. This is especially true when per capita GNP data are adjusted in accordance with the Kravis purchasing power parity indices for each country and transformed into logarithms, so as to give less weight to improvements in spending power at higher levels of income and thus capture the notion of diminishing marginal utility of income. (This means that the "happiness" derived from an additional dollar of income is greater at lower than at higher levels of income.)[7] However, unlike composite index approaches, per capita income indicators have the disadvantage of not identifying outlier cases where social progress is either above or below the normal levels attained in other countries for comparable per capita incomes.

Social indicators also have limitations: they fail to shed light on the less readily measurable elements connected with social well-being, such as people's fears, sufferings, conditioned wants, and satisfaction with life. With respect to personal suffering and societal injustice, for example, social indicators can attest to Governments' enactment of legal measures abolishing bondage, caste systems, racism, and ethnic, religious and other forms of discrimination. But more subtle forms of inquiry would be necessary to determine if and to what extent there persisted a legacy of lingering stigma. Similarly, although social statistics might show that rural households in a given area lived in rudimentary shelter, lacked piped water and latrines, and had no access to schools or health clinics, the assumption that such households felt severely deprived or discontented would be unwarranted if, in fact, food supplies were adequate, living conditions were not associated with high levels of debilitating diseases, local life did not require literacy, and community and family relations provided reasonable levels of happiness and satisfaction.

Indicators derived from surveys of the poor often portray that population as extremely deprived, but findings of this kind will be incomplete if they do not take note of corresponding behavioural responses, such as the population's resiliency and capacity to adapt to, and to cope with, misfortune and adversity. Thus, social as well as economic indicators can provide no more than partial and incomplete glimpses of the complex and sometimes contradictory realities that determine and shape the quality of life of both individuals and societies.

## B.  SOCIAL RESPONSES

Human beings have certain universal innate sentiments, such as kinship patterns that hold children dear and forbid murder and incest. They have moral senses of sympathy, fairness, self-control and duty that have made it possible for the human species to evolve over time.[8] In addition, all human beings have needs ranging from basic physical ones, for food and shelter, for love, belongingness, self-actualization, and other sustenance of the human spirit and of self-identity. Each of these elements is in its own way critical to a sense of personal well-being; emotional development, for instance, is retarded and the risk of developing mental disorders is greater in cases where persons are socially isolated and lonely. What may be surprising, however, is the extent to which objective improvements in life opportunities, as measured by indicators of purchasing power, health and education, are not matched by corresponding increases in level of psychological satisfaction and sense of well-being. As can be observed in table 11.2, the difference between how the poor and the economically well-off rate their quality of life is not as great as the difference in their income levels.

Attitudes and tastes are a product of internalized values and social experiences that vary according to cultural background and expectations. Thus, happiness need not rise with improvements in material and physical well-being. Someone's satisfaction with life is unlikely to increase as a result of material improvements if aspirations rise even more rapidly, as can happen when the incomes of reference groups are fast-growing. In the case of the sampled population groups in table 11.2, respondents tended to compare their situation with a reference norm derived from their prior and ongoing social experience. According to the survey, people in higher income groups were happier, on average, than those in lower income groups, but the association between income and happiness was more ambiguous across individual countries. This suggests, reasonably enough, that people are more influenced by national reference groups than by standards of living in other countries when they assess their own quality of life. What does happiness involve? The respondents overwhelmingly emphasized immediate personal concerns, such as adequacy of income, family matters and health, rather than broader national or social issues such as pollution and the threat of war.[9]

*Table 11.2*

Level of personal happiness among lower- and higher-income groups in 12 countries, circa 1960[a]

| Country | Happiness rating[b] lower-income group | higher income group | Per capita gross national product 1989 dollars[c] | Size of national sample |
|---|---|---|---|---|
| Japan | 4.3 | 5.8 | 23 810 | 972 |
| United States | 6.0 | 7.1 | 20 910 | 1 549 |
| Germany | 3.0 | 4.9 | 20 440 | 480 |
| Yugoslavia[d] | 4.3 | 6.0 | 2 920 | 1 523 |
| Brazil | 3.9 | 7.3 | 2 540 | 2 168 |
| Cuba | 6.2 | 6.7 | 2 000 | 992 |
| Poland | 3.7 | 4.9 | 1 790 | 1 464 |
| Panama | 4.3 | 6.0 | 1 760 | 642 |
| Dominican Republic | 1.4 | 4.3 | 790 | 814 |
| Philippines | 4.1 | 6.2 | 710 | 500 |
| India | 3.0 | 4.9 | 340 | 2 366 |
| Nigeria | 4.7 | 5.8 | 250 | 1 200 |

Sources: R. Easterlin, "Does economic growth improve the human lot? Some empirical evidence", in *Nations and Households in Economic Growth*, P. David and M. Reder, eds. (New York, Academic Press, 1974), p. 102, table 5.

a   Responses concerning people's hopes, fears, and general level of happiness were obtained through the use of a self-anchoring striving scale. The scale yielded ratings by each respondent, based on his or her subjective evaluation of level of happiness on a scale ranging from 0 (worst possible life) to 10 (best possible life).
b   Ranging from a minimum of 0 to a maximum of 10.
c   Figures drawn from the World Bank and (for Cuba) from United Nations Development Programme (UNDP).
d   Data refers to the Socialist Federal Republic, which was composed of six republics.

Happiness and other subjective entities are not decisive barometers of quality-of-life-related progress and achievements. However, if large numbers of people become, on balance, unhappy and frustrated with their circumstances and prospects, alienation may grow and lead to various forms of social disruption which in turn can reduce the quality of life of the general population. This appears notably to be the case in most developed market-economy countries, where substantial improvements in living standards and material well-being have been accompanied by a weakening of the social fabric reflected in the rise in homicide, crime, drug abuse, suicide, divorce and illegitimate births. These trends call into question the assumption that economic progress invariably induces social progress and that through the combined effects of both forms of progress a better quality of life is achieved.

Incomes since the 1960s have risen in real terms, for instance, enabling most households to have a car and better housing. In addition, technological improvements have increased life expectancy, augmented physical comfort, reduced the drudgery of household chores, brought varied forms of leisure-time entertainment into the home and eliminated the most difficult and unpleasant tasks in the workplace. Productivity growth has made it possible for employees to work shorter weeks and enjoy longer vacations. Likewise, the proportion of people's normal life spent in employment has fallen substantially as more years have been spent in formal schooling and improved pension and social security provisions have enabled people to retire earlier.[10] Furthermore, over the course of several decades, social security systems have helped reduce poverty, poor health and insecurity among vulnerable groups. In the past several years, however, the impact of the psychology of plenty seems to have diminished in countries where economic growth has slowed; the appeal of the counter-culture has faded as young people vie for fewer jobs with good career prospects; and parents are expressing concern that the living standards they grew up with may be beyond the reach of their children when they become adults.

In past decades along with material progress have come growing social problems and a fraying of the social fabric. The growth in imprisonment, homicide and drug abuse shown in the table applies mainly to low-income groups. These are often racial or cultural minorities, for whom drugs are generally associated with escapism, violence with alienation, and crime with, among other things, the economics of supporting a drug habit. As for suicide, the incidence appears likewise to be highest among the urban poor.[11] Although declining slightly among older people, suicides have risen among the young, particularly those who abuse drugs or are emotionally vulnerable to the pressures of a stressful social, school or work-place environment.[12] Similarly, the incidence of severe depression has grown substantially, especially among young people. The principal reason postulated is psychological stress associated with the erosion of family cohesion and the waning of religious beliefs that traditionally helped buffer people against life's set-backs.[13]

Generally, secular individualism has helped fuel the increase in sexual freedom and short-term cohabitations outside marriage.[14] The rise in divorce and births out of wedlock partially reflects the diminished role of the family as an institution of economic survival, the growth in the competing choice and opportunities that women in particular face in their lives, and in some cases the perverse effects of well-meaning social and fiscal policies.[15] Marriage is no longer the only socially accepted path to female adulthood. While certainly not an outworn arrangement, marriage is no longer indispensable to women to gain the security, respectability and social standing long advocated by traditional social institutions such as the family, religion, neighbours, custom, law, school and the workplace.

The fraying of the social fabric reflected by the rise in divorce and births out of wedlock, however, is likely to stabilize and reverse course when social trends reach extreme levels with respect to social norms. This has already happened with divorce rates in the Netherlands and the United States.[16]

Progress as well as retrogression has been noted in the social trends of the developed market-economy countries. Notwithstanding recent violence by the nationalist right against immigrants, tolerance and openmindedness have been growing in those countries as ignorance, prejudice and fixed beliefs wane. The counter-culture movement of the 1960s and 1970s, for instance, raised the consciousness of the general population regarding the perils of environmental degradation, the tragedy of war and the unjust biases that underlie gender inequality. Movements created by groups with grievances have played an essential role in reducing overt discrimination on ethnic, religious, gender-related, sexual preference-related, and other grounds, as reflected by gains achieved by those groups in social and workplace acceptance. The influence of the media and increased access to higher education have helped reduce blind prejudice against and cultural absolutism concerning, among other things, suicide, divorce and births out of wedlock.

Ambiguous trends in living standards and social ills have not been limited to the developed market-economy countries. Despite policies of egalitarianism and cradle-to-grave security in the countries of Eastern Europe and the former Soviet Union, rates of divorce, alcohol consumption, intentional homicides and suicides were respectively 7, 22, 29 and 29 percentage points higher in those countries in the 1980s than in the OECD countries.[17] These statistics suggest a pattern of alienation partly due perhaps to frustration over low consumption and living standards that did not improve with time; discontent over the lack of individual freedoms, of a sense of personal responsibility, and of opportunities for better pay; and a cynical attitude towards Socialist ideals as access to desired goods, quality service, and various privileges and entitlements became increasingly conditional on Party membership, useful connections and exchange of favours and bribes.[18]

Trends reflecting the relationship between material progress and social malaise comparable with those observed in developed countries cannot with certainty be said to have existed in the developing ones. Bear in mind the diversity of challenges and problems faced by developing countries, and remember the limited and generally poor quality of their statistical data on changes in the social fabric. But the separation of workplace and home, and other factors that have eroded extended-family support structures, have been amply documented, as have the high incidence of lone-parent families and the proliferation of homeless street children in many third world cities.[19]

Cultural patterns that bound individuals into webs of mutual dependency are being frayed as individual-centred interests gradually undermine systems of kinship, ritual and obligation.[20] Rising levels of homicide and crime are a problem, especially in large cities. In these cities poverty and too few opportunities for gainful work exist in close proximity to the conspicuous consumption and the modern lifestyles that give rise to material aspirations that cannot be realized by people with low incomes. Indeed, in the course of development, crime in the developing countries has shifted increasingly to the lower strata of urban societies, where the impact of assault, theft and property violations has surpassed that in the developed countries.[21] However, offsetting factors, including the all-consuming struggle to overcome adversity and simply survive, gives the third world at least a sense of urgency, and a purpose and meaning to life, often lacking among wealthier people and in more prosperous and economically secure societies. Moreover, the goal of upward mobility motivates most people in the third world, in particular rural-urban migrants and low-income urban households aspiring to middle-class status, and provides them with a purpose in life.

## C. CONCLUSIONS

Substantial progress has been made in living conditions throughout the world in recent decades. Although unequally divided between rich and poor, the improvements in some developing countries have been especially important and rapid. Material well-being has also improved in many industrialized countries. However, as indicated by the findings of polls measuring people's psychological satisfaction and sense of well-being, satisfaction with the quality of life has lagged behind objective improvements in living conditions. In addition, there is evidence in many countries of rising levels of crime, drug addiction, suicide and family breakdown, with instances of social malaise especially evident in the countries where living standards are high. This paradoxical combination of material progress and social deterioration conveys the ambiguous nature of the quality of life in many countries.

The question why material and social progress so often diverge does not yield an easy answer, but partial explanations may be offered at least for developed market-economy countries. For instance, because rapid technological changes in post-industrial societies involved a need for employable work skills and attitudes, those changes have contributed to the disaffection of the members of the labour force who, though lacking such skills and attitudes, have consumption wants that the economic system promotes but the social welfare system does not satisfy.

Among the economically better-off, the trend towards increased security, affluence and social tolerance has provided more life options. Those options may erode the willingness of individuals to put up with the frustrations encountered in work and family situations.[22] Women have been fragmented by the conflicting demands of work and home. A loss of deeper values can be partly attributed to consumerism, alienation, drugs and the decline of both traditional institutions and a distinct social culture.

As for the needs of the human spirit and the self, for love and a sense of accomplishment, for example, no amount of economic growth and technological progress can satisfy them. Finally, changes in human nature can take a long time, and they sometimes branch off in misguided directions before eventually becoming adaptations to changes in the economy and technology.

To focus too much on signs of social malaise, however, is to risk losing sight of what matters most: the huge disparity in physical and material well-being that continues to exist between the poor and the well-off of the world. No doubt a person who is a member of a dominant class and financially well-off has opportunities, powers, privileges and a source of solace in a stressful world that a poor person lacks. The grievances of people who have satisfied all of their objective needs seems trifling to people who do not have enough to eat. To equate, within the hierarchy of human needs, the whines of the materially well-off with the anguished cries of the poor is to trivialize the importance of what is basic and in urgent need of attention.

In the long run the subjective aspects of the quality of life may play an important positive role in facilitating social change and human development. Dissatisfaction with present conditions can turn into a catalyst or critical impulse for social progess. Although safeguarding freedom and human rights should not be a pretext for tolerating clearly negative, antisocial behaviour, collective human growth and adaptation to change are more likely to occur if diverse values and approaches to life are pursued, even if for a time that process includes divisive and in some cases regressive social trends. Psychological costs will be incurred as people struggle to accommodate contradictory normative systems within their lives, but an adaptive process that leads to a new synthesis of social values holds better prospects in the long term of personal growth and an improved quality of life than defensive postures aimed merely at maintaining the status quo ante in a rapidly changing world.

## Notes

[1] A simple index has been proposed to capture the fact that as longevity grows, it becomes more difficult to increase life expectancy. The index consists in the ratio of the increase in life expectancy to the shortfall of the base-year from some target figure, say 80 years. Applying the ratio to table 1, for example, one obtains an improvement in the figure for life expectancy at birth of 0.42 for low-income countries, 0.36 for middle-income countries, and 0.55 for high-income countries. For details, see A. Sen, "Public action and the quality of life in developing countries", *Oxford Bulletin of Economics and Statistics*, vol. 43, no. 4 (1981), pp. 287-319.

[2] Of the numerous efforts at developing comprehensive indices of the quality of life across countries, some have been characterized by high levels of complexity and ambition. For instance, in D. Slottje, G. Scully, J. Hirschberg and K. Hayes, *Measuring the Quality of Life Across Countries: A Multidimensional Analysis* (Boulder, Colorado, Westview Press, 1991), a large number of measures were selected; weights were alternatively determined by rank of attributes, principal components of attributes and hedonic representation of the attributes. Sensitivity analysis of the different weighing specifications was then used to calculate relative rankings for each index; the average rank for each country was calculated over all the different indices; and the various indices were ranked to obtain the final index of the quality of life. See A. Sen, *The Standard of Living* (Cambridge, Cambridge University Press, 1987). Quality-of-life indices need to capture differing dimensions of happiness, utility (satisfying of one's desires), choice, achievement and ability to achieve. However, operationalizing the concept is complicated by the need to obtain consensus on a wide array of objective attributes that yield utility; the difficulty of knowing how individuals or groups weigh the attributes of quality of life from which they derive utility; problems of identifying and measuring the environment in which people live and its importance to the utility they derive from the physical dimensions of the quality of life; and the lack of objective weights for combining various freedom-of-choice properties. Most quality-of-life and related indices have been simpler and have focused primarily on statistical data including estimates of life expectancy at birth, adult literacy and real per capita GDP. Based on a range of values for each of the composite indicators, a deprivation index for each country has typically been calculated, in terms of the extent to which country falls short of a specified maximum value. Originally elaborated in M. Morris, *Measuring the Condition of the World's Poor: The Physical Quality of Life Index* (Elmsford, New York, Pergamon Press, 1979), the same index has been further

refined (see UNDP, *Human Development Report* (New York, Oxford University Press), various editions). The Human Development Index elaborated in these reports adjusts per capita income in accordance with the Kravis purchasing power parity indices for each country, and converts the figures into logarithms in order to capture the notion of diminishing marginal utility of income. See also P. Dasgupta, "Well-being: foundations, and the extent of its realization in poor countries", World Institute for Development Economics Research (WIDER) Working Paper, no. 80 (Helsinki, September 1989); and A. Kelley, "The Human Development Index 'handle with care' ", *Population and Development Review*, vol. 17, no. 2 (June 1991), pp. 315-324.

[3] An extended discussion with illustrations of the application of a political freedom index can be found in UNDP, *Human Development Report, 1992* (New York, Oxford University Press, 1992), chap. 2. The general conclusion reached is that personal security, rule of law and political participation are lacking much more in developing than in developed countries, whereas gaps in freedom of expression and in particular equality of opportunity are less pronounced.

[4] For example, see Aristotle, *Nicomachean Ethics*, J. Thompson, trans. (London, Penguin Books, 1976). For extended discussions of this Aristotelian principle, see J. Rawls, A Theory of Justice (Oxford, Oxford University Press, 1972), p. 414; and B. Williams, *Ethics and the Limits of Philosophy* (London, Fontana and Collins, 1985), chap. 3.

[5] Indicators for measuring political freedom and civil rights have been elaborated in C. Taylor and D. Jodice, *World Handbook of Political and Social Indicators*, vol. 1 (New Haven, Yale University Press, 1983), tables 2.1 and 2.2.

[6] For an index correlating improvements in political freedom and human rights with economic and welfare growth, see P. Dasgupta, op. cit.

[7] See A. Kelley, op. cit.

[8] For a scholarly and provocative analysis on whether there is an innate universal moral sense, see J. Wilson, *The Moral Sense*, (The Free Press/Macmillan, New York, 1993).

[9] See R. Easterlin, "Does economic growth improve the human lot? Some empirical evidence", in *Nations and Households in Economic Growth*, P. David and M. Reder, eds. (New York, Academic Press, 1974), p. 102, table 5.

[10] Retirement age dropped by three years, from 62 to 59, and the age of completion of formal education rose from 18 to 20 in the OECD area between 1969 and 1989. See O. Marchand, "Une comparaison internationale des temps de travail", *Futurables*, nos. 165-166 (May-June 1992), p. 38.

[11] For an analysis of suicide characteristics among widely varying socio-economic groups, see R. Petrovis, "The diffusion and characteristics of suicides", *Yugoslav Survey*, vol. XXXII, no. 3 (1991).

[12] See C. Pfeffer, *The Suicidal Child* (New York, Guilford Press, 1992).

[13] According to the findings of comparable research designs in Edmonton, Canada; Munich; Florence; Paris; Christchurch, New Zealand; and Los Angeles, New Haven, Baltimore, St. Louis and Piedmont County in the United States, between 1960 and 1980, there was a trend of increasing incidence of major depression over time in all sites, with, in all cases, a substantial increase in the cumulative rates of major depression with each successively younger birth cohort. As major depression is believed to result from a combination of psychological stress and biological vulnerability, the studies concluded that stresses that could trigger such vulnerability had grown over time. Postulates given for why younger generations were at increased risk included stress related to the breakdown of family life, erosion of structure supports in the community and waning of beliefs in religion, which have long been emotional buffers against the sense of hopelessness leading to depressive episodes that can result from personal set-backs and failures. See Cross-National Collaborative Group, "The changing rate of major depression: cross-national comparisons", *Journal of the American Medical Association*, vol. 268, no. 21 (2 December 1992), pp. 3098-3105.

[14]It has been found, based on data from the European Values Studies, that approval of sexual freedom and partnership outside marriage are positively associated with secular individualism. Frequent church attendance, on the other hand, is strongly correlated negatively with cohabitation outside marriage. See R. Leshaeghe and J. Surkyn, "Cultural dynamics and economic theories of fertility change", *Population and Development Review*, vol. 14, no. 1 (1988), pp. 1-45.; and E. Carlson, "Couples without children: premarital cohabitation in France", in *Contemporary Marriage: Comparative Perspectives on a Changing Situation*, K. Davis, ed. (New York, Russell Sage Foundation, 1985), pp. 113-130. In the United States the rise in premarital intercourse, increases in out-of-wedlock child-bearing and the growing incidence of short-duration cohabitation are viewed as outcomes of the decline of parental authority. See, for instance, R. Rindfuss and A. Vandenheuval, "Cohabitation: a precursor to marriage or an alternative to being single?", *Population and Development Review*, vol. 16, no. 4 (1990), pp. 703-726; and L. Bumpass, "What's happening to the family: interactions between demographic and institutional change?", *Demography*, vol. 27, no. 4 (1990), pp. 483-498. More recently, fear of acquired immune deficiency syndrome (AIDS) may also be a factor behind rising trends of cohabitation in large cities of the United States.

[15]In the United States, for instance, the bearing of illegitimate children and the maintaining of lone-parent families are unintentionally encouraged among the poor by welfare measures that reward unemployed single mothers for each additional child. See G. Duncan and W. Rodgers, "Lone-parent families and their economic problems: transitory or persistent?", in OECD, *Lone-Parent Families: The Economic Challenge*, OECD Social Policy Studies, no. 8 (Paris, 1990). In Sweden, where, as of 1985, 68 per cent of all unions were consensual and 32 per cent were marital (*Statistik Arsbok '92*, vol. 78 (Stockholm, Statistika Centralbyran, 1992), marriage has been discouraged by high progressive tax rates that hurt married couples filing jointly more than persons filing separately. In other respects, cohabitation in Sweden is similar to marriage in the sense that most cohabiting unions are of long duration and include child-bearing and rearing. See, for instance, B. Hoem, "Early phases of family formation in contemporary Sweden", *Stockholm Research Reports in Demography*, no. 47 (University of Stockholm, 1988).

[16]Divorce rates in the Netherlands, after rising by 65 per cent between 1975 and 1985, fell by 18 per cent between 1985 and 1989 (the most recent year for which data were available). See Netherlands Central Bureau of Statistics, *Statistical Yearbook of the Netherlands, 1991* (The Hague, SDU/Publications, 1991). Divorce rates in the United States, after rising by 127 per cent between 1960 and 1984, declined by 4 per cent between 1984 and 1987 (the most recent year for which data were available). See United States Bureau of the Census, *Statistical Abstract of the United States*, 111th edition (Washington, D.C., 1991).

[17]During 1985-1987, annual divorce rates as a percentage of the total population age 25 and above were 4.8 in Eastern Europe and the former Soviet Union compared with 4.5 in the OECD countries. Per capita adult consumption of spirits (litres) averaged 4.4 per cent annually in Eastern Europe and the former Soviet Union and 3.6 per cent in the OECD countries during 1980-1985. Intentional homicides per 100,000 persons during 1987-1988 amounted to 4.9 in Eastern Europe and the former Soviet Union and 3.8 in the OECD countries. Suicides per 100,000 persons during 1987-1988 totalled 18.8 in Eastern Europe and the former Soviet Union and 16.6 in the OECD countries. There were insufficient data on illegitimate births, prisoners and drug crimes in Eastern Europe and the former Soviet Union to make comparisons with the OECD countries. See also UNDP, *Human Development Report, 1991* (New York, Oxford University Press, 1991), p. 176, table 28.

[18] See W. Brus and K. Laski, *From Marx to the Market: Socialism in Search of an Economic System* (Oxford, Clarendon Press, 1989), pp. 10-11 and 36-37; J. Kornai, *Contradictions and Dilemmas* (Budapest, Corvina and MIT Press, 1985), pp. 125-138; M. Matthews, *Privilege in the Soviet Union* (London, Allen and Unwin, 1978); and E. Makrzycki, "The legacy of real socialism and Western democracy", *Studies in Comparative Communism*, vol. XXIV, no. 2 (June 1991), pp. 212-213.

[19] See document A/46/454, entitled "International cooperation for the eradication of poverty in developing countries".

[20] For instance, the convention of arranged marriages is yielding in many developing countries to a trend towards more marriages based on love. This is lamented by elders for undermining old, traditional bonds of loyalties, obligations and social stability. Two factors contributing to that trend have been an older first-marriage age and, in some countries, exposure to television soap operas and foreign movies. See W. Jankowiak and E. Fisher, " A cross-cultural perspective on romantic love", *Ethnology*, vol. XXXI, no. 2 (April 1992), pp. 149-155.

[21] See Centre for Social Development and Humanitarian Affairs, *Trends in Crime and Criminal Justice 1970-1985, in the context of Socio-economic Change: Results of the Second United Nations Survey of Crime Trends, Operations of Criminal Justice Systems and Crime Prevention Strategies* (United Nations publication, Sales No. E.92.IV.3), pp. 49-56.

[22] This point was brilliantly discussed by D. Riesman in his foreword to the sixth edition of D. Riesman, N. Glazer and R. Denney, *The Lonely Crowd* (New Haven, Yale University Press, 1963).

# PART III

Emerging social issues
and dilemmas

# 12

## Public institutions

MAJOR economic and social institutions throughout the world are being called into question in a manner unforeseen even a few years ago. Some of the most fundamental institutions of society are undergoing change in Eastern Europe and the successor republics of the former Soviet Union. In developing countries, policy reforms include the transformation of both economic and political institutions. In market-economy countries, increasing attention has been directed to the role of economic institutions in technological progress and to mechanisms for maintaining international competitiveness. Everywhere there has been a sharp retreat from governmental control and regulation of economic activity, even though it is well understood that no market economy can exist without a public sector. The most fundamental of institutions, the family, has begun to take new forms. Non-governmental organizations have gained far more prominence than ever before. International organizations have come up against new challenges, and the international community has been slow in responding.

The most dramatic changes are taking place in the economies in transition. Fundamental economic and social institutions are being redesigned. The State is being divested of the means of production. Laws have been enacted to establish private ownership and are being implemented. Entire mechanisms for providing social security are being newly designed. Totalitarian governments are having to limit their spheres of activity and intervention in the life of individuals and in associations of individuals. Centrally planned economies are being transformed into market-driven economies.

Limiting the economic role of the State is a feature common

to all economies. In developing countries this has implied reducing ownership of enterprises, removing administered prices and liberalizing international trade. In developed countries, while there has been some selling of State-owned enterprises, the most striking feature has been deregulation. All economies have experienced a shift towards using policy instruments that work through the market, and Governments are contracting out activities that they finance.

The way governments are formed and how they conduct their business have also been changed. Periodic popular elections of the legislature and the head of the executive branch have replaced military rule and single-party governments in several countries. Powers of government have been separated, especially with a view to establishing a judiciary independent of the executive and the legislature. Strong demands have been made for greater transparency in the functioning of government.

The emergence of the market in the economy has made the function of entrepreneurship all the more important.

These dramatic changes in institutions have been preceded by academic inquiries over a long time into the nature and significance of institutions in the economic and social development of societies.[1] They have been identified as "sets of rights and obligations affecting people in their economic lives".[2] Property rights are perhaps the clearest case here. Property can be held in numerous ways, determining among other things the distribution of its yield. The most active concerns are with alternatives to the State ownership of property and their consequences for economic and social development, as well as for civic society.

Alternative institutional arrangements, for example, through legally enforceable contracts, may also reduce uncertainty and provide greater flexibility in the allocation of resources. A functioning financial market encourages a more efficient allocation of resources. As an economy becomes more complex because of the division of labour, innovations and improvements in institutions become necessary to reduce transaction costs among the myriad agents in the economy. Institutional innovations thus become an instrument for reducing transaction costs, much the same way as advances in technology help reduce transformation costs.

## A. GOVERNMENT AND THE ECONOMY

For either ideological or pragmatic reasons, the role of Government increased in virtually all economies during the twentieth century, especially in the developed market economy countries. (see table 12.1). As the 1980s progressed, claims for limiting the role of government vastly increased. In developed market economies the major macroeconomic policy preoccupation became one of controlling inflation rather than of combating depression. Income creation by Governments by spending beyond their revenue was seen as a major

*Table 12.1*

Government current expenditure on goods and services
as a percentage of GNP at current market prices 1870-1965

|                | 1870 | 1913 | 1938 | 1965 | 1960-1989[a] |
|----------------|------|------|------|------|--------------|
| Belgium        | —    | —    | —    | 12.8 | 39.5 |
| Canada         | 4.6  | 8.1  | 10.9 | 13.8 | 34.1 |
| Denmark        | —    | —    | 9.3  | 13.8 | 41.2 |
| France         | —    | —    | 13.8 | 13.3 | 39.2 |
| Germany        | 5.9[b] | 8.7 | 23.1 | 15.5 | 37.8 |
| Italy          | 8.1  | 9.7  | 15.7 | 14.7 | 34.1 |
| Japan          | 6.8[c] | 9.1 | 25.0 | 9.3 | 19.5 |
| Netherlands    | —    | —    | 11.4 | 15.9 | 44.2 |
| Norway         | 3.8  | 6.3  | 9.9  | 17.0 | 38.9 |
| Sweden         | 4.7  | 5.6  | 10.4[d] | 19.3 | 45.1 |
| Switzerland    | —    | —    | —    | 11.8 | 25.4 |
| United Kingdom | 4.9  | 7.0  | 13.0 | 16.7 | 36.8 |
| United States  | 3.7[e] | 4.2 | 10.1 | 17.4 | 30.5 |

Sources: Angus Maddison, *Economic Growth in Japan and the USSR*, (New York, W.W. Norton & Company, Inc., 1969), p. 13, table 5; and *OECD Historical Statistics*, 1960-1989 (Paris, Organisation for Economic Cooperation and Development, 1991), p. 67, table 6.4.

a   1960-1989 average; current disbursement by Government as a percentage of GDP.
b   1871-1890.
c   1879.
d   1938-1939 average.
e   1869-1878 average.

villain of the piece. Citizens whose marginal rates of taxation had risen substantially, as in Sweden, the United Kingdom and the United States, voted against further increases. In the centrally planned economies, in addition to the political unacceptability of government ownership of all means of production, there was massive popular dissatisfaction with scarcities, queuing and deterioration of economic and social conditions. The State in these economies was to have served the public interest by correcting market failures. Instead, it was found to have let conditions deteriorate well beyond those in most market economies.[3]

In developing countries, governments as the source of inflation-generating money income, especially in Latin America, came to be identified as a main source of economic instability. Stabilization policies generally required that government spending be curtailed. Government-owned enterprises made no return on the capital invested in most instances and were a permanent drain on government financial resources. Where these enterprises were not open to competition, inefficiency was rampant. Government enterprises were not leaders in technological innovation, with rare exceptions. Regulations of economic activity generally created incentives for acquiring large fortunes out of rentier income rather than productive activity. In addition, the behaviour of economic agents was governed by bureaucrats, whose objectives in relation to those enterprises were different from those of entrepreneurs.[4] Most damaging, these controls stifled initiative, eliminated competition and obstructed the flow of ideas conducive to economic development.

In many developing countries the immediate reason for reducing the size of government was a policy package accepted by Governments in negotiations with the International Monetary Fund and the World Bank on economic reforms.

### 1. *Curbs on government expenditure*

One of the most salutary effects of disciplining the financial conduct of government has been that in many countries inflation has been brought under control. Consumer price inflation had been

7.0 per cent in major industrial countries in 1982; it was brought down to 3.2 per cent in 1992. However, there is fear that massively larger expenditure by the Government of Germany in the process of integrating the economy of the former German Democratic Republic may engender inflationary processes. In developing countries, price inflation in 1991 at 75 per cent was two and a half times that in 1981. Yet compared with 477 per cent in 1990, that was a dramatic improvement. The improvements between 1990 and 1991 were most marked in Latin America, with a deterioration in Africa and Asia. In deep contrast, price inflation in European centrally planned economies took a markedly upward trend in 1991, except in Poland, where the rate of growth of consumer prices fell from 584 per cent in 1990 to 70 per cent in 1991.[5] In economies where prices had been stable for a generation or more, the increase was disturbing to the public.

The longer term social benefits of price stability are numerous, besides the conditions conducive to more rapid economic growth that such stability permits. Since the nature of inflation is that the value of money (and near money assets) falls in terms of other assets, all those who hold money will lose command over resources to others in the economy. The longer money is held, the larger will be the losses. Since the poor hold little money for short periods and the rich hold only a small proportion of their total assets in money, losses will be incurred by those in the middle. The value of the major asset owned by the poor, their labour power, does not rise to compensate for a fall in the purchasing power of money, especially where they are not organized in trade unions, so their real earnings will fall in a time of inflation.[6] Therefore, rising inflation has ominous consequences for maintaining the social fabric in the previously centrally planned economies. Emerging price stability in developing countries portends less inequity and social strife.

## 2. Sale of enterprises

Governments have been divesting themselves of the ownership and management of enterprises as part of the process of reducing their economic functions. In the economies in transition, the privatization of small units has been highly successful. More than 15,000 small enterprises were auctioned off in the former Czechoslovakia in 1991; in Poland about 60,000 small units were leased or sold to the private sector during 1990-1991 and 70 per cent of retail trade was in private hands by mid-1992.[7] Hungary is currently auctioning small enterprises to the public. In Romania, as well as in some of the States of the former Soviet Union, the sale of small enterprises started in 1992.[8]

A quasi-private sector emerged in China as a result of farm reforms and experiments with other changes since 1979. In rural areas the introduction of a contracting system and family farming, free marketing of farm products and permission to establish small-scale enterprises led to a growth in farmers' income. Township and village enterprises reabsorbed the surplus labour squeezed out from the land. By 1990 "collective enterprises" produced 54 per cent of industrial output while the share of State-owned enterprises declined from 80 per cent in 1979 to 46 per cent in 1990.[9]

Two thirds of the "collective enterprises" are township and village enterprises owned by workers or local governments through holding companies. Personally owned enterprises are still few in number, except in the coastal provinces, where their role is more significant. There, private enterprises have been established jointly with foreign capital.

Selling large enterprises to the private sector has been more questionable. In the economies in transition, legislation has provided a legal basis for the private ownership of enterprises and the employment of labour for profit.

Bulgaria adopted a Law on Privatization in 1992, establishing the National Privatization Agency. Under the law, 20 per cent of the shares of all enterprises sold to the private sector must be transferred to a national mutual fund to cover restitution claims and for subsequent distribution to the public at large. A further 20 per cent is reserved for employees who can buy them at 50 per cent of the market price.[10] Romania prepared 23 State enterprises in a variety of sectors for a pilot privatization programme. The establishment of five Private Ownership Funds was approved by Parliament in 1992 and they are being set up. The Russian Federation started a mass privatization programme on 1 October 1992, when every man, woman and child received a voucher worth 10,000 roubles.

In Poland the Government preferred rapid and wide-scale privatization. In July 1991, 400 enterprises were chosen for sale to private sources. These enterprises accounted for about 25 per cent of total industrial sales and around 12 per cent of total industrial employment in the country.[11]

In Hungary several privatization campaigns have resulted in a significant reduction of the share of State assets in the economy and in a much more diversified ownership structure. By September 1991 the share of the State-owned assets in the economy fell below 50 per cent.[12]

In Germany the Treuhandanstalt (a public trust fund for the administration of State property) responsible for privatizating State enterprises in the former German Democratic Republic had sold nearly 9,500 enterprises by October 1992 out of 12,000 assigned to it.[13]

Several factors have stood in the way of rapid privatization in the economies in transition. First, an assets market for enterprises is generally part of a complex and sophisticated set of markets, including those for goods, labour and money. Each of these markets would have its own organizations, such as stock exchanges, money markets and commodity markets. They would all be governed by a set of commercial laws and a system of courts. The markets would determine prices, including interest rates, and therefore the net present value of assets. Laws and legal procedures would provide the means of enforcing contracts. In the absence of a functioning market for labour and social safety nets, it is natural that Government, enterprise managers and workers in large enterprises would resist changes in ownership which could deny livelihood to large numbers, and engender political opposition to these changes. There is also the problem of knowledge and familiarity with entrepreneurial activity. In the centrally planned economies where private entrepreneurship was not totally wiped out and State ownership came after the Second

World War there were some remnants of entrepreneurship skills, whereas in the former Soviet Union, after more than two generations of Socialist economy, such skills were much rarer.

The changeover to a new economy and society is also hampered by the weight of values and norms espoused and cultivated under Communist rule. Although it failed to create a "new man",[14] the average person absorbed the ideological principles of equality, social security and solidarity. Those principles were heavily emphasized through education and the mass media. Society was expected to provide not simply equality in opportunities but outcomes as well. Knowledge of functioning of markets was scant, except where there was contact with "market socialism".

Higher education was geared to training specialists in industry, in particular heavy industry. Economics education focused mostly on the theory of socialism and skills required within that scheme. The economics curriculum varied considerably among countries. Polish and Hungarian students had better access to knowledge about markets even in the late 1950s and 1960s than did the former Soviet or Romanian students. The latter's familiarity with markets, competition, banking and exchange rates was abstract and inadequate to operate under real market conditions.

The strength of these habits of mind and values is reflected in findings from recent surveys and opinion polls. Rejection of the social costs of economic reforms is as common as support for markets and capitalism. Although most respondents agreed that incompetent workers should be dismissed and understood that incomes would be unequal, they also expect the State to continue welfare programmes on the same scale as earlier and actively interfere to limit high incomes and reduce differences between the rich and the poor. According to the overwhelming majority of respondents, the State should also continue to provide employment to all those wanting to work.[15]

These inherited attitudes and skills are, in general, more a liability than an asset in the process of transition to market economies in all countries in the region. The attitudes towards work, learning and innovating, profit, competition, welfare and social justice are not typical for a market economy.

Workers now as before are primarily concerned with wage increases; their demands are often unrelated to improvements in work efficiency. When part of the Polish company, Wedel, was acquired recently by Pepsico, most workers believed that the major change in their enterprise under new management would be a rise in wages to a level closer to those in the United States.[16] Bureaucrats in institutions in some countries that have already replaced the old structures, such as planning commissions or branch ministries in Hungary, still operate within the old schemes. A new class of private businessman seems to be more interested in arbitrage and marginal trade than in longer term investments and searching for opportunities to innovate. Recent studies of the adaptability of Polish managers to competitive market conditions suggest that many of them, especially those in monopolistic enterprises, continue their passive attitudes of the past with respect to the acquisition of new skills, the search for new clients and markets, the development of new products and cutting costs.[17] The State is often considered the saviour of failing enterprises. Demands for negotiation with Government on plans to save the aircraft industry or inefficient steel mills are cases in point.

Developments in economies in transition so far show that it is indeed a slow and difficult process.[18] The formal elimination of old laws, regulations and other institutions has not produced a new market system. Nor have new values been widely understood and accepted by workers, farmers, managers of privatized enterprises and bureaucrats.

They will change under the pressure of a new competitive environment, new education curricula and experience. The process will be lengthy and socially painful in all countries of the region. The moral claims of the major social groups that initiated the transition, workers and farmers, cannot be matched by adequate rewards, at least in the short and the medium terms, as the costs of transition occur much earlier than the benefits.

The centrally planned economies of Asia — China, the Lao People's Democratic Republic, Mongolia and Viet Nam — have followed different paths of institutional reform. The functions of the State have remained intact. The former dominant political parties continue to be in power. Large-scale industries remain in the public sector. Agriculture and small-scale enterprises function in the private sector under various institutional arrangements. The exchange rate has been determined largely by market forces. Attempts at price liberalization have been made. Output has increased at markedly high rates in agriculture and in small-scale industry in China and Viet Nam. Industrial output dependent on imports from the economies in transition in Europe has fallen in Mongolia and Viet Nam because of difficulties both in supply in these economies and of financing after the breakdown of earlier arrangements. Viet Nam began to export rice in 1985 and other exports have grown. Exports from the Lao People's Democratic Republic to Thailand have also grown. These favourable changes have not been accompanied by the kind of institutional changes common in economies in transition in Europe.

There is no one market model to follow. A variety of options exist, ranging from the United States to Japan and to the Republic of Korea. They have gradually evolved their own version of markets and capitalism, depending on their history and culture. The market systems that will evolve in the economies now in transition would differ from all these and exhibit their own characteristics. Replicating the entire political, legal and economic institutional infrastructure of the United States would not be easy in the economies in transition. The emphasis on equality and solidarity in the former Socialist countries points to the need for combining market mechanisms, parliamentary democracy and limited forms of private ownership of the means of production.[19]

More than 50 developing countries are pursuing programmes of privatization. Several have enacted special legislation and established organizations to complement these programmes.

In Ghana the Divestiture Implementation Committee, created in

June 1988, is responsible for the preparatory work on privatization. In Egypt a Public Sector Company Law was enacted in 1992 to provide legal provisions for the privatization of government-owned enterprises.[20] In Chile a special administrative structure established in 1974 was integrated in a public holding company and made responsible for all transfers of public enterprises to the private sector.[21]

So far, privatization in developing countries has been on a modest scale. The most wide-scale privatization programmes have been in Chile and Mexico. The total number of State-owned enterprises in Mexico fell from 1,155 (majority holding) in 1982 to 132 in January 1992.[22]

In Chile, five large agro-industrial companies were transferred to private enterprises during the period 1985-1989. Sixteen State-owned industrial enterprises were also sold to the private sector. Sixteen financial intermediaries and six transport and telecommunication companies were also privatized. In Brazil, only a few small companies were privatized during 1980-1989 and the plan was to sell another 22 in 1992. However, violent public protests erupted against the transfer of USIMINAS, the largest steel mill in Latin America, in October 1991, indicating that popular support for privatization was not enthusiastic.

In Africa, Ghana, Guinea, Côte d'Ivoire, Niger, Nigeria, Senegal, Togo and Uganda have been enthusiastic about the privatization of government enterprises.[23] India has actively implemented a privatization programme. In 1991, 17 out of 244 central government enterprises were partially divested. In 1992 the Government decided to offer to the public shares in another 20 public companies.[24] The Malaysian Privatization Plan of 1990 identified 147 government entities as privatization candidates. Of these, 37 were due for sale in the following two years.[25] In the Philippines, one of the largest State-owned enterprises to be sold to the private sector was Philippine Airlines.

In African countries, as in the economies in transition, one of the main impediments to the sale of public assets to the private sector has been the rudimentary nature of securities markets and a lack of potential buyers. Only five stock exchanges are operating in sub-Saharan Africa. One of the major reasons that large-scale enterprises were started by the public sector in the first place was the inability of private sector enterprises to raise capital on the required scale at a reasonable cost. Where capital markets are better developed, as in most of Asia and Latin America, other factors have stood in the way of rapid privatization. One of these is opposition by the employees of the threatened enterprises, who reasonably fear retrenchment or reductions in the privileged conditions of employment they enjoy in State enterprises. In some of these instances, the enterprises have been handed over to private sector managers with ownership resting in the government.

Still other public enterprises await financial sructuring before being put on the market for sale to the private sector. Enterprises loaded with debt or banks with large non-operating assets wait to be put on a sounder financial footing before their net worth can be properly established and buyers can find them attractive.

### 3. Minimalist government

The development experience of successful developing economies in the twentieth century does not support a minimalist approach by government. In many of these economies, the State was highly interventionist, especially during the early phase of industrialization. For example, Governments in both the Republic of Korea and Taiwan Province of China were highly protective and interventionist. The Republic of Korea intervened in investment allocation through import substitution programmes, credit allocation via the State-controlled banking system and subsidization. It also intervened massively in the acquisition and spread of technology and in attracting foreign direct investment.[26] Singapore provided similar protection to infant industries.

Public enterprises also played prominent roles. In the Republic of Korea and Taiwan Province of China, the contribution of public enterprises to gross capital formation was substantial. In Taiwan Province of China, the share of public enterprises in industrial production during 1953-1962 was about 50 per cent and industrial output grew by 11.7 per cent per annum. Public enterprises accounted for 25 per cent of gross domestic capital formation in the Republic of Korea during 1974-1977 and GDP in real terms grew by 13 per cent per annum.[27]

Government participation in technology transfer in both Korea and Taiwan Province of China was functional, intensive and targeted. Governments intervened by providing tax incentives, institutional support, funding and direct guidance. They set up research establishments in selected activities and sponsored relevant research projects. An instructive instance of such intervention in Taiwan Province of China is in the design and production of semiconductors. In 1974, the Government set up the Electronic Research and Service Organization (ERSO) to develop semiconductor design and production. By 1985, United Micro-electronics, a subsidiary of ERSO with private sector participation, was in full production of 256K dynamic random access memory chips, close to the frontiers of technology.[28]

Governments promoted technology transfer by employing high-quality foreign experts, training national personnel both at home and abroad, providing incentives to local firms to develop local technology and to foreign firms to transfer technology to local producers. Where contracts were given for turnkey projects, Governments insisted that local engineers participate in all stages of design and engineering. In establishing production facilities under licence, local firms were provided guidance, information and assistance in bargaining.[29] Governments of the Republic of Korea, Singapore and Taiwan Province of China were assiduous in building organizations to support industrial development and national technology strengths. Governments imposed high-quality standards and supported training, information collection, technology diffusion, testing and research institutes.

These successful efforts need to be contrasted against failures in other countries. Heavy protection of domestic industry and ubiquitous Government intervention in the economy in India and the

Philippines in Asia, in most of Latin America and in Africa have not raised the rates of economic growth and social development in the same way as the economies in East Asia. The development process in Africa has been seriously undermined by market imperfections. Governments have contributed little to correct them. Where political power has been exercised by select groups such as the military or urban elites, as in Latin America, or by those with an interest in continuing current policy regimes, it has been difficult for Governments to perform their normal functions competently.

## B.  FEATURES OF GOVERNMENT AND DEVELOPMENT

These contrasts emphasize the significance of certain features of Government. First, government intervention in the market should be limited to what it does best. This has implications for government ownership of enterprises, taxation, deficit financing, regulation and subsidies. However, the responsibility of Government for social security, social protection, the reduction of inequality in the distribution of income and the provision of physical and social infrastructure cannot be minimized. These are not functions that the market performs best, although market instruments can be used by the Government. The less sophisticated markets would make it all the more necessary for Governments to shoulder these responsibilities. The extent to which outcomes are satisfactory will be determined by the competence of the Government.

The second feature is that Governments are held accountable to the public. The periodic election of the legislature and the chief executive gives the public an opportunity to approve of the policies and conduct of the Government. For such an election to be meaningful, the public must have a choice between alternative political parties, that the public is well informed of alternative policies and that the elections are fair and open. In recent years, the United Nations itself has either conducted or supervised such elections in Angola, Nicaragua and Namibia. Eminent persons from outside the country have been invited to attest to the fairness of elections in a few other countries.

An efficient executive is the third feature. Its emergence requires good education, fair means of recruitment and promotion, training, adequate remuneration and the establishment of sound traditions of public service. Deterioration of pay and conditions of service in many countries in Africa has made the retention of highly competent persons very difficult. At lower levels, public sector workers have taken up other activities to eke out their incomes. In several instances inadequate pay has enticed government employees to obtain illegal compensation from persons who stand to benefit from the decisions made by them. The discretion available to them in highly regulated economies has made it feasible to obtain such gratification. To the extent that training and equipment can improve efficiency in the executive branch, this is an area for technical cooperation activities. Much of the capacity-building activities financed by the United Nations Development Programme has been in this area.

A fourth feature is an impartial judiciary. This is especially important for the emergence of markets since the enforcement of contracts depends finally on the presumption that the courts will decide cases impartially between parties to conflicts, and the rest of the judicial system will enforce these decisions. A judiciary independent of other branches of Government is necessary to ensure that individuals can exercise their rights against an executive which might abuse its power and against legislation which may attempt to encroach on them. These assurances depend on the rule of law rather than the arbitrary decisions of the executive or the judiciary itself.

The fifth feature is that processes be transparent. A literate and vigilant public would help immensely to ensure that the conduct of the Government remains transparent. Governments must function in a language the public understands. The information media should be free to report and comment on government activities and have adequate access to these processes. Open government would also provide opportunities for the public to participate in formulating policies and monitoring their implementation.

Political, administrative and constitutional changes in developing countries in recent years have generally contributed to better governance. In Latin America and the Caribbean, except Haiti, military rule has been replaced by popularly elected Governments. In Asia, there have been parallel changes, except in Myanmar where the military rules, ignoring the results of elections to the legislature in 1990.

In Africa the process of change is more variegated. Military rule and one-party political systems prevail in several countries. A number of elections to the legislature and of the chief executive were scheduled for the end of 1992. In Algeria, Botswana, Namibia, Senegal and Tunisia several political parties compete for power. Several other countries, including Nigeria, are moving towards establishing multi-party systems. Even countries with a single political party have experienced demands for reforms, permitting greater political competition, administrative reforms within the existing framework of law and constitutional reforms to check the powers of the party and the State.[30] Multi-party elections were planned in Kenya at the end of 1992.

The African Charter for Popular Participation in Development and Transformation (Arusha 1990)[31] recognized that the political context of socio-economic development was characterized, in many instances, by an over-centralization of power and impediments to the effective participation of the overwhelming majority of the people in social, political and economic development.

The extent of political transformation aimed at reducing these shortcomings varies from country to country. In several countries, including Cameroon and the Congo, the process started with increased scope for political competition within the single ruling party. In other countries, restrictions on political activity and on the press were eased and new political publications have emerged. In Madagascar, a law enacted in March 1990 allowed independent political parties and four opposition parties to be formed rapidly. In Cape Verde, constitutional reforms ending single-party rule and legalizing opposition parties were a first step towards parliamentary elections in January 1991.[32]

These liberal and democratic forms of Government are desirable in themselves in preference to totalitarian and autocratic forms. The massive disaffection of the public in economies in transition from Communist party rule is clear testimony of that preference. However, there is no evidence from recent experience that the features discussed above are necessary for rapid economic growth and social development.

Some of the fastest growing economies in Asia, both developed and developing, have not been multi-party democracies in practice. Sustained rapid economic growth in some of them has taken place in a strongly coercive atmosphere. Multi-party democracy is quite new in several of these countries. In some, although there are competing political parties, one party has been in power without interruption for 20 to 30 years. In others, military rule has gone hand in hand with rapid economic growth. In a few, political accountability has been poor and senior politicans have been accused and convicted of corruption. In contrast, in the two countries in Asia that have adopted democratic forms, namely India and Sri Lanka, the pace of economic growth has been moderate.

In Latin America, periods of recent military rule, as in Brazil and Chile, have also been periods of rapid economic growth. In Chile, the last period of military rule was also one of economic liberalization.

In contrast the severe restrictions on economic well-being in Africa make tasks of political liberalization much more difficult. As the economic space in which individuals and groups can move becomes restricted, those who stand to lose power and economic privileges are less likely to be willing to share power with others. Economic revival and growth in these countries would contribute immensely to the process of political liberalization.

## C. CONCLUSIONS

The change and development of institutions are important not only for the promotion and preservation of human rights but also for economic and social development. Representative forms of Government and limits to their authority are essential components of these changes. They may have less to do with rapid economic and social development. Where interventions in economic and social life become impediments to good governance, each society has to decide where to draw the line beyond which Government may not encroach.

Since all economies are mixed economies, the quality of government intervention is an important consideration. In economies where markets are rudimentary, the development of markets itself is an important function of Government. Protection of the environment, construction of physical infrastructure, primary health care and education, the regulation of banking and finance industries, the eradication of poverty and the reduction of inequality in the distribution of income, and the provision of social protection and security are functions of Government. The enactment and administration of laws and regulations and the maintenance of peaceful conditions in which entreneurship can thrive are primary responsibilities of Government. In technologically backward economies, Governments must take the initiative in undertaking research and training.

It is now clearer that in performing these functions, Governments would do well to use market instruments to ensure that as many of them as feasible are subject to competitive forces. It is also necessary that users of these facilities pay for them both to avoid waste and to finance their maintenance and expansion. Where administrative competence is scarce, the use of market instruments would have an added advantage.

The quality of Government will depend on the competence of its bureaucracy. Proper training, adherence to merit in appointment and promotion and adequate wages are essential to recruit and retain competent personnel. International cooperation has been a significant means of providing training. Much room exists for both expanding and improving the quality of such cooperative action.

New insights into the significance of institutions in the economy seek to demonstrate that they govern costs of transactions in the economy while technology governs costs of transformation. The extent and the speed of technology change itself is determined to some degree by institutional arrangements. Economic, political and social institutions bear a much heavier burden of responsibility for human well-being than was previously thought.

## Notes

[1] See, especially, R. C. O. Matthews, "The economics of institutions and the sources of growth", *The Economic Journal*, vol. 96 (December 1986), pp. 903-918. See also Douglass C. North, *Institutions, Institutional Change and Economic Performance* (Cambridge, Cambridge University Press, 1990); Oliver E. Williamson, *The Economic Institutions of Capitalism* (New York, Free Press, 1985); John L. Campbell and others, eds., *Governance of the American Economy* (Cambridge, Cambridge University Press, 1991).

[2] Matthews, loc. cit., p. 905.

[3] Murray Feshback and Alfred Friendly, Jr., *Ecocide in the USSR* (New York, Basic Books, 1992).

[4] Anne Krueger, "Government failures in development", National Bureau of Economic Research, Working Paper No. 3340, 1990.

[5] "The world economy in 1992 — An update: note by the Secretary-General" (E/1992/INF/8).

[6] Eliana Cardoso, "Inflation and poverty", National Bureau of Economic Research, Working Paper No. 4006, March 1992.

[7] European Bank for Reconstruction and Development, *A Changing Europe, 1991* (London, 1992), pp. 42-43.

[8] *Privatization International*, no. 49 (October 1992), p. 16.

[9] Lue Goguan, *Issledovaniya Ekonomicheskoi Reformi Gossudarstvennoi Sobstvennosti v Kitae*, Seria Ekonomicheskaya, no. 2 (Moskva, 1990).

[10] *Privatization International*, no. 49 (October 1992), p. 16.

[11] Poland, Ministry of Ownership Changes, *Mass Privatization: Proposed Programme* (Warsaw, June 1991), p. 4.

[12] "Privatizacios kutatointezet: szonda ipsos", *Barometer of Privatization*, no. 91/1 (Budapest, October 1991), p. 1.

[13] Leslie Colitt, "Optimists repeatedly disappointed", *Financial Times*, 26 October 1992, p. x.

[14] For a discussion of how these issues were seen in the early days of communism, see Sidney and Beatrice Webb, *Soviet Communism: A New Civilization?* (New York, Charles Scribner and Sons, 1936), in particular, vol. II, *Social Trends in Soviet Communism*. For a discussion of later experience, see W. Brus and K. Laski, *From Marx to the Market: Socialism in Search of an Economic System* (Oxford, Oxford University Press, 1989), pp. 10-11 and 36-37.

[15] According to an opinion poll in Poland, 85 per cent of the respondents believed that incomes should depend on individual qualifications and competence; at the same time, 39 per cent wanted the State to limit the wages of those earning the most and 72 per cent to limit profits of private enterprises; almost 70 per cent of the respondents were of the opinion that the State should be concerned about reducing income differences (see W. Morawski, "Reform models and systemic change in Poland", *Studies in Comparative Communism*, vol. XXIV, no. 3 (September 1991)).

[16] Joanna Solski, "W Wedlu wierza ze zarobia jak w Ameryce", *Polityka*, November 1991.

[17]See Janusz M. Dabrowski and others, "Polish state enterprises and the properties of performance: stabilization, marketization, privatization", Central School of Planning and Statistics (Warsaw)/Center for International Affairs, Harvard University (mimeo), May 1991, pp. 38-41 and 44. For a more pessimistic view, see, for example, Richard A. Jenner and Joseph Gappa, "Learning under fire: adaptability of Polish managers to competitive market conditions", *Journal of World Trade*, vol. 25, no. 2 (April 1991).

[18]The slow nature of assimilating new values and attitudes is discussed by David S. Landes in "Why are we so rich and they so poor", American Economic Association *Papers and Proceedings*, vol. 80, no. 2 (May 1990), and, in particular, by Amitai Etzioni, who analyses this issue in relation to the former Soviet Union in "How is Russia bearing up", *Challenge*, May-June 1992.

[19]Pranab Bardhan and John E. Roemer, "Market socialism: a case for rejuvenation", *Journal of Economic Perspectives*, vol. 6, no. 3 (summer 1992), pp. 101-116.

[20]*The Banker*, July 1991, p. 7.

[21]O. Bouin and Ch.-A. Michalet, *Rebalancing the Public and Private Sectors: Developing Countries Experience*, OECD, Development Centre Studies (Paris, 1991), pp. 235-236.

[22]See *The Divestiture Process in Mexico*, Secretariat of Finance and Public Credit (Mexico City, Hacienda, 1991).

[23]C. Vuylsteke, *Techniques of Privatization of State-Owned Enterprises: Methods and Implementation*, vol. 1 (Washington, D.C., World Bank, 1988), pp. 177-180.

[24]*Privatization International*, no. 49 (October 1992), pp. 1 and 25.

[25]*Privatization International*, no. 42 (March 1992).

[26]Alice H. Amsden, *Asia's Next Giant: South Korea and Late Industrialization* (Oxford and New York, Oxford University Press, 1989), pp. 12-13.

[27]See S. Short, *The Role of Public Enterprises: An International Statistical Comparison — Public Enterprises in Mixed Economies: Some Macroeconomic Aspects*, R. Floyd and others, eds. (Washington, D.C., International Monetary Fund, 1984).

[28]For an instructive study, see Robert Wade, *Governing the Market: Economic Theory and the Role of Government in East Asian Industrialization* (Princeton, Princeton University Press, 1991); see also Erich Weede, "The impact of democracy on economic growth: some evidence from cross-national analysis", *Kyklos*, vol. 36 (1983), p. 21.

[29]Sanjaya Lall, *Explaining Industrial Success in the Developing World: Current Issues in Development Economics*, V. N. Balasubramanyam and Sanjaya Lall, eds. (London, Macmillan, forthcoming).

[30]Goran Hyden and Michael Bratton, eds., *Governance and Politics in Africa* (London, Lynne Rienner, 1992), p. 36.

[31]A/45/427, appendix II, para. 6.

[32]Hyden and Bratton, eds., op. cit.

# 13

## Ethnic conflicts and national disintegration

A GREAT escalation of violent conflict has taken place in the world since the end of the cold war — in the former Soviet Union, in Eastern Europe and in Asia and Africa. In the period 1989-1990, there were 33 armed conflicts with more than 1,000 casualities (table 13.1) Only one of those conflicts was fought between nation States. The rest were all civil wars — conflicts between ethnic, religious or other groups in one and the same nation-State.[1]

The casualities in these conflicts have been high. The number of people killed in the former Yugoslavia in recent ethnic and religious conflicts up to mid-1992 was close to 6,000. In India during 1989-1991, the number of people killed in ethnic conflicts was reported as 12,261.[2] Millions of people have had their livelihoods and homes destroyed and been driven forth as refugees or displaced persons.

The conflicts are destroying conditions necessary for economic and social development and siphoning off resources from the urgent tasks of feeding, educating and housing desperately poor populations. Ethnic strife in Somalia and the former Yugoslavia has prevented humanitarian assistance from reaching people in conditions of extreme hunger, sickness and homelessness. More than 2 million refugees and displaced persons were fleeing from the former Yugoslavia at the end of 1992. The cohesion of States is being threatened in many instances by brutal ethnic, religious, social, cultural and linguistic strife.[3] In the wake of the cold war, these local conflicts have emerged as the most common or imminent threats to peace.

*Table 13.1*

Parties to major armed conflicts in the world, 1990

| Country or area and year formed[d] year joined[a] | Parties to conflict | Casualties[c] (including 1990) |
|---|---|---|
| **Africa** | | |
| Angola | | |
| 1975/1975 | National Union for the Total Independence of Angola (UNITA) | 1975-1989: 25,600[d] |
| 1975/1975 | Liberation front for Cabinda (FLEC) | |
| 1975/1975 | National Front for the Liberation of Angola (FNLA) | |
| Chad | | |
| 1982/1987 | Islamic Legion | |
| 1989/1989 | Mouvement patriotique du salut | |
| 1973/1979 | Libyan Government (Aozou Strip) | |
| Ethiopia | | |
| 1970/1971 | Eritrean People's Liberation Front (EPLF) | 1962-1990: 500,000[e] |
| 1976/1976 | Tigray People's Liberation Front (TPLF) | |
| 1975/1980 | Ethiopian People's Democratic Movement | |
| 1977/1977 | Oromo Liberation Front (OLF) | |
| 1974/1975 | Ethiopian People's Revolutionary Party (EPRP) | |
| 1975/1975 | Afar Liberation Front (ALF) | |
| Liberia | | |
| 1989/1989 | National Patriotic Forces (NPLF) | 1989-1990: 10,000-13,000 |
| 1990/1990 | Independent National Patriotic Forces (INPLF) | |
| 1990/1990 | Economic Community of West African States (ECOWAS) Monitoring Group (ECOMOG) | |
| 1990/1990 | Government of Burkina Faso | |
| Morocco | | |
| 1975/1976 | Polisario | 1975-1989: 10,000-13,000[f] |

| Country or area and year formed[d] year joined[a] | Parties to conflict | Casualties[c] (including 1990) |
|---|---|---|
| **Mozambique** | | |
| 1975/1976 | National Resistance Movement | 100,000 (civilian)[g] |
| **Somalia** | | |
| 1981/1981 | Somali National Movement (SNM) | 1981-1990: 50,000-60,000 |
| 1989/1989 | Somali Patriotic Movement (SPM) | |
| ../1990 | United Somali Congress (USC) | |
| **South Africa** | | |
| 1950/1984 | African National Congress (ANC) | 1984-1990: over 7,750 [h] |
| 1979/1983 | Inkatha versus ANC | |
| 1990/1990 | White rightist groups | |
| **Sudan** | | |
| 1980/1983 | Sudanese People's Liberation Army | 1983-1990: over 33,000 (military) |
| 1990/199 | Military factions | |
| **Uganda** | | |
| 1986/1986 | Uganda People's Democratic Movement (UPD) | 1986-1990: over 11,000 (military) |
| 1987/1987 | Uganda People's Army (UPA) | |
| 1987/1987 | United Democratic Christian Movement (UDCM) | |
| **South Asia** | | |
| **Afghanistan** | | |
| 1978/1978 | Mujahideen based in Afghanistan, Republic of Iran, Pakistan | 1978-1990: 1,000,000[i] |
| **Bangladesh** | | |
| 1971/1982 | Parbattya Chattagram Jana Sanghati Samiti (JSS) Shanti Bahini (SB) | 1975-1990: 1,200-3,000 |
| **India** | | |
| 1947/1981 | Khalistan Commando Force | 1983-1990: over 19,800 |
| 1947/1982 | Jammu and Kashmir Liberation Front | |
| 1990/1990 | Hizbul Mujahideen | |
| 1988/1988 | Bodo Student Union/Bodo Voulantiers Force | |
| 1967/1967 | Naxalites, People's War Group | |

*(continued)*

*Table 13.1 (continued)*

| Country or area and year formed[d] year joined[a] | Parties to conflict | Casualties[c] (including 1990) |
|---|---|---|
| **Myanmar** | | |
| 1948/1949 | Karen National Union | 1948-51: 8,000<br>1950: 5,000 |
| 1948/1948 | Kachin Independence Army | 1981-1984: 400-600 yearly |
| 1949/1949 | Mon State Party | 1985-1987: over 1,000 yearly |
| 1965/1965 | Shan State Army | 1988: 500-3,000 |
| 1989/1989 | Burma National United Party | |
| 1989/1989 | Noom Suk Harn | |
| 1989/1989 | National Democratic Army | |
| **Sri Lanka** | | |
| 1976/1983 | Liberation Tigers of Tamil Eelam | |
| 1969/1987 | People's Liberation Front (JVP) | |
| **Pacific Asia** | | |
| **Cambodia** | | |
| 1975/1979 | Democratic Kampuchea (Khmer Rouge) | 1979-1989: 25,300[j] |
| 1979/1979 | Khmer People's National Liberation Front (KPLNF) | |
| 1979/1979 | Front Uni pour un Cambodge Indépéndant Neutre, Pacifique et Coopératif/Armée Nationale Sihanoukiste (FUNCINPEC/ANS) | |
| **Indonesia** | | |
| 1975/1975 | Revolutionary Front for an Independent East Timor (Fretilin) | 1975-1990: 15,000-16,000 (military)[k] |
| ../1989 | Aceh Merdeka | |
| ../1989 | National Liberation Front of Aceh | |
| **Lao People's Democratic Republic** | | |
| 1975/1975 | United Lao National Liberation Front (ULNLF) (1980) and other | 1975-1990: over 1,000[l] |

| Country or area and year formed[d] year joined[a] | Parties to conflict | Casualties[c] (including 1990) |
|---|---|---|
| **Philippines** | | |
| 1968/1986 | New People's Army | 1972-1990: over 37,500[m] |
| 1982/1986 | Reform Army Movement | |
| 1972/1986 | Mindanao National Liberation Front | |
| 1990/1990 | Military faction | |
| **Central and South America** | | |
| **Colombia** | | |
| 1949/1978 | Fuerzas Armadas Revolucionarias de Colombia | 1980-1990: over 8,500[n] |
| 1965/1978 | Ejército de Liberación Nacional (ELN) | |
| 1968/1977 | Ejército Popular de Liberación (EPL) | |
| **El Salvador** | | |
| 1976/1979 | Farabundo Martí Front for National Liberation (FMLN) | 1979-1990: 76,000 |
| **Guatemala** | | |
| 1967/1968 | Guatemalan National Revolutionary Unity | 1962-1990: 20,000-60,000 |
| **Nicaragua** | | |
| 1981/1981 | Contras | 1981-1990: over 30,000 (military) |
| **Peru** | | |
| 1980/1981 | Sendero Luminoso | 1981-1990: 11,500-20,000 |
| 1984/1986 | Movimiento Revolucionario Tupac Amaru (MRTA) | |
| **Middle East** | | |
| **Iran** | | |
| 1961/1980 | Kurdish Democratic Party | 1980-1989: 5,000-6,000[g] |
| 1975/1980 | Patriotic Union of Kurdistan | |
| **Israel/Palestine** | | |
| 1964/1964 | Palestine Liberation Organization (PLO) groups or related groups | 1948-1990: over 11,000 December 1987–December 1990: 900-1,000 |

*(continued)*

*Table 13.1 (continued)*

| Country or area and year formed[d] year joined[a] | Parties to conflict | Casualties[c] (including 1990) |
|---|---|---|
| **Lebanon** | | |
| 1975/1975 | Lebanon Army (Aoun) | 1975-1990: 150,000 |
| 1985/1985 | Lebanese Forces (Gaegea) | |
| 1979/1979 | Amal | |
| 1975/1975 | Islamic Resistance/Hezbollah | |
| 1964/1964 | Palestine Liberation Organization (PLO) | |
| 1959/1965 | Al Fatah | |
| 1969/1969 | Democratic Front for the Liberation of Palestine (Hawatmah) | |
| 1967/1968 | Popular Front for the Liberation of Palestine (Habash) | |
| 1968/1968 | Popular Front for the Liberation of Palestine — General Command | |
| 1968/1975 | Palestine Popular Struggle Front Lebanese Forces | |
| 1974/1976 | Fatah Revolutionary Council (Nidal) | |
| 1977/1977 | Palestine Liberation Front (Yaqoub) | |
| 1961/1975 | Syrian Socialist Nationalist Party | |
| 1975/1975 | Lebanese National Resistance Front | |
| 1975/1975 | Popular Nasserite Organization | |
| 1975/1975 | Lebanese Baath Party | |
| 1978/1978 | South Lebanese Army | |
| 1976/1976 | Government of Syrian Arab Republic | |
| 1978/1982 | Government of Israel | |
| **Turkey** | | |
| 1974/1984 | Kurdish Worker's Party | 1984-1990: 2,000-2,500 |
| **Europe** | | |
| United Kingdom of Great Britain and Northern Ireland | | |
| 1969/1969 | Provisional Irish Republican Army (IRA) | 1969-1990: 2,800 |

Source: Stockholm International Peace Research Institute (SIPRI), *World Armaments and Disarmament Yearbook 1991.*

Notes: Two dots (..) indicate that year of formation of a conflict is unknown.

a    Year formed is the year in which a party to the conflict last formed the relevant policies or the year in which a new party, State or alliance involved in the conflict came into being. Year joined is the year in which the armed fighting last began or the year in which armed fighting recommenced after a period for which no armed combat was recorded. For conflicts with very sporadic armed combat over a long period, the year joined may also refer to the beginning of a period of sustained and exceptionally heavy combat.

b    Parties to conflict are those that have come into conflict with similar other organizations of the Government of the country. Only those parties active during 1990 are in this column.

c    The figures for deaths refer to total battle-related deaths during the conflict. The figures exclude, as far as data allow, civilian deaths owing to famine and disease. Military and civilian refer to estimates, where available, of military and civilian deaths; where there is no such indication, the figure refers to total military and civilian battle-related deaths in the period or year given.

d    Figures refer to the period up to 1989. During January–October 1990, the Government and UNITA claimed to have killed over 1,800 of each other's soldiers, but each admitted only to having incurred small losses. According to the Government, UNITA in addition killed 1,720 civilians during the same period.

e    The 500,000 deaths refer to the Eritrean conflict and include both military and civilian deaths. It is unclear whether the figure includes all deaths in connection with the conflict, (in other words, not only battle-related deaths).

f    Figures for the period up to 1989. Military activity during 1990 was low.

g    Figures are for the period up to 1989 since figures are not available for 1990.

h    Including deaths connected with the struggle between ANC and Inkatha supporters.

i    The figure is likely to include all deaths in connection with the conflict, that is, not only battle-related deaths. According to Soviet sources, the total number of Soviet troops killed in the period 1979 to 15 February 1989 was 15,000. Figures for the total number of deaths during 1990 are not available.

j    For figures for battle-related deaths in this conflict before 1979, see *SIPRI Yearbook 1990.* Regarding battle-related deaths during 1979–1989, the only figure available is from official Vietnamese sources, indicating that 25,300 Vietnamese soldiers died in Cambodia. An estimated figure for the period 1979–1989, based on various sources, is over 50,000, and for 1989, over 1,000. Figures for 1990 are not available.

k    The 15,000 to 16,000 military deaths refers to the East Timor conflict. No reports are available for the number of deaths in East Timor during 1990.

l    This currently low-level conflict has since 1975 produced over 1,000 battle-related deaths. Higher figures have been reported, but there is no agreement regarding their accuracy.

m    Not including casualties from Mindanao conflict.

n    Politics-related deaths (that is, excluding deaths resulting from fighting between Government and cocaine cartels). The figure does not include October–December 1990.

o    Including the 2,000 NLA (Iranian National Liberation Army) deaths (in 1988) in the war between Iran and Iraq.

## A. ETHNIC AND RELIGIOUS DIVERSITY OF NATION-STATES

Most nation-States contain more than one ethnic or religious group. In the old nation-States of Europe, the sharp differences among ethnic groups have for the most part melted away in the course of nation-building and economic development. Those activities moved and mixed people, promoted a common language and culture, stimulated inter-marriage and created an industrial society with new social classes having a strong interest in national stability. Even in those States, however, bitter language feuds continue (in Belgium, for example), and old feuds survive in various forms. This is attested by the fierce terrorism of the Provisional Irish Republican Army (IRA) in Northern Ireland and in the rest of the United Kingdom of Great Britain and Northern Ireland, the debate about devolution in Scotland and the ethnic claims of marginal communities, such as the Basques in Spain and the Tyroleans in Italy.

The most spectacular case of a multi-ethnic nation-State is the United States of America, where waves of immigration have created a dynamic web of semi-integrated communities. Although the scars left by the oppression of the original Indian population and the enslavement of transplanted Africans still mark the political life of the nation, its integrity is not in doubt.

In other parts of the world, some nation-States such as China and Japan are relatively homogeneous in ethnic composition. Brazil, although more diverse, has also succeeded in merging its several groups into thriving communities. The newer nation-States are generally much more diverse and have not yet had the benefit of experiencing those forces that tend to reduce the sharpness of ethnic differences. A full survey of ethnic conflicts in nation-States will not be presented here, but some of the situations currently claiming the attention of the world will be briefly reviewed.

### 1. *Africa*

Africa presents by far the most varied and complex ethnic diversity of all continents. Virtually all the States of Africa contain a large number of ethnically distinct communities, tribes or language groups, and ethnicity is also an important factor in African society. Ethnically homogeneous countries include Lesotho, Somalia and Swaziland. In Africa, ethnicity is often a key factor determining affiliation in political parties and participation in public office, the army or trade unions. Many ethnically diverse States, such as Ghana and the United Republic of Tanzania, are thriving communities where ethnicity is not a disrupting factor.

Conflict among ethnic groups has been reflected in recurrent civil, border and secessionary wars and in the tendency of political divisions to take on an ethnic dimension. Civil strife and internal insecurity have been a main obstacle to progress in Angola, Chad, Ethiopia, Somalia and the Sudan for many years. The 36-year-old civil war in the Sudan between the Muslim north and the Christian south has been a serious deterrent to growth and development. During the period 1960-1976, after the granting of independence to many countries, 21 internal and border wars of major proportions were fought in Africa. In the 1980s, 10 more were added to the list. It continues to grow because of new conflicts in the 1990s.

The drawn-out ethnic conflicts in Burundi and Rwanda involve groups that live in several nation-States.[4] Some of these groups live in Uganda, the United Republic of Tanzania and Zaire as well as in States in the Great Lakes region. The Government of Rwanda came to be controlled by the Hutu, who made up about 85 per cent of the population. After about 10,000 of the Tutsi were massacred, the survivors escaped to neighbouring countries. There they attempted a major invasion of Uganda. In February 1991, Burundi, Rwanda, Uganda, the United Republic of Tanzania and Zaire agreed to end the conflict.

The Tutsi hold government power in Burundi, although they are a minority of the population. In 1972 an attempt was made by the Hutu population to gain control of the Government. This was unsuccessful and led to an estimated 100,000 casualities among the Hutu population. Recently, initiatives have been taken to open up opportunities in a more equitable manner, but ethnic conflict remains a prominent feature of social and political life in the Great Lakes countries.

Nigeria has an estimated 250 identifiable ethnic groups.[5] Each distinct group was governed as a separate administrative unit under British indirect rule. The Act of Amalgamation, passed in 1914, was the first step towards the creation of modern Nigeria. The next step was the Richards' Constitution of 1946 which established a Federation of three regions — east, north and west — and the Federal Territory of Lagos. When Nigeria became independent in 1960, this federal structure was retained in recognition of the regional diversity of the country.

Ethnically-based cultural organizations became the stepping-stones towards political parties. The northern region contained 54 per cent of the population and covered two thirds of the surface area. In the first elections in independent Nigeria, 174 seats out of 312 in the Congress were allotted to that region. The Northern Peoples Congress (NPC) could form the central government without other support. The extreme manifestation of regionalism was the threat of secession. In July 1967 the eastern region's proclaiming itself the Republic of Biafra started a civil war that lasted until January 1970. In the aftermath of the civil war, the victorious federal authorities showed great statesmanship and sought to rebuild a reunited and more just Federation.

Another aspect of Nigeria's diversity is reflected in the mounting religious strain. The inclusion of the *shariah* (Islamic law) into the constitution in 1988 became the object of strong controversy. The last decade has seen Muslim-Christian violence occurring over many other ostensibly innocuous issues.[6] The most recent Muslim-Christian riots took place in April/May 1991 at Bauchi and in October 1991 at Kano.[7]

One approach to the political problem has been to increase increase successively the number of constituent States in the federal structure to permit each large ethnic group to gain control of the State apparatus governing it.[8] With the creation of more States, minorities also gained direct access to power in the Federation.[9]

The successful completion of a national census in 1991, not feasible earlier because of ethnic rivalries, and the peaceful election of governors and State legislatures on 15 December 1991 augur well for the future.

The national rail network moving people and goods throughout the nation has been a powerful force for unity.[10] The freedom of movement permitted by a united Nigeria has prompted people to move in search of economic opportunities, and this has resulted in the geographical mixing of ethnic groups. With a total labour force of 37 million and unemployment at 3 to 5 million (figures for 1986), one of the main focuses of national integration will concern the success people have in finding work regardless of their ethnic origin. The set-backs to Nigeria's economic and social development during the 1980s have seriously limited this prospect.

The most flagrant ethnic divisions exist in South Africa, although the policies of apartheid are now being abolished. The division in Angola between two warring factions is not based primarily on ethnic conflict; nevertheless it is supported by such conflict. In Chad, the separation between Arabs and Teda-Daza (called Goranes by the former) has been feeding political rivalry even though both communities share the same Islamic faith.

The Sudan has been the victim of ethnic and religious conflict and civil war almost from the time it gained independence in 1955. The population in the north (about 40 per cent of the total), considers itself of Arab descent and is mostly Muslim. The population in the south is of Nilotic origin and comprises followers of Christianity and other faiths. The emergence of Islamic fundamentalism has further complicated the situation. The entire population is divided into 19 major ethnic groups and 597 subgroups. There are 115 languages, the dominant ones Arabic and Dinka.

War between ethnic groups in the south and the central government of the Sudan began in 1955. Periodic clashes have been frequent not only in the south but also in the west, among the Nuba mountains. Conflicts grew in violence in 1983 as the 1984-1985 drought hit particularly hard.

The creation of paramilitary forces each distinct in ethnic composition has created a situation in the western and southern provinces that is almost anarchic. While the main southern military organization is the Sudan People's Liberation Army, a number of armed militia whose membership is exclusively Muslim are active. Extrajudicial executions by the military on a massive scale have been reported in the south.

In contrast, Somalia is united by one language and by one religion, Islam, but divided into a large number of relatively small groups, each one fighting the other. The country has had no stable Government since rebel forces in January 1991 overthrew the Government of President Barre.

This collapse of civil society has taken place in a country that has fought a war during 1977-1978 with the Western Somali Liberation Front and Ethiopia. Two decades of recurring drought have ruined much livestock and many agricultural activities. The civil war has destroyed irrigation systems and seed stocks, drastically reducing harvests. About 60 per cent of the physical infrastructure and 80 per cent of social services have been rendered non-operational.

When the civil war erupted in 1988, 450,000 Somali nationals became refugees in Ethiopia. An estimated 300,000 people died of starvation and as a result of the war since November 1991. Children account for a large proportion of the dead. Another 1 million children are estimated to run the risk of severe malnutrition.

## 2. India

India is a country of immense cultural diversity. It has adherents of the six major world religions. Indians speak 14 major languages, each with a flourishing literature. Besides these, there is Sanskrit, an ancient language with a rich literature in which Hindu rituals are conducted, while English is common among small proportions of all linguistic groups. The Hindu population is also divided into castes.

The federal constitution provides for a strong central government and a substantial measure of autonomy for the constituent units, designed to accommodate the existing diversity and guarantee each minority its cultural, religious and linguistic distinctiveness.[11] The constitution also contains special provisions for improving economic, cultural and social conditions among castes and tribes listed in a separate schedule.

To provide autonomy to a larger number of linguistic and ethnic groups, the number of constituent units in the Federation has been increased to comprise 25 States and 7 centrally administered Territories. A system of local self-government, known as *panchayati raj*, has also been introduced. The progressive division of constituent units has been carried out largely on the basis of language.

Caste has been a major cause of sporadic localized conflict. Legislation against caste distinctions has been in force since 1950. To assist underprivileged castes, a policy of affirmative action was adopted. Under this policy, 22.5 per cent of seats in institutions of higher learning and in public employment were set aside for the members of scheduled castes and tribes. Their economic and social conditions have improved substantially.

India's strong democratic traditions enable these social groups to compete for opportunities opened up by economic development. However, sections of the rest of the population see in this process a denial of equal opportunity for all. Widespread protests against the reservations policy broke out in August 1990 in northern India, after a decision by the Government to set aside an additional 27 per cent of jobs in central public services for the backward classes.[12]

Religious conflicts between the Muslim and Hindu populations have been common. There were over 100 million Muslims in India in 1991, more than in any other country except Indonesia and Bangladesh. Muslims in India have had to reconcile their allegiance to a secular, although Hindu-dominated India, with their own religious and cultural traditions. Recently there has also been a growing tendency for politicans and political groups to be affected by religious divisions. Conflicts between religious groups in Jammu and Kashmir, and between separatist groups and the central government, have been prolonged and destructive. Some of this violence in recent years may have less to do with ethnic conflicts than with the work of extremists and terrorists. Every Hindu-Muslim disturbance in India causes concern in Pakistan about the safety of Muslims there. This concern and the dispute over Jammu and Kashmir have impeded the development of friendly relations between the two countries.

The long-term dominance of the Indian National Congress produced exceptional conditions conducive to the management of ethnic, religious and caste conflicts. It permitted a high degree of cooperation between the central and state governments, as most issues involving the central government and the States were handled inside the Congress. Industrialization has created an integrated national economy. Power and water-supply systems provide services to several ethnic groups. A national system of rail and road transport carries people and goods across the whole of India. An all-India cadre of managers in Government and in private business draws expertise from every region. The emergence of a national system of mass communication — demonstrating the reach of newspapers, radio, cinema and television — has nurtured the growth of a national consciousness.[13] In workplaces, government offices and the armed services, members of different ethnic groups function harmoniously.[14] Rapid economic growth, evident in India during the 1980s, would, were it to continue, provide excellent conditions for the taking root of national integration.

## 3. *Latin America and the Caribbean*

Although countries of Latin America and the Caribbean contain several ethnic groups, those countries are generally not marked by violent ethnic conflict. To the indigenous population of Amerindians (*indios*) in South America have been added, over the centuries, European colonists and immigrants, and immigrants from Africa, China, India and, most recently, Japan. The offspring of mixed unions among these groups are separately identified as mestizos, born of the union of Amerindians and Europeans; mulattos, born of the union of Africans and Europeans; and zambos, born of the union of Amerindians and Africans. Over the centuries, a process of ethnic integration (*mestizaje*) has been producing mestizo culture, which has served as a cushion for easing ethnic tension and creating opportunities for open dialogue among the several groups. More recently, it has been realized that the identity of indigenous people needs to be recognized and nurtured.

The mestizo population and the populations of European origin form a large cultural majority in Latin America. The assimilation of Spanish traditions to indigenous ones has produced a Ladino culture, with which the mestizo population identifies itself. Some countries have favoured the immigration of people of European origin, thereby strengthening the latinity of their cultures and substantially ignoring the *indio* influence.[15] These processes of ethnic and cultural assimilation have been far from perfect or complete. The extent to which the mestizo population has been assimilated into the Ladino culture varies from place to place. In Peru, for instance, the massive urbanization that has taken place during the past few decades has enabled the gradual access of mestizo populations to Spanish language skills and some access of those populations to creole patterns of consumption. The mestizos are designated as belonging to a cholo subculture.[16] Both mestizo and *indio* populations belong to that subculture. They are poorer than the elite and far removed from it. The furthest removed are the *indio* populations from the Amazon in Bolivia, Brazil,[17] Colombia, Ecuador, Peru and Venezuela; they live in cultural isolation from the rest of national society.[18]

In Caribbean countries, ethnic differences, distinguished by colour of skin, have always been important in defining social hierarchies.[19] Trinidad and Tobago has a highly diverse ethnic composition including Creoles who are descendants of Whites, browns and Blacks. People of Indian origin who came to Trinidad and Tobago to work in the sugar plantations are 41 per cent of the population. Each segment, Creole and Indian, has its own stratification. Tensions between the two major ethnic groups exist in several fields of activity, including the political.

The differences are even more acute in Central American countries. The *miskitos*, an indigenous people of Nicaragua, were forcibly relocated to prevent their being caught between the warring factions, the Sandinistas and the Contras.[20] About 22,000 escaped to refugee camps in Honduras. In Nicaragua the major conflict was between ideologies rather than ethnic groups.[21] That conflict and natural disasters battered the country for 20 years beginning in 1970.

In Guatemala, half the population are descended directly from the Mayas, and the other half are mainly mestizo; the economic and social division between them is sharp. The *indio* populations have a distinctly lower standard of living and are relatively isolated from the mainstream of the economic, social and political processes.[22]

Only recently has the sharp dualism involving Ladino and *indio* cultures on the one hand and the "indigenous problématique" on the other been recognized. Differences are not limited to the narrowly cultural. Access to land and other resources, and to education and health services, the use of indigenous languages in the conduct of official affairs, and self-determination in the management of public affairs at the local level are among the rights claimed by indigenous peoples in Latin America. International recognition of those rights is reflected in the Convention concerning Indigenous and Tribal Peoples in Independent Countries (No. 169), adopted by the International Labour Organisation in 1989. Consequent to this Convention, an Agreement establishing the Fund for the Development of the Indigenous Peoples of Latin America and the Caribbean[23] was signed in July 1992.

Ethnic diversity in Latin America and the Caribbean has generally not led to violent confrontation. By establishing a dialogue for the elaboration of policies with the participation of the several groups concerned, by improving access to employment, education and training, social security and health, and by increasing respect for fundamental rights to freedom, it has been possible to avoid the worst forms of conflict. The peculiarity of the Latin American region consists in tendencies towards the assimilation of diversities in a wider common culture. The validity of that approach has been questioned because it is inimical to preserving the identity and survival of distinct ethnic groups.

### 4. *The former Soviet Union*

The Russian empire and the Soviet Union that succeeded it were the results of a long history of expansion of territories in Eastern Europe, Siberia, Central Asia and the Caucasus and their inclusion within one nation State. Populations of completely different ethnic origin, culture, language, religion and economic development had been brought together under the tsars.[24] The October revolution inherited this gigantic pluralism. Some counts identify at least 128 ethnic groups.[25]

The problem of nationalities was one of the first that the leaders of the Soviet Union had to face after the Russian revolution. Great efforts were devoted to the integration of the republics and the promotion of Russian as a common language. The republics were highly integrated economically. In 1989, more than 60 per cent of the net material product of each of the three Baltic republics was sold in other Soviet republics; among the Central Asian republics, this proportion varied from 29 to 50 per cent. The lowest figure (18 per cent) was that for the Russian Federation.[26] Railways, highways and air traffic all connected the far-flung parts of the Soviet Union to one another. The Administration concentrated power at the centre. The Communist party was itself a strong binding force.

Yet ethnic animosities came out into the open during the last few years of the Soviet Union. When the central government replaced local cadres with officials from the centre in 1986, strong negative reactions were sparked in Kazakhstan, the Transcaucasian republics and the Baltic republics. The worsening of ethnic conflicts in Armenia and Azerbaijan, and of those between Abkhazes and Georgians, and the violence perpetrated in the Central Asian republics against Russian immigrants were all signs of impending disintegration.[27]

Perhaps because the binding forces all emanated from the centre, the end of the Communist regime coincided with the end of the

unitary Soviet State. The disintegration of the Soviet Union, anticipated by the separation of the Baltic republics in September 1991,
took place in December 1991, when the Commonwealth of Independent States was established. The dynamism of the Soviet economy had come to an end by this time, and its collapse removed
whatever incentives the constituent republics may have had for
holding themselves together.

### 5. *The former Yugoslavia*

The former Yugoslavia was similar to the former Soviet Union
in that it contained many nationalities and one dominant nationality — the Serbs — but different in that it was a comparatively new
State. It was formed in the aftermath of the First World War (1914-
1918) to combine the existing States of Serbia and Montenegro
with territories that had been part of the Austro-Hungarian empire
(Croatia and Slovenia) and ones that more recently had been part
of the Ottoman empire (such as Bosnia and Herzegovina, which
had been annexed by Austria-Hungary as late as 1908).

The new State, then, did not have the historic traditions and
unity enjoyed by the older States in Europe. In fact, the new country lay along the fault lines of some of the most important divisions in European history — between Christianity and Islam and
between Orthodoxy and Roman Catholicism. However, the Orthodox Serbs, the Catholic Croats and the Muslims lived together
peacefully until the outbreak of the Second World War (1939-
1945), when a separatist movement emerged.

During the war, national unity was strengthened in the course
of the common anti-Fascist struggle. The design of the new State, a
federation of six republics and two autonomous provinces, was
aimed at allowing different ethnic and religious groups to live
together on an equal footing, including equal participation in government at all levels. However, with the death of Marshall Tito and
the discrediting of one-party rule, the bonds that had held the
republics together disintegrated.

The various republics became determined to attain independence, but the nationalist emotions that surfaced, which were ruthlessly exploited by politicans, made compromise and a peaceful unbinding of the federation difficult. The consequences have been ethnic conflict and barbarity — "ethnic cleansing", detention centres where civilians are murdered and indiscriminate shelling of civilian populations — on a scale that is scarcely imaginable.[28]

## B. RELIGIOUS FUNDAMENTALISM

The rise of fundamentalist and revivalist religious movements has also been the cause of new conflict. The great religions have no national boundaries and bind together people of divergent national and ethnic groups. Conflicts have in recent years come into the open between Muslim and Christian populations in many countries of Africa, Eastern Europe, West Asia and the Philippines; between Muslims and Hindus in India, Pakistan and Bangladesh; among the Sikhs, Hindus and Muslims in India and Pakistan; between Muslims and Christians and between Orthodox Christians and Roman Catholics in the former Yugoslavia; between the Jews and their predominantly Muslim Arab neighbours; between Christians and Muslims in Lebanon; among factions of Muslims in parts of West Asia and Northern Africa; and between Catholic and Protestant communities in Northern Ireland.

Revivalist tendencies among Hindus and Sikhs in India; a new trend associating Buddhism with nationalism in Thailand and Sri Lanka; and recent waves of renewed Confucianism in Japan, the Republic of Korea and Taiwan Province of China are all matters of concern.[29]

Religious persecution is seldom the cause of religious conflicts today. More commonly, the social and economic differentiation among groups adhering to various religions fuels antagonism among them. The issues involved are access to power and sharing of economic and social well-being. The conflicts have intensified where religious differences have coincided with ethnic ones and discrimination with respect to the distribution of economic well-being and access to political power is perceived to exist. Internal dissensions have often been exploited by parties outside the country to further their own objectives.

Fundamentalist and revivalist approaches to religion are not limited to Islam, although the term Islamic fundamentalism is used more commonly than others. Although those approaches are not homogeneous across religions and countries, they share common features. First, they assert their identity in the face of invading religious, social and economic forces (in the case of Islam, those from Europe and North America especially). Some groups in society stand to gain from the assertion of such values while others stand to gain from change. Second, the values fundamentalist and revivalist approaches espouse are not limited to those of religious life but apply as well to individual and social behaviour. Those approaches try to ensure that the family and its function in society, the division of roles according to gender, questions of social justice, the administration of justice, financial transactions and the exercise of political power are all governed by religious considerations.

## C. FACTORS CONTRIBUTING TO DISINTEGRATION AND INTEGRATION

Conflict is not the inevitable consequence of ethnic diversity. Ethnicity is "one of those forces that is community-building in moderation, ... community-destroying in excess".[30] The perpetuation of discrimination and injustices against ethnic or religious groups, cumulative memories of offences and humiliations whether real or imagined individual acts of violence or exploitation, remote and ineffective governments, physical and cultural isolation in the absence of transport and communications and a common language and the sudden demise of an authority that had previously kept order have all contributed to the spread of ethnic conflict and violence in recent years. The affordability and easy availability of powerful firearms have increased the destructive power of these conflicts manyfold.

Most ethnic conflicts arise from fissures buried deep in the past. The antagonism between the Sinhala and the Tamil in Sri Lanka, between Mende and Temne groups in Sierra Leone and between Croats and Serbs in the former Yugoslavia are only a few cases in point.

In the formation of nation-States in Eastern Europe after the Second World War, several ethnic groups were often aggregated in the same State. History brought together people of different ethnic backgrounds within one nation-State, as in the former Yugoslavia. They were held together by powerful central mechanisms, such as the Government of the former Soviet Union and the Communist party, or single-party governments, such as those in several States in Africa.

Colonization created new boundaries, often dividing ethnic groups among colonies or clustering several ethnic groups. Ancient kingdoms were grouped together with stateless rural societies and administrtive boundaries were erected that had no historical precedents.[31] In several instances, people were more loyal to ethnic and tribal groups than to central national authorities. Government efforts to generate a national consciousness were frustrated by the predominance of kinship awareness.

The authority of a distant government will not prevail in fragmented economies.[32] Ethnic linkages within the immediate surroundings of the family and the village may be more immediate and useful. Opportunities for ethnic integration are scarce. Loyalty is given to sociopolitical units smaller than the nation-State. Ancestors are more relevant than official institutions. The absence of roads, railways and common means of communication makes this isolation stronger. Means of transport and communication and a common language to link ethnic groups are essential in binding them together.

Major examples of disintegration have been the breakaway from Pakistan of Bangladesh and the breakup of the former Czechoslovakia, Soviet Union and Yugoslavia. Similar changes have occurred in large federal States, such as India and Nigeria, when constituent States multiplied in number.

The factors promoting the integration of nation-States are often economic, although there is no evidence that large national economies necessarily grow consistently faster than small ones. The fastest-growing economies in the world include China and Indonesia as well as Hong Kong, the Republic of Korea, Malaysia, Singapore and Thailand. Factor movements are easier within national boundaries than between them, although short-term capital now moves rapidly among nation-States with almost complete freedom.

One of the most powerful factors making for closer integration within a society is the perception by all communities that the standard of living is rising and the opportunities for betterment are open to all. Even when the benefits of growth are not distributed uniformly among ethnic communities, they tend to diffuse ethnic tensions when each community perceives that it is moving up the ladder of social and economic well-being, with an increasing number of individuals gaining access to higher levels of such well-being. Where development is stunted and economic space becomes too limiting to permit mobility, there is a tendency for conflict among groups to arise. Benefits from coexistence are often ignored, each group seeking improvements in economic and social well-being at a cost to others.

In contrast, in affluent multi-ethnic societies such as Switzerland and the United States, tensions among ethnic groups seem to be absorbed with much less destructive force. Even there, however, persistent economic hardship among selected ethnic groups does erupt into violence, as it did in Los Angeles in April 1992; hitherto welcome immigrant workers have become, as in France, Germany and Italy, targets of hate and violence.

The collapse of binding ties, such as strong centralizing governments and a single nationwide political party (in the former Soviet Union, for example) and of military rule (for example, in Ethiopia and Somalia) has suddenly unleashed ethnic conflicts. Authoritarian rule not only suppressed open debate on political and social issues but also kept in check divisive tendencies. The earlier repression of antagonisms left a situation without mechanisms for consultation and compromise among antagonistic ethnic groups.

Pluralistic democracies have shown a capacity to absorb ethnic conflicts and avoid breaking up into separate new States. Separatist movements in Canada, Western Europe and India have not yet led, in spite of sometimes violent demonstrations, to the emergence of breakaway nation-States. Frequent dialogue between political opponents, respect for minorities, local autonomy and decentralization of powers contribute to the diffusion of tensions and have been achieved in the large federal States of India and Nigeria.

## D. INTERNATIONALIZATION OF CONFLICTS

Ethnic and religious conflicts are not merely of local relevance.[33] Swift communication ensures such rapid and wide diffusion of information concerning violent events as may generate support among particular groups or touch off initiatives to provide humanitarian assistance. There is easy access to international markets for weapons. The Arab-Israel confrontation and apartheid in South Africa have a worldwide impact, creating tensions in distant areas and generating solidarities, flows of funds and political support. The internationalization of ethnic conflicts is a threat to world peace.

An ethnic conflict in a given country is internationalized when people who live in different, often contiguous countries and are of the same ethnic origin or religious affiliation as some party to the conflict feel a solidarity with that party based on common kinship.[34] The distribution of the Kurds in Turkey, the Islamic Republic of Iran, Iraq, the Syrian Arab Republic and the former Soviet Union; of the Basques in both Spain and France and of the Tamils in Sri Lanka, India and Malaysia are cases in point. People of Russian origin live in substantial numbers in virtually all the constituent republics of the former Soviet Union; and now that the latter have become nation-States, the treatment of the minorities therein becomes a matter of concern to all Russians and to the Russian Government. Ethnic conflicts in Burundi and Rwanda, though occurring in different nation-States, mostly involve members of the same groups. Because members of some of those groups live in the

United Republic of Tanzania, Uganda and Zaire as well as in the States of the Great Lakes region, they have been in one way or another drawn into the conflict.

People of a given ethnic origin or religious faith may derive support even in far distant places — from fellow Sikhs in Canada and the United States, fellow Palestinians in various Islamic countries, fellow Basques in Central America and fellow Armenians in the United States, for example.

The interest of groups in the fate of kindred groups in neighbouring States may involve Governments in domestic conflicts and may internationalize those conflicts. The intervention of the Governments of Greece and Turkey on behalf of the Greeks and Turks in Cyprus and of the Government of India on behalf of the Tamils in Sri Lanka, in accordance with the bilateral agreement between India and Sri Lanka, illustrates this point.

The United Nations has intervened over the years both to reduce conflict and to establish peace and provide humanitarian assistance. The contexts in which these interventions take place have changed recently. The Security Council, in resolution 743 of 21 February 1992, decided to establish a United Nations Protection Force (UNPROFOR) as an interim arrangement to create the conditions of peace and security required for the negotiation of an overall settlement of the Yugoslav crisis. UNPROFOR has also been an essential instrument in enabling humanitarian assistance to be delivered to the people affected by the conflict. The Council, in resolution 746 of 6 October 1992, requested the Secretary-General of the United Nations to establish an impartial Commission of Experts to examine and analyse various information, with a view to providing the Council with its conclusions on the evidence of grave breaches of the Geneva Convention and other violations of international law committed in the territory of the former Yugoslavia.

Regional intergovernmental organizations have intervened both to bring about peace in areas of conflict as well as to provide humanitarian assistance. The Organization of African Unity, the League of Arab States and the Organization of the Islamic Conference have tried to bring about national reconciliation and unity in Somalia. The European Union and the Conference on Security and Cooperation in Europe have both been active in seeking a political settlement to conflicts in the former Yugoslavia and in providing humanitarian assistance. In spite of these efforts, however, the conflicts and losses of life have continued.

Ethnic and religious conflicts also become questions of international concern when intergovernmental and international voluntary organizations step in to provide humanitarian assistance, as well as information on the violation of human rights. The United Nations Children's Fund (UNICEF), the Office of the United Nations High Commissioner for Refugees (UNHCR) and the World Food Programme (WFP) are prominent among those organizations that provide humanitarian assistance. Among voluntary organizations, the International Committee of the Red Cross is the most prominent. In matters regarding human rights, the Commission on Human Rights and Amnesty International have been the most active.

## E. SELF-DETERMINATION, THE NEW NATIONALISM AND SEPARATISM

Among the purposes for establishing the United Nations was the need to develop friendly relations among nations based on respect for the principle of equal rights and self-determination of peoples.[35] The large-scale process of decolonization after the Second World War was based on this principle of self-determination. One of the main principles invoked by ethnic groups within existing nation-States in the course of establishing new ones has been that of self-determination. Both as a matter of practical importance and as a means of maintaining peace, it is necessary to identify those features that entitle peoples to self-determination. Within the new nation-States formed in Eastern Europe and the former Soviet Union, numerous claims are being put forth by peoples on behalf of forming new nation-States. In some cases the process can be harmonious, as when the Czechs of Bohemia and Moravia and the Slovaks of Slovakia decided in a 1992 referendum to form two separate nation-States.

In other parts of the world, despite much strife and the existence of long-standing claims, there has been (except for the emergence of Bangladesh in 1973) no splintering of nation-States. The claims of Sikhs in India and Tamils in Sri Lanka have not ended with the establishment of new nation-States. Despite complaints about the arbitrary boundaries drawn up by colonial rulers in Africa, nation-States have not broken up into smaller ones.

Claims for succession have been put forward by Catholics in Northern Ireland, by Catalans and Basques in Western Europe, and by Quebeckers in North America.

Major problems arise when an ethnic group claiming statehood lives intermingled with others and not in a well-demarcated area. Serbs, Croats and Muslims live in ethnically mixed communities in the former Yugoslavia, where attempts to consolidate a territory under one ethnic group have resulted in mass expulsions, genocide, "ethnic cleansing" and open war. Such experiences have not been an exception in modern history. The most egregious instance was the expulsion and extermination of Jews from Nazi Germany. The partition of colonial India into two States resulted in the forceful transfer of massive populations. The breakup of the former Yugoslavia has generated a process of "ethnic cleansing" that recalls earlier atrocities. Administratively defined frontiers of the constituent republics of the former Yugoslavia did not follow ethnic lines. Croatia has a significant Serbian minority; and in Bosnia and Herzegovina, Croats, Serbs and Muslims have lived side by side over many generations. Attempts by each ethnic group to "cleanse" itself of people belonging to other groups have brought about catastrophically inhuman conditions.

Dangers of a similar nature cannot be ruled out in several instances. Special efforts need to be made to defuse tension and ensure respect for human rights. The three Baltic States of Estonia, Latvia and Lithuania contain large Slav populations. Many of the republics of the former Soviet Union are multi-ethnic States, as are several States in Eastern Europe.

The principle of self-determination has sometimes failed to be an instrument of peace. To build a new nation, nationalist movements used to aim at integrating different groups of a geographical area under one flag, thereby overcoming differences in language, tradition, ethnic grouping and religious affiliation. Now these movements can be seen in some instances to be moving in the opposite direction.[36] Several nationalist movements have become divisive and emphasize differences among communities, by stressing ethnic factors, religious affiliations and the common historical background of smaller groups. Ethnic control over government becomes the goal of such nationalistic aspirations. This new nationalism will be associated with ethnic solidarity and separatism, contrary to past experience.

## F. CONCLUSIONS

The spread and intensification of ethnic and religious conflicts in a period when ideological rifts have abated and pluralistic democratic forms of government have become more common has come as a surprise to many. It is all the more surprising at a time when many nation-States are actively trying to become integrated to achieve greater prosperity. The removal of authoritarian rulers was expected to result in claims for self-determination by communities that had been kept together by force in the past. That a new community would be sought in ethnic and religious kinship was not expected. In large federal States, such as India and Nigeria, there has been a tendency for the constituent political entities to be identified by linguistic and ethnic characteristics. The alignment of political forces along religious lines has introduced further sources of conflicts in a number of countries. Even when the vast majority of people in a nation-State follow the same major religion, new forces demanding stricter adherence to the tenets of that religion and the application of religious precepts to wider spheres, including economic and political domains of society, have created tension and conflict.

The use of force has proven unfit to resolve these conflicts. The use of force destroys much that is valuable in the economy and in society and does not create conditions for cooperation. Decentralization of authority with all groups sharing power has worked in many instances. Democratic forms of government hold out opportunities for such diffusion of power. The enlargement of economic opportunities tends to reduce conflicts as all groups perceive the benefits of life together. Physical infrastructure that ends isolation and integrates communities into larger markets and into units of greater social interaction would greatly help movement in these directions.

Many ethnic and religious conflicts have called forth action at the international level aimed at working out solutions to the problems involved. One part of the international effort is concerned with mitigating the disastrous consequences of violence and destruction. An inherently more difficult part is concerned with finding political solutions to the conflicts. Both regional and world-wide intergovernmental bodies have become engaged in this task. Voluntary international organizations have played an outstanding role in providing humanitarian assistance.

The formation of ethnically homogeneous nation-States established on the principle of self-determination carries with it the danger that other compelling factors may be overlooked in the process. Some of the most powerful forces pushing smaller political entities to unite to form large nation-States in the nineteenth century were economic. Moves towards unity in Western Europe after the Second World War have been driven by similar forces. Recent advances in technology provide facilities that can bring people physically closer together than they were at any time in the past.

## Notes

[1] See K. Lindgren and others, "Major armed conflicts in 1990", in Stockholm International Peace Research Institute (SIPRI), *World Armaments and Disarmament Yearbook*, 1991 (Oxford, Oxford University Press), p. 345.

[2] *News India* (New York), vol. 22, no. 49 (6 December 1991), p. 6. Estimate up to 19 November 1991.

[3] See document A/47/277-S/24111, entitled "An Agenda for Peace: preventive diplomacy, peacemaking and peace-keeping. Report of the Secretary-General pursuant to the statement adopted by the Summit Meeting of the Security Council on 31 January 1992", p. 3.

[4] The Tutsi, sometimes called the Hima, live in both countries and speak their own dialect, although the dialect is part of the same Bantu languages spoken by the people of the region. In Rwanda the monarchy used to be in the hands of a Tutsi dynasty, while in Burundi the power was in Hutu hands, or, more exactly, the hands of an aristocratic subgroup called Ganwas, although the Hutu king (mwami) used to marry his daughters to the most aristocratic families of the Tutsi. See F. Gaulme, "Le facteur éthnique dans les Etats africains", *Etudes* (Paris) (février 1987), pp. 149-158.

[5] Eghosa E. Osaghae, "Ethnic minorities and federalism in Nigeria", *African Affairs*, vol. 90, no. 354 (April 1991), p. 238; see also James S. Coleman, *Nigeria: Background to Nationalism* (Berkeley, University of California, 1958), p.15.

[6] Among the more recent serious religious riots were those in December 1980 in the city of Kano, in which some 1,000 people, including 50 policemen, died (see *Africa Recorder* (New Delhi), 29 January-11 February 1981; p. 5559. Another riot occurred in October 1982 in Maiduguri, resulting in 452 casualities, including 100 policemen. The riots later spread to Kaduna, leading to 44 deaths.

[7] The cause of the latest round of communal riots (1991) was a Muslim demonstration (against the visit of the German evangelist preacher, Reinhard Bonnke, touring the north of the country) that went out of control. Much property was destroyed and thousands of Christian refugees had to seek shelter in police and army barracks. See "Nigeria: Country Report, no. 4, 1991", *The Economist Intelligence Unit* (London), pp. 9-10.

[8] See Eghosa E. Osaghae, "Ethnic minorities and federalism in Nigeria", *African Affairs*, vol. 90, no. 354 (April 1991), pp. 235-258, for a discussion of the impact of the creation of States on the forces of regionalism.

[9] Members of the minorities were eventually appointed to many senior positions in the federal Government, both in the military and the civil service. These positions included Chief of Staff, Supreme Headquarters, Chief of Air Staff and Federal Commissioner for external affairs, for defence, for education, for information and for labour.

[10] See A. H. M. Kirk-Greene, *Lugard and the Amalgamation of Nigeria* (London, 1969), p. 6; also Emme O. Awa, *Federal Government in Nigeria* (University of California, 1964), p. 45.

[11] Government of India, Ministry of Law, Justice and Company Affairs, *Constitution of India* (New Dehli, 1977), articles 25-30.

[12] The decision was based on recommendations in the *Mandal Commission Report*, submitted in 1980, investigating the conditions of the socially and educationally backward classes. See *Reservation for Backward Classes: Mandal Commission Report of the Backward Classes Commission, 1980* (Dehli, Aklank Publication, 1991).

[13] Robert L. Hardgrave, Jr., "The Northeast, the Punjab and the regionalization of Indian politics", *Asian Survey*, vol. XXIII, no. 23 (November 1983), p. 1173.

[14] It is estimated that Sikhs make up about 10 per cent of the Indian army, and constitute a somewhat higher percentage of the officer corps; these are much higher proportions than that of Sikhs in the total population. See Christopher Shackle, *The Sikhs*, no. 19 (London, Minority Rights Group, 1984), p. 13.

[15] See Rodolfo Stavenhagen, *The Ethnic Question — Conflicts, Development and Human Rights* (Tokyo, United Nations University, 1990), p. 50.

[16] See Carlos Franco, "Nación, Estado y clases: condiciones del debate en los '80s", in GEOSUR, IX, no. 97/98 (mayo-junio 1988), p. 13.

[17] For a critical assessment of the racial relationships between the black and the non-black population in Brazil, see Jan Fiola, *Race Relations in Brazil: A reassessment of the "Racial Democracy", thesis*, Occasional Papers Series, no. 24 (University of Massachusetts at Amhearst, Latin American Studies Program, 1990).

[18] For an analysis of the indigenous movements in the Amazonian region, see Jean-Pierre Chaumeil, "Les nouveaux chefs, pratiques politiques et organisations indigènes en Amazonie péruvienne"; and Christian Gros, "Colombie: Nouvelle politique indigèniste et organisations indiennes", both in *Problémes d'Amérique Latine, La Documentation Française*, 1990, no. 96, in addition to the large literature on the Brazilian Amazonian populations.

[19] See Colin Clarke, ed., *Society and Politics in the Caribbean* (Oxford, Macmillan, 1991), pp. 6-7 and 47-73.

[20] The *miskitos* are an indigenous people who live in the Atlantic coast department of Zelaya in Nicaragua and in the department of Gracias a Dios in Honduras. See Institut Catala d'Antropologia, *Los Miskitos* (Madrid, Iepala Fundamentos, 1986), p. 23. *Miskito* territory was occupied by the Nicaraguans in 1894. No cultural integration was ever implemented.

[21] See Alison Rooper and Hazel Smith, "From nationalism to autonomy: the ethnic question in the Nicaraguan revolution", *Race and Class*, vol. XXVII, no. 4 (spring 1986), pp. 12-13.

[22] See Azzo Ghidinelli, "La mitad de Guatemala discriminada" and Ana Lorena Carrillo, "India y Ladinas. Los asperos caminos de las mujeres en Guatemala", both in *Nueva Sociedad*, no. 111 (enero-febrero 1991).

[23] A/C.3/47/11, annex.

[24] For an analysis of these processes, see M. N. Pokrovskii, *Russkaia istoriia s drevneishikh vremen (Russian History from the Earliest Times)*, 7th ed., 4 vols. (Moscow, 1924-25), partly available in English (up to 1739) under the title *History of Russia from the Earliest Times to the Rise of Commercial Capitalism*, J. D. Clarkson and M. R. M. Griffiths, eds. (New York, International publishers, 1931). See also Walter Kolarz, *Russia and her Colonies* (Archon Books, 1967), pp. 5-7; and Bohdan Nahaylo and Victor Swoboda, *Soviet Disunion — A History of the Nationalities Problem in the USSR* (New York, The Free Press (Macmillan), 1990).

[25] See Valevii Tishkov, "Glasnost and nationalities within the Soviet Union", *Third World Quarterly* (Ottawa, 1989), no. 11(4), p. 19.

[26] *World Economic Survey*, 1992 (United Nations publication, Sales No. E.92.II.C.1), p. 29.

[27] See Helene Carrere d'Encausse, *La gloire des nations ou la fin de l'Empire Soviétique* (Paris, Fayard, 1990); and B. Nahaylo and V. Swoboda, op. cit.

[28] See report on the situation of human rights in the territory of the former Yugoslavia, prepared by Mr. Tadeusz Mazowiecki, Special Raporteur of the Commission on Human Rights, pursuant to paragraph 15 of the Commission resolution 1992/S-1/1 and Economic and Social Council decision 1992/305 (A/47/666-S/24809), annex.

[29] For an analysis of these cases, see *Fundamentalisms Observed*, Martin E. Marty and R. S. Appleby, eds. (Chicago, University of Chicago Press, 1991).

[30] See Youssef M. Choueiri, *Islamic Fundamentalism* (Boston, Twayne Publishers, 1990).

[31] See Donald L. Horowitz, *Ethnic Groups in Conflict* (Berkeley and Los Angeles, University of California Press, 1985), pp. xii-xiii.

[32] See A. A. Mazrui, *The Africans — A Triple Heritage* (Boston-Toronto, Little, Brown and Company, 1986), p. 179.

[33] See M. Said, "Integration as a mode of ethnic conflict resolution in Africa", *International Interactions* (Garden and Breach, Science Publisher, Inc., 1981), vol. 8, no. 4, p. 357.

[34] See D. L. Horowitz, *Ethnic Groups in Conflict* (Berkeley and Los Angeles, University of California Press, 1985), p. 5.

³⁵ For an analysis of general conditions favouring this phenomenon and a specific analysis of the internationalization of ethnic conflicts in South and South-East Asia, see K. M. deSilva and R. J. May, eds., *Internationalization of Ethnic Conflict* (London, Pinter Publishers, 1991), International Centre for Ethnic Studies, Sri Lanka, in association with the Friedrich Ebert Stiftung.

³⁶ A nation has been characterized as an abstraction, an invention, an imagined community. See Benedict Anderson, *Imagined Communities: Reflections on the Origin and Spread of Nationalism* (London, Verso Editions, 1983).

# 14

# Social consequences of advances in technology

THE spectacular technological changes of recent years have given rise to a flood of speculation about their economic and social consequences. The potential of the new technologies has evoked visions of extraordinary prosperity and comfort, but at the same time those technologies have inspired vivid apprehensions about technologies-related unemployment and about a widening gulf between industrially advanced and less developed countries.

The range of responses, extending from visions of technological utopianism to deep distrust, has accompanied industrial society for at least 200 years. Looking back over the record, one must conclude that both hopes and fears have been justified. Technological growth has been the driving force behind the economic growth that has transformed living conditions throughout the world. But the social change that has accompanied this transformation has been painful for those whose way of life was wiped out by what Joseph Schumpeter called the creative destruction of economic growth. Moreover, parts of the developing world have been relatively untouched by technological change and remain so to this day. It is only reasonable to expect that recent technological change will have similar mixed impacts — hurting some people in the short run, perhaps benefiting more in the long run (albeit some more than others) and leaving yet others unaffected.

The tendency among commentators is to consider today's new technologies — especially in the fields of electronics, biotechnology and new materials — so spectacular as to be overshadowing the past completely and ushering in a new era. That tendency was also characteristic of the writings and commentaries of the past, but we now know that economic growth (for all the hyperbole and rhetoric) is a gradual process even when it is highly dynamic.

These qualifications notwithstanding, there is much in the new technologies to capture the imagination and suggest the opening of new vistas. It must be stressed, however, that so far there is no evidence of major macroeconomic effects, such as a conspicuous rise in overall productivity. Furthermore, social consequences have on the whole so far eluded measurement: the high rate of unemployment in industrialized countries cannot be ascribed to the new technologies and other consequences tend to be two-edged and difficult to grasp in terms of numbers.

The following account is therefore in the nature of a summary of information about the new technologies, including more or less speculative discussions about their possible effects.

One of the most visible consequences of such advances has been the knitting together of all parts of the world, whether in news-gathering, data flows, financial transactions or the exchange of other types of information. The new technology has effectively broken down national boundaries with regard to the flow of information. Computer-assisted design and manufacture have become an efficient means of producing commodities for discriminating consumers. They have probably reduced the comparative advantage of labour-cheap economies in producing certain of those commodities. Numerically controlled machines and computer-controlled tools have changed the skill levels of the labour force, skilling some of its members and deskilling others. Productivity has risen substantially in certain secretarial and clerical jobs, and management is receiving powerful assistance from computers and information systems.

Some of these consequences are likely to affect women adversely. Others are changing organizational structures. Still others are contributing to the decentralization of work in contrast with the factory system, whose tendency to gather workers together in large numbers enabled them to organize as a countervailing power.

The new technology is affecting homes: they are becoming workplaces into which enormous amounts of information can be fed. Through advances in that technology, new types of software are competing with human intelligence so as to increasingly undertake more of the very functions that have been considered unique to that kind of intelligence. The new technology is enabling a whole range of new experiments and forms of data analysis contributing significantly to the advancement of knowledge.

Biotechnology has wide applications in crop agriculture, animal husbandry, the discovery and production of pharmaceutical drugs, the practice of medicine, human reproduction and many other areas. The capacity to alter and otherwise affect genes has created a technology with far-reaching consequences. Only a few of them are yet visible. That much of the new knowledge is being discovered and retained (through private ownership) by private corporations enables those corporations to earn fees from every new application. In contrast, green revolution technology was mostly public property and available to farmers at little cost.

The new technology also challenges long-accepted legal norms regarding ownership, as in the case of genes that are taken from a person and altered by a technician, with copies subsequently sold on the market. Similar ethical and legal problems are emerging from the new mechanics of human reproduction. A society's capacity to identify the function of each gene and substitute others enables that society to write its own preferences with regard to animal and human biology and, eventually, personality. Such practices are starkly contrary to processes of natural evolution and also challenge deeply held humanistic views about equality among humans.

Advances in the material sciences have made feasible the application of some of the above-mentioned technology. At the same time, those advances have caused economies in the consumption of natural materials and led to the constitution of substitutes for those materials, in some instances damaging the economic fortunes of producers in developing countries.

## A. INFORMATION TECHNOLOGY

1. *Spread of the technology*

The core information technology is associated with semiconductor chips and with programs to instruct them to perform specific functions. Semiconductor chips use light or electron beams to etch tightly packed miniature electronic circuits on to silicon wafers. One unique characteristic of chips has been their continuing decrease in cost and increase in capacity. In 1975 a chip had one kilobyte (1K), or 1,000 bytes, of memory. By 1979, this figure had risen to 16K; by 1981, to 64K; and by 1983, to 256K. In 1990, 4 megabytes (4M) and 16 megabytes (16M) were available and 64 megabytes had already been announced, although their mass-scale production was a few years away.[1]

Nanoelectronics, under development for use when the limits of silicon are reached (in roughly three-chip-generations time, or 5 to 10 years), promises further and much larger capacities. It could give rise to shirt-pocket super computers, as well as memory chips able to store the entire contents of the United States Library of Congress on a 12-inch-wide silicon disk.[2]

In 1991 an IBM chip sold for $4.50, so that 1K of memory, equivalent to that of the first computer (electronic numerical integrator and calculator (ENIAC)), now costs just $0.0045. It is expected that, in future, price per memory unit will drop further.[3] The cost of the information handling and storing power that 40 years ago was available to only a few select scientists has come down to an order of magnitude that makes it affordable by virtually any developing country inhabitant.[4] Current predictions indicate that price trends of personal computers will go the way of radios and calculators, turning them into widely used, affordable consumer electronic devices.[5] If the improvements in micro-electronics technology had occurred in the aeronautics industry, an airplane in 1980 would have carried 500,000 passangers, on an air ticket costing less than one penny, at a speed of 20 million miles per hour.[6]

These characteristics of technology help it to achieve massive penetration into the economy. In 1985, in the United States, there were more computers, including those imbedded in various devices, than people. In the same year, over 400 million microprocessors, that is, computers on a chip, and 4 million discrete computers were produced worldwide.[7] In 1991 there were about 3 billion computer devices in the world and, in the year 2000, there will be about 10 billion, roughly one for each man, woman and child alive. In 1989, chip sales worldwide stood at $48.9 billion[8] and were expected to more than double, to $110 billion, by 1994. In the first half of the 1980s, the world market for software and computing services had doubled, from $28 billion to about $55 billion, and was forecast to reach $163 billion in 1991 and $340 billion in 1996.[9]

Computer devices are also being increasingly interconnected through a rapidly developing and pervasive communications network. Global communications had by 1987 become the world's fastest-growing industry.[10] The emerging Integrated Services Digital Network (ISDN), a vast network of data girdling the world, is developing an interconnected system that is growing at an exponential rate.[11] Much of this equipment operates in developed countries. The combined Latin American and African market for data transmission equipment, including satellites, constituted 5 per cent of the United States and European share in 1980, dropping to 4 per cent in 1990.[12]

The spread of communications technology is less rapid than the spread of computer-based devices for several reasons. Telecommunications were conveniently delivered by copper wire, which was costly to string along, especially in rural areas, and telecommunications facilities in developing countries were by economic necessity concentrated in urban centres. New technologies based on fibre optics are rapidly replacing copper wires in the industrialized countries. These carry heavy volumes of communications traffic and promise a major transformation within the next decade. That promise has been partially realized in several countries where a large array of services are delivered to the home, providing the customer with a wide spectrum of options.

Telephone systems in developing countries would need to

install new digital equipment to use computer technology. One ambitious program uses digital technology to connect India's 600,000 villages.[13] Both fibre optics and digital technology are expensive innovations to install, so in the short term their widespread use in developing countries will probably be restricted to urban areas.

Currently available technologies based on wireless systems provide communications at relatively reasonable cost.[14] Techniques of pooling channels to maximize available capacities in radio transmission are being developed in both developed and developing countries, including India. Cellular phone technology is being adopted in several developing countries, Malaysia among them, as a cost-effective strategy.[15] Eastern European countries, including the former Czechoslovakia, Hungary and Poland, are examining cellular systems as a quick and inexpensive solution to the problem of establishing communications facilities.[16]

## 2. Spread in developing countries

The introduction of the new technology in manufacturing is more questionable in developing countries. Even in developed countries, the adoption of some components, such as computer-integrated manufacturing, has been slower than what was envisaged in the 1970s. While there have been some spectacular gains in productivity, those gains have not always been pervasive. The new technology requires a general spread of scientific knowledge and technical know-how among workers. Since that technology advances rapidly and the equipment involved requires adaptation for specific tasks, almost continuous training is needed. The use of complex and vulnerable machinery can be sustained only with a stable, reliable, competent, responsible and motivated labour force. Since adequate returns on investments in this equipment can be made only with high-capacity use, significant down time because of power failure and breakdowns in communications and transport networks tends to reduce returns on the investment. For these and many other reasons, the adoption of the new technology in manufacturing can be expected to be quite limited except in a few developing countries (and in selected sectors in those economies).[17]

The Republic of Korea is one of the first three chip manufacturers in the world with some of its core semiconductor technologies, like that involving DRAM (dynamic random access memory) chips, only a few years behind those of Japan. Brazil, China, India and Malaysia also manufacture semiconductors. Some of this manufacturing has occurred primarily with local investment, as in Brazil, China, India and Korea. In other countries, notably Malaysia, the investment has been carried out by transnational corporations. In several countries, computers and computer-imbedded devices are being assembled from imported chips.

Cheap information technology devices could supplement the information and knowledge needs of several traditional callings in developing countries. Thus cheap hand-held user-friendly computing devices could advise farmers on the optimal mix of fertilizer, seed and water after data about prevailing conditions are keyed in. Such cheap devices, based for example on the idea of a spreadsheet, could also be used in a variety of economic activities such as retail trading, as is now being done in developed countries. Personal computers (PCs) are beginning to be used in a variety of tasks in developing countries, most commonly in administration.[18] Expert systems could also supplement the activities of professional workers in many areas, including health, industrial process control and education.[19] Computers and suitable software can also perform the functions of collecting and classifying a large body of knowledge prevalent in societies in developing countries, much of it still transmitted orally and in danger of rapid extinction as younger generations eschew the callings of their parents.[20] In fact, expert systems may be the only realistic means of capturing that knowledge in time.

Where telecommunication links exist between developed and developing countries, a new type of global worker, the so-called electronic immigrant, can be expected to emerge.[21] The precursors of that type of worker under another technology were those who keyed in data for firms in developed countries. As that work is now undergoing automation, with scanners reading the material, such a trend is being partially reversed. The new type of professional worker, telecommuting over thousands of miles, will encompass a spectrum of skills situated at much higher levels. In the United States, telemarketing has already been carried out from Jamaica, and insurance claims for American firms have been processed in Ireland.[22] Professionals in relatively cheap labour markets could be hired to perform remotely a variety of computer-based tasks, including word processing, computer programming and analytical work on certain scientific problems.

Software costs little compared with the production of semiconductor chips and computers. In 1990 an estimated 300,000 persons were engaged in computer software production, and that figure is expected to double by the mid-1990s.[23] This expansion could very well be siphoned off to developing countries.[24] An illustrative case is that of software production in India. It has grown rapidly. In 1990, software exports reached $100 million and were poised to grow further. Although the largest producer was a private sector company with 60 per cent of the share, the medium-sized companies were growing at an annual rate of 72 per cent, and small companies were growing even faster.[25]

### 3. *Effects on organizations*

Information technology, being pervasive and generic, has changed social relations in the workplace. Some workers using the new technology have come under more rigid control. For example, truck-drivers who enjoyed the freedom of the road have come to be effectively controlled. Computers have been used to monitor use of time and intensity of application to work, for example, by counting the number of strokes a worker produced on a keyboard.[26]

The application of information technology has resulted in a continuation of the process of deskilling associated with mechanization since the industrial revolution and, in the opposite direction, has necessitated the adoption of new skills. Thus, print industry workers in developed countries today typically work at a video monitor. Hitherto skilled work, such as typesetting, proofreading and layout, has been replaced by jobs involving lower-level skills. The contrary process of upgrading skills is affecting secretaries, who are now interrogating databases, producing reports, advising customers and otherwise enlarging their spheres of autonomy.

A group especially vulnerable to the process has been women, who account for the vast bulk of clerical staff in developed countries. In the United States, employment in the insurance and banking industries was expected to fall by 40 per cent and 20 per cent respectively between 1980 and 2000.[27] The majority of those affected would be women. In several areas where women have worked traditionally, they are expected to be replaced by new developments connected, *inter alia*, with voice recognition, optical character recognition and artifical intelligence.[28]

The flexibility provided by the new technology has allowed certain jobs in developed countries, especially those of women, to be transferred to the home, that is, telecommuted. In the new home-computing environment, workers, who are mostly women, are paid by the piece, not by the hour. They earn less than half their office counterparts and also do not have the benefits that are common to office jobs, entailing a loss of the traditional workers' rights that had been won after decades of struggle.[29]

The widespread adoption of computers in offices has tended to change the structure of organizations. By gaining access to information through a computer, workers can sometimes make decisions that were previously made by managers. A significant number of jobs have been redesigned, and this has led to the performance of several functions by the same person following a parallel acquisition of multiple skills, with many middle-level managers losing their functions and the organizational pyramids flattening further towards a broader base of skilled clerical workers.

As more services become tradeable across political frontiers using new communication techniques and networks, new elements vital to developing countries will emerge, encompassing questions of cultural identity and vulnerability.[30]

Video cassettes are a powerful means of introducing foreign cultures into countries. The capacity to receive television broadcasts across continents with the help of satellites keeps at least some populations of developing countries in touch with the major broadcasting centres of the world. Although the concept of a television-connected global village was premature in the 1960s, it is becoming a reality now.

The emergence during the last decade of enterprises whose principle business was worldwide television broadcasting testified to the opportunities opened up by the new technology. Pictures from television broadcasts convey the horrors of war, disasters and famine. So it is now conceivable to speak of the formation of world public opinion in such a way as could not be achieved by previous media. These broadcasts also bring, at least to some parts of the populations of developing countries, pictures of well-being in, and lifestyles of, developed countries. All of this may stimulate a demand for new material goods.

## 4. *Employment*

To what extent the new technology displaces jobs and creates them is still uncertain. It is evident that some skills are displaced and new ones created. There is some evidence that information technology reduces labour input per unit of output. For example, in the United States banking industry, several companies required that one human worker be displaced every time an automated teller was put into use.[31] In the United Kingdom of Great Britain and Northern Ireland, the use of word processors reduced office staff in several companies by up to 50 per cent and in blue-collar work two jobs were lost for each robot used. In the 1990s, robots were expected to displace 100,000 workers in the United States.[32] On the other hand, many jobs have been created with the new technology.

The new technology is being applied across a whole spectrum of economic activities, ranging from professional to white-collar work and from the work of skilled craftsmen to that of unskilled manual labourers. Over the last few years the areas encroached upon by computer devices have tended to spread to encompass skills of increasingly higher levels. It is useful to list those areas to indicate the breadth of the spread.

Some of the first applications of the new technology were in the military. Because the speed at which modern battle occurs makes it impossible for human commanders to keep track unaided of all that is happening and to respond appropriately, battle management expert systems have been used as adjuncts in decision-making. At a lower level, information technology has displaced junior commanders performing virtual staff functions in a military organization. In addition, a whole range of skilled activities of soldiers, sailors and airmen have been informatized with a vast range of chip-based weaponry ranging from automatic guns to automatic sensors, automatic pilots, guided missiles and automatic responses to attacking missiles.

The new technology has changed office work from the highest to the lowest level. A broad range of management skills has been replaced by expert systems. Applications of information technology-based artificial management (AM) include scheduling and forecasting, personnel management and procurement.[33] Computers have also been used in long-range business and economic forecasting. Recent artificial intelligence (AI) systems, including neural systems and genetic algorithms, have outperformed human systems in tracking market performance.[34]

In manufacturing, the whole chain of skills is being fully or partly replaced with computers and related equipment. Thus, CAD (computer-assisted design) and CAM (computer-assisted manufacture) have transferred some of the work of engineers to computer programs. In CAD, computer graphics at a terminal are used to design, draft and analyse a product to be manufactured. Among the many successful applications of CAD have been printed circuit boards, aircraft and automobiles, with dramatic gains in the productivity of engineers and architects.[35]

Robotic devices have fully or partly replaced unskilled workers, cutting costs and often producing, at much less risk to worker's health and safety, better-quality work than earlier. It is forecast that in the 1990s as many as 40 to 50 per cent of all workers in the United States will be using daily some sort of electronic terminal.[36]

## 5. *Social interactions*

Information technology is a generic technology. Its effects will be far-reaching, intruding into almost every economic and social niche. Of all the major technologies to emerge since the industrial revolution, information technology, with the possible exception of biotechnology, will have the most far-reaching effects. Because of its rapid price drop, further microminiaturization and other unique characteristics, the penetration of information technology will be extremely rapid. As it penetrates different sectors and niches, it is rearranging the several human and material elements that it encounters. As it moves across the social landscape, it is cutting a broad swath across the landscape and reshaping it. In turn, the social landscape is itself moving into the technology, moulding it in particular ways. A dynamic interaction between the two is resulting.

The new technology questions some of the most cherished self-perceptions of humans. Questions are being raised relating to human problem-solving and mental processes, and to what it means to be uniquely human. Some of these questions extend to the core religious and philosophical assumptions of human society. Thus, while in many senses a technology of social liberation, the new technology is ultimately not a comfort-producing one: disturbing elements are at its core. However, the logic of intertwined social and technological systems is driving it forward almost inexorably. An important task then would be to influence this most plastic of technologies so that it can reflect the best social aspirations and knowledge systems of the world's different cultures.

## B. BIOTECHNOLOGY

### 1. *Uses of new biotechnologies*

The new biotechnology, by interfering with the activity of

organisms at a deep biological level, uses those organisms to bring forth new products. It differs from traditional biotechnology in that it achieves its objectives by modifying or using the genetic material of organisms in a direct manner, at the level of the cell or gene.

Characterizing biotechnology at the cellular level are the techniques of tissue culture, and, at the level of the gene, those of genetic engineering. Tissue culture is a relatively cheap technique that allows cells from one plant to propagate thousands of plants having an identical genetic structure.[37] Also, under the new technology, two or more cells can be fused to become a single cell with characteristics different from the original cells, so as to produce hybirds from organisms that are widely different genetically.[38]

Genetic engineering — also called recombinant deoxyribonucleic acid (DNA) technology — allows for combinations of genes that have been artifically put together and were unknown previously. For example, the process of recombination allows a piece of genetic material, or DNA, from one species to be inserted into the DNA of a second species.[39] The application of the new biotechnology to the plant kingdom can result in plants that are resistant to selected diseases, insects and herbicides and have the capacity to grow in selected harsh climates.

Microbial organisms that are genetically engineered will be able to control plant pests and influence the nutrient uptake of plants.[40] By transgenic techniques, plants can be given genes from bacteria that code for insect-killing proteins, thus ensuring plant protection.[41] Similarly, plants have been developed that are "vaccinated" against commonly occurring viruses.[42, 43] By transferring those genes that confer a nitrogen-fixation ability, a kind of self-fertilization of plants is possible, with enormous consequences for agriculture now using artifical fertilizers.

In the immediate future, one can also expect to benefit from bacteria and fungi designed to live intimately with plants so as to prevent attacks by pathogens. One can also expect engineered plants that could create their own antibiotic antibodies against pests and diseases. Plants are also being engineered to tolerate specific herbicides so that the herbicides could kill weeds and have no effect on the plants themselves.[44]

Genetic engineering techniques have also been used to improve the nutrient content of foods, for example, their protein composition.[45] The new technology can change the maturation and ripening cycles of particular plants, permitting longer storage without special facilities.[46] Through genetic modification, plants have been changed to produce useful products, such as economically important peptides[47] and proteins.[48] Through a similar approach, plants are expected to become factories for the production of important pharmaceuticals, such as anticlotting agents and growth hormones,[49] human serum albumin (HSA)[50] and antibodies.[51]

Key genetic technological changes that increase productivity of farm animals include those involving bovinesomatotropin (BST), a pituitary hormone in cattle that increases milk production.[52] Some of the most far-reaching effects of animal biotechnology are occurring through developments in animal reproductive technology, including the ability to create (by mixing the genetic endowments even from entirely different species) animals with genetic changes that will help them resist diseases better, yield better-quality products, grow faster and reproduce themselves with greater efficiency.[53] Animals have also been genetically altered to yield cheap and useful pharmaceutical products, such as human growth hormones in their milk.[54] Substances such as insulin, tissue plasminogen activator (a blood-clot-removing agent) and factor IX (a substance that is missing in some haemophiliacs) have been produced through this process.[55]

The new biotechnology has widespread applications in the health sector. New vaccines can be developed, using recombinant DNA techniques. A one-shot vaccine is a distinct possibility. In this vaccine, genetic elements drawn from a variety of viruses are strung together, against a spectrum of diseases.[56] Highly specific, inexpensive diagnostic techniques that are affordable even in poor countries are being developed.[57]

The new technology offers the possibility of avoiding genetic diseases and of developing medicines that are narrowly targeted and without side-effects. Examples of the latter would include mono-clonal antibodies that can target specific antigens and have already been used successfully in therapies for a wide variety of disorders, such as paediatric tumours,[58] in neutralization of the tetanus toxin,[59] in reduction of mortality in patients suffering from potentially fatal septic shock[60] and (acting as molecular "scalpels") in removal of the opaque cells after cataract surgery.[61] This large list illustrates the range of possibilities that exist with monoclonal antibody therapy.

Sharply focused targeting of medicines through genetic means, for example, in treating cancers, is also being developed. Tumor-infiltrating lymphocytes that home in on tumour cells[62] and antibod-ies that take poisonous chemicals directly to cancer sites, leaving healthy cells intact,[63] reflect such development. Growth factors, a set of targeted remedies that help heal wounds quickly, smooth wrin-kles, destroy cancer cells, restore function to paralysed limbs and generally enhance the immune system, are likely to be derived from products of bioengineering patterned after natural growth factors.[64]

Gene probes identify specific genes, and their major applica-tions are in infectious disease diagnosis, forensic testing, paternity testing and identification of genetically transmitted diseases. In future they could be used in determining the risk of developing dis-eases of genetic origin and in diagnostic testing for cancers.

The list of medical disorders that have been identified as being of genetic origin has been growing steadily. The detailed map of human genes being made by the Human Genome Initiative would allow for the systematic and exact identification of most disease-causing genes. With the availability of techniques that could repair those genes, the possibilities for medical intervention would be enhanced dramatically.[65] The first instance of human gene therapy was approved in 1990.[66] At the end of 1991, trials of cures for three additional genetic diseases were approved in the United States.[67]

The mapping of the human genome now under way, may, when once applied and turned into a biotechnology, have a more far-reaching effect on humans than all other biotechnology products. The Human Genome Initiative aims at identifying approximately 3 billion base pairs and 100,000 genes in the 46 chromosomes that constitute human genetic material. It is a search for the ultimate answers to the chemical underpinning of human existence.[68] Several attempts are also being made to map plant genomes, permitting the identification of individual plant genes that could then be transferred from organism to organism to replicate desired characteristics.

The new biotechnology may thus dramatically alter the most fundamental biological endowments of plants, animals and humans.

## 2. Spread of applications

Because biotechnology operates through living organisms or their products, its activities are limited to materials that can be biologically manipulated. The economic applications of biotechnology pervade agriculture, forestry, mining, chemicals, drugs and food, and health care.[69]

The new biotechnology yields an array of products that require less material, energy and labour input than those of earlier technology.[70] In this sense, it substitutes indirectly for labour. There are possibilities for using biological material such as proteins and other large molecules, rather than silicon, for electronic circuits.[71] In this event, the new biotechnology will directly substitute for labour.

The biotechnology industry emerged into the commercial field not much earlier than 1980. The forecasts at that time, with their promise of quick profits, were for rapid growth reflected in initial investor euphoria in market economies.[72] Biotechnology was also the fastest-growing scientific discipline worldwide in the 1980s, judging by the number of scientific papers published.[73] Since then, however, only a handful of distinct products have come to market. Substantial underestimates were made of the time needed to get a product to market. One reason for the delay was that time was needed to procure products' approval for use, taking into account their effects on planetary life, including human life.

In the 1990s this picture is likely to change. As many drugs were expected to enter production in 1991 as in the entire previous decade.[74] Accordingly, in 1990-1991 biotechnology stocks did not suffer the fate of many others at the New York Stock Exchange. On the contrary: in 1991 in the United States, the leading country in the field, 35 biotechnology companies made public offerings, bringing in $1 billion from investors.[75] Although still burdened with high research and development costs, many biotechnology firms entered 1990 with sizeable growth in sales and revenue.[76] About 75 per cent of biotechnology firms in the United States now have products for sale. Total sales in 1991 exceeded $2 billion.

A range of new biotechnology products was expected in the 1990s in manufacturing, environmental protection and agriculture. Within the first decade of the twenty-first century, the impact of biotechnology in the economic and social field is expected to become comparable with that of information technology.[77]

## 3. *Impact on developing countries*

The new biotechnology, because of its heavy research and development components and market potential, is at the moment concentrated in developed countries. The advances expected in those countries can have repercussions for some crops in developing countries. However, since research is concentrated mostly on developed country crops, the impact on productivity in agriculture in developing countries is yet small.

Perhaps not more that 10 developing countries have the capacity to undertake research on genetic engineering. Those countries with a nucleus of competent researchers in plant biotechnology would be able to exploit tissue culture methods on a much larger scale.[78] However, it is possible to use the products of genetic engineering — seeds, say, that have been genetically engineered elsewhere — in many developing countries.

The development of new seeds through genetic engineering is taking place largely in multinational corporations in developed countries. National research centres and international centres of the kind that spearheaded green revolution technologies are noticeably absent in genetic engineering.[79] Those that develop new biotechnologies establish private rights to them, with the right to exclude others from using them except through payment of fees.[80]

The new biotechnology presents the agricultural planners with a new option. Despite spectacular gains in yields from improved seeds, the principal approach so far has been to provide heavy infrastructure. The new biotechnology working at the level of genes permits the development of seed that meets the demands of the immediate environment. Seed development to suit a given environment is thus an alternative that must be assessed against the development of heavy agricultural infrastructure.

Until 1990 no transgenic crops competed with developing countries' products on the market. However, experimental results suggested that genetically engineered rape-seed, tobacco and rubber would be available in five years. Several other clonally propagated crops were expected to be commercially available within the next five years. Clonal propagation was under development for another 35 vegetables, trees, shrubs and flowering plants.[81]

With the seed market becoming saturated in industrialized countries, the new markets for the companies concerned are in developing countries. A few large companies today dominate the production and commercialization of seeds of selected crops.[82] As they compete in developing countries and introduce a few biotechnologically produced seeds, a shrinkage in genetic diversity is taking place as old seeds are replaced. Many petrochemical and pharmaceutical companies have either completely taken over seed-producing companies or become major shareholders. One result of this is the development of particular seeds that will not be sensitive to the particular herbicide that a given firm manufactures, allowing for the herbicide's exclusive application and hence ensuring the sale of both seed and herbicide by the same company.

4. *Property rights*

In a ruling that was protested by animal welfare environment activists, farmers and religious groups, the United States Patent and Trademark Office ruled in 1987 that all genetically engineered multicellular organisms, including animals but excepting humans, could be trade-protected.[83] Generally, the area of patents for biological material has become one of great contentiousness. Recently, biotechnological firms have sought patents to genetic material existing naturally but whose process of extraction was discovered by them.[84] Genentech successfully claimed exclusive ownership to "natural" TPC (tissue plasminogen activator), a blood-clot-dissolving enzyme that occurs naturally, but the patents for whose extraction remained with the company.[85]

The largest set of problems connected with ownership of naturally occurring biological material would come with attempts to patent human genetic material. This could result ultimately in patenting by researchers working on the Human Genome Project of sections of genetic material as they are decoded. Such patents have been obtained in the United States, even without a knowledge of what the patented sequences actually code for.[86] No international consensus has emerged on this issue. It will have a profound effect on the entire human species. Opinion has been generally more circumspect in Europe than in the United States. In late 1991 the National Ethics Committee in France issued guidelines opposing the patenting of the human genome, declaring it the common heritage of humanity.[87] It also called for open access to genome data banks.

With work on the Human Genome Project accelerating in the coming years, concerns regarding ownership of and access to the new genetic material become a vital global issue. Such concerns relate to determining what constitutes the common biological heritage of humanity (most of whose members live outside the regions where the genome is being researched) and to provide incentives for the institutions engaged in this vital research. This is an area where the widest possible debate has to be entered into on the most urgent basis.

The concerns are even more far-reaching. The tropical countries have the greatest biological diversity and hence the largest store of naturally occurring genetic material. Special concern has been felt about attempts to extend the scope of international property rights to include those of plant breeders. Some developing countries have objected to the proposal on trade-related aspects of intellectual property rights (TRIPS) in the General Agreement on Tariffs and Trade (GATT). It was seen as neglecting the need to control abusive practices and as impeding the free flow of scientific and technological information.[88]

The effects of the involvement of multinational corporations in the new technologies are also being felt in the field of indigenous knowledge. Developing new biotechnology material requires access to a variety of useful genes. Of the 265,000 species of plants on earth, only 1,100 have been thoroughly studied, and 40,000 probably have medicinal and nutritional uses for humans.[89] Plant breeders using the new biotechnology will need access to this pool of genetic diversity. Although these plants remain unknown in developed countries, indigenous farmers, pastoralists and traditional healers have identified their uses over the centuries. This knowledge is now being gathered by multinational corporations. The particular gene responsible for a desired property could later be isolated and incorporated in a new genetically engineered plant. Moreover, the patented plant or seed could then be fed back as a commercial product (replacing the existing flora of a particular developing country), possibly into the same groups that had identified the desired trait in the first place.[90]

The knowledge that is patented comes from two sources: the farmer who originally identified the plant's useful properties and the scientist who isolated and incorporated the gene. Under present arrangements, it is only the scientist who is rewarded. This problem is now a subject of deep debate in several United Nations organizations, including the World Intellectual Property Organization (WIPO). It has profound implications for farmers' incomes and the relative global distribution of income.[91]

Some talented and skilled scientists in developing countries are languishing without access to the most basic equipment and literature. They are close to biotechnology's largest source of raw material, namely, tropical forests, and have easier access to local knowledge than others. Biotechnology could bring about a synergistic combination of developing country raw material, trained developing country scientists and developed country capital and knowledge. Such a synergistic combination would also have the unintended consequence of increasing the access to resources of developing country scientists and curbing the brain drain.

## 5. *Environment*

The new technology could reduce polluting chemicals by reducing the use of pesticides; however, genetic engineering of plants also carries certain ecological risks. Traits from new plant varieties conferring pest resistance, if introduced into other plants through either escape of the engineered crop or crossing the new plants with wild plants could have a serious impact on cultivated crops. Herbicide-resistant genes could also be exchanged between domesticated plants and wild weeds, resulting in the need for larger doses of chemicals to control the newly resistant weeds.[92] New types of weeds could then emerge and become a threat to agricultural systems. To destroy a weed that had incorporated a gene for herbicide resistance would now require more dangerous chemicals. Similarly, insect-resistant traits might then lead to the rapid evolution of pest species. The existence of weeds with a new trait that made them withstand their usual enemies would tend to reduce genetic diversity.

The new technology, through the genetic engineering of new organisms, could also pose a threat to the environment. The threat of this possibility has resulted in strict control over experimentation and release of new organisms in most developed countries. Such strict enforcement in developed countries may encourage companies to seek safe havens in those developing countries that lack awareness of the problems involved and have minimal (or no) control protocols. This would be a repetition of earlier practices of using developing countries as test beds for experimental medicines, as well as for dumping toxic wastes. Testing medicines in the developing world also seems to be occurring in the genetics field, as exemplified in the testing of genetically altered vaccines.[93]

In developing countries, there is generally a lack of both public awareness concerning the issues involved and trained scientific personnel. Regulatory mechanisms are vital in developing countries but these have to take into account the twin objectives of encouraging industry and protecting the public interest. Local awareness-raising exercises, combined with international cooperation, appear essential.

## 6. *Biotechnology and ethics*

Through the use of amniocentesis and chorionic villus sampling, the future diseases, health, parentage and sex of the foetus may be assessed. Because this knowledge can be used to terminate a pregnancy, these diagnostic procedures are assuming the evaluative function of determining those humans that are more valuable than others, and those that would be a potential burden to their community. When further diagnostic procedures — such as those at the level of the gene — become widespread, the list of human traits that could be rectified will constitute a reality.

With the new technology a total gene screen of embryos has become a distinct possibility.[94] The use of amniocentesis to test for the sex of the foetus (with subsequent abortion if the sex is female) — a precursor of mass genetic screening — has been adopted in some developing countries.[95] This could lead to attempts to "perfect" offspring, which would then contain socially desirable characteristics and have undesirable characteristics excised.[96] The genome, altered by excision of undesirable genes and incision of desirable ones, then becomes in fact a map of society's wishes. A particular society's definition of the correct, the beautiful and the desirable can, through reproductive technology, be mapped in the embryo. This type of intervention calls seriously into question the notion that we are born equal and are not created by society.[97]

Feminism, as an important social movement, has over the last few decades developed a formal body of literature with a distinct orientation to social problems. However, advances in embryology, tissue transplants and intervention at the point of the creation of human life are now calling into question several of feminism's social assumptions. Some of these key questions have arisen as a result of radical intrusions into reproductive processes through such techniques as sex preselection, surrogate motherhood, flushing of embryos, *in vitro* fertilization, surrogate embryo transfer and cloning, and (in the future) genetic manipulations.

Some of these advances are a continuation of a process of liberating women from biological determinism. The new technology increases the capacity of women to break their links with both the animal origins of, and the patriarchal control over, reproduction. Yet these pro-interventionist arguments are now under attack owing to the elaboration of horror-inducing scenarios concerning control over the reproductive function.

The new techniques of reproduction raise generally a question of how socially a parent is to be defined. Who are the parents of a child brought forth by *in vitro* fertilization (from an egg that, donated by Mrs. A, is then combined with a sperm from Mr. B and implanted in the uterus of Mrs. C) and given up for adoption (to Mr. D and Mrs. E)? These complicated social and ethical issues can be expected to intensify and their incidence to increase in the near future, when it will be possible for genetic characteristics themselves to be incised into or excised out of chromosomes.

The social and medical implications of the new technologies have been discussed largely in the developed countries; this discussion has therefore occurred within the context of certain social, cultural and ethical assumptions that may not necessarily be universal. Clearly, wider discussion, especially in developing countries, is called for.


## C.  CONCLUSIONS

The wave of advances in technology now sweeping developed countries are of a generic character — as those in steam technology were — and they are having similarily pervasive economic and social consequences. The advances differ in three principal respects, however, from those in earlier technologies. First, they are extremely close to advances in scientific knowledge in a way that the changes behind the industrial revolution were not. Consequently, there is close collaboration between universities and research laboratories, and the new inventions. Secondly, the production, running and maintenance of the new equipment require labour with far more scientific knowledge than earlier. The new technology is therefore unlikely to be available at reasonable cost in societies where the recent disciplines of molecular biology, microbiology, biochemistry and modern physics are not being firmly pursued. Thirdly, the new technology changes fast. Equipment and the programmes to run them become obsolete in two to five years, and rapid obsolescence calls for new investment. These factors handicap developing countries in adopting the new technology. Among those countries, the ones with high investment ratios and a strong science and technical education framework stand to gain while others lag behind.

Research and development expenditure in advancing new technology is quite high. Where Governments do not finance research and development, none but the largest corporations can afford the outlay on developing the core technology. Even the largest corporations have tended to pool resources in order to deal with the most advanced work. The average small- or medium-sized enterprise in developing countries cannot participate in this core development of technology. In fact, there may be a legitimate role for Governments in financing some of this activity. However, small-scale enterprises in developing countries could do exceedingly well in writing software and applying certain techniques in biotechnology.

Private sector enterprises are prominent in developing, with the new biotechnology, both new seeds responsive to specific chemicals and pharmaceutical drugs. The rights of those enterprises to intellectual property do provide incentives to innovation. Keepers of traditional knowledge also have valid claims to the payment in connection with such innovation. It is still a matter of debate where the interests of the public lie.

Information technology has knit the world closer together. News of events travels instantaneously, creating a bond between diverse people in a manner inconceivable a generation ago. Currency transfers take place on a massive scale. Prices in the principal share and commodity markets are closely linked. All these developments have eroded national boundaries separating economies and cultures. They have also reduced the authority of Governments, increased the power of multinational enterprises and strengthened solidarity among non-governmental organizations.

The new technology raises difficult moral and ethical questions regarding fundamental relationships, for example, between parents and children, because it raises unprecendented questions about reproduction and raising children. It also makes it potentially feasible to write society's current preferences into the genetic makeup of a population in a manner hitherto undreamed of.

The technologies discussed above are poised to have major impacts on economic, social and ethical issues. Before such pervasive effects are realized, it is necessary that those techniques be, as widely as possible, the subject of intensive discussion.

## Notes

[1] *Japan Economic Journal* (23 June 1990); and Eric Hannah and Jeffrey Soreff, "Single chip computers", *Interdisciplinary Science Review*, 8, no. 1 (1983).

[2] Phillip Yam, "Atomic turn-on", *Scientific American* (November 1991), p. 20; and Otis Port, "Creating chips an atom at a time", *Business Week* (29 July 1991), pp. 54-55.

[3] *The Economist* (23 February 1991), p. 68.

[4] Arthur Anderson, "Trends in information processing technology", *ATAS Bulletin*, no. 3 (1986), p. 17, Centre for Science and Technology for Development, United Nations, New York.

[5] "PC's — what the future holds", *Business Week* (12 August 1991), pp. 58-64.

[6] G. Osborne, *Running Wild. The Next Industrial Revolution* (New York, McGraw-Hill, 1979).

[7] Kari Kairamo, "Longer-term impacts of information and communication technologies", in *Interdependence and Cooperation in Tomorrow's World* (Organisation for Economic Cooperation and Development, 1987).

[8] *Electronic Weekly* (23 May 1990).

[9] Susume Watanbe, *International Division of Labour in the Software Industry: Employment and Income Potentials for the Third World* (International Labour Organisation, 1989), p. 4.

[10] *Business World* (1987), p. 8.

[11] Ian Miles, R. Muskens and W. Grupelaan, *Global Telecommunications Networks/Strategic Considerations* (Doordech, Kluwer Academic Publications, 1988); and Koji Kobayashi, "Integration of computers and communications, C + C: the influence of space technology", *Interdisciplinary Science Reviews*, vol. 8, no. 1 (1983).

[12] Juan F. Rada, *Information Technology and Services* (International Labour Organisation, 1986), p. 58.

[13] John Williamson, "The rural telecom dilemma", *Telephony* (24 July 1989).

[14] August Blegen, "Data communication: a user's perspective", *Telecommunications* (January 1991).

[15] Williamson, op. cit., p. 28.

[16] Deborah Pfeffer and Czatdana Inan, "The times they are a-changing", *Telephony* (7 January 1991).

[17] See Karl. H. Ebel, "Computer-integrated manufacturing: a new menace for developing countries", *International Labour Review*, vol. 130, nos. 5-6 (1991), pp. 635-644.

[18] "New information technologies and development", *ATAS Bulletin*, No. 3 (June 1986), pp. 66-73, Centre for Science and Technology for Development, United Nations, New York.

[19] United Nations Industrial Development Organization, *The Impact of Expert Systems* (1986), p. 11.

[20] Chris Bird, "Medicines from the rainforest", *New Scientist* (17 August 1991), pp. 34-39.

[21] Joseph N. Pelton, "Telepower: the emerging global brain", *The Futurist* (September-October 1989), p. 12.

[22] John Burgess, "White collar jobs go offshore", *New York Herald Tribune* (7 October 1991).

[23] "Computer software: programming the future", *The Economist* (30 January 1988).

[24] United Nations Centre on Transnational Corporations, *Transnational Corporations and the Transfer of New and Emerging Technologies to Developing Countries* (New York, 1990), p. 51.

[25] *India Abroad* (17 July 1991).

[26] Michael Wessels, *Computer, Self and Society* (Englewood Cliffs, New Jersey, Prentice Hall, 1990), p. 43.

[27] Roessner and others, *The Impact of Office Automation on Clerical Employment, 1985-2000: Forecasting Techniques and Plausible Futures in Banking and Insurance* (London, Quorum Books, 1985).

[28] Amin Rajan, *Information Technology in the Finance Sector: An International Perspective* (World Employment Programme, International Labour Organisation, 1990).

[29] Ruth Perry and Lisa Greber, "Women and computers: an introduction", *Signs: Journal of Women in Culture and Society*, vol. 16, no. 1 (1990).

[30] United Nations Centre on Transnational Corporations, *Transborder Data Flows: Access to the International On-line Data Base Market* (New York, 1983).

[31] Barbara Garson, *The Electronic Sweatshop: How Computers are Transforming the Office of the Future into the Factory of the Past* (New York, Simon and Schuster, 1988).

[32] H. A. Hunt and T. L. Hunt, *Human Resource Implications of Robotics* (Kalamazoo, Michigan, W. E. Upjohn, 1983).

[33] Eliezer Geister, "Artifical management and the artifical manager", *Business Horizons*, vol. 29, no. 4 (July/August 1986); and Peter Di Giammarino and Matthew Kuckuk, "The movement of advanced decision support and strategic systems", *Bankers Magazine*, vol. 174 (May/June 1991).

[34] T. Francis, "Expert system tools are Wall Street's newest creation", *Wall Street Computer Review* (June 1989); and B. Arthur, J. Holland and R. Palmer, "Using genetic algorithms to model the stock market", in *Proceedings of the Optimisation in Financial Services Conference* (London, IBC Technical Services Ltd., 1991).

[35] Wessels, op. cit., p. 32.
[36] E. Giulano, "The mechanization of office work", *Scientific American* (September 1982).
[37] United Nations Development Programme, *Plant Biotechnology including Tissue Culture and Cell Culture* (New York, 1989), p. 15.
[38] John Farrington, ed., *Agricultural Biotechnology: Prospects for the Third World* (London, Overseas Development Institute, 1989), p. 11.
[39] Mark. D. Dibner, "Factories of our future", *Consumers' Research* (April 1989).
[40] *Bio Technology: Economic and Wider Impacts* (Organisation for Economic Cooperation and Development, 1989), p. 25.
[41] *Agricultural Research* (March 1990), p. 2; James Cook, "Biological pest control", *Agricultural Research* (March 1989); and Ingrid Wickelgren, "Please pass the genes", *Science News*, vol. 136, no. 8 (19 August 1989), pp. 120-124.
[42] United Nations Development Programme, *Plant Biotechnology . . .*, p. 24.
[43] Anderson Walter Truett, "Food without farms", *The Futurist* (January-February 1990).
[44] Wickelgren, op. cit.
[45] Henry J. Miller and Stephen J. Ackerman, "Perspectives on food biotechnology, *FDA Consumer* (March 1990).
[46] *Manufacturing Chemist* (April 1989).
[47] *Science News* (15 April 1989).
[48] *Chemistry and Industry* (6 March 1989).
[49] *European Chemical News* (6 November 1989).
[50] Ibid.
[51] Miller and Ackerman, op. cit.
[52] George E. Seidel, "Biotech on the farm: geneticists in the pasture", *Current* (October 1989).
[53] *New Scientist* (14 April 1990).
[54] Ibid.
[55] Barry R. Bloom. "Vaccines for the Third World", *Nature*, vol. 342 (November 1989).
[56] *Bio Technology . . .*, p. 68.
[57] *Medical World* (10 April 1989).
[58] *New Technology Japan* (January 1990).
[59] *European Chemical News* (30 April 1990).
[60] *McGraw-Hill's Biotechnology News Watch* (16 April 1990).
[61] *New Scientist* (20 January 1990).
[62] *New Scientist* (1 April 1989).
[63] Manny Ratafia, "Growth factors: poised to revolutionize health care", *Medical Marketing and Media*, vol. 23, no. 1 (January 1988); Manny Ratafia, "How biotechnology will change human therapeutics", *Medical Marketing and Media*, vol. 23, no. 12 (October 1988); and *European Chemical News* (28 May 1990).
[64] *New Scientist* (8 September 1990); and *Nature*, vol. 345 (7 June 1990).
[65] Rick Weiss, "First human gene-therapy test begun", *Science News*, vol. 138, no. 12 (22 September 1990).
[66] *US News and World Report* (4 November 1991), p. 70.
[67] James D. Watson, "The human genome project: past, present and future", *Science*, vol. 248, (April 1990).
[68] *The New York Times* (6 February 1990).
[69] *Bio Technology . . .*, p. 53.
[70] Neil Gross, "Biochips: life mimics electronics", *Business Week* (15 June 1990), p. 94; and Michael Conrad, "The lure of molecular computing", *IEEE Spectrum*, vol. 23, no. 10 (October 1986), pp. 55-60.
[71] Michael Gianturco, "Bullish on biotech", *Forbes*, vol. 146, no. 6 (17 September 1990).

[72] Andy Coghlan, "Boom time for biotechnology", *New Scientist* (11 January 1992), p. 11.

[73] Andrew Evan Serwer, "Biotech stocks are poised to take off", *Fortune*, vol. 121, no. 6 (12 March 1990).

[74] Ann Thayer, "Industry leaders bullish on biotech outlook", *Chemical and Engineering News*, vol. 68, no. 19 (7 May 1990).

[75] *Scientific American* (January 1992), pp. 134-136.

[76] *Chemical Marketing Reporter* (25 September 1989).

[77] *Monoclonal Antibodies Markets: An International Market Analysis* (Theta Corporation, 1990).

[78] Ibid.

[79] Albert Sasson, *Biotechnologies and Development* (Paris, United Nations Educational, Scientific and Cultural Organization, 1988), p. 262.

[80] *Trade and Development Aspects* . . .

[81] *Trade and Development Aspects* . . .

[82] Sasson, op. cit., p. 261.

[83] *Patenting Life* (Washington, D.C., Office of Technology Assessment, 1989).

[84] R. Weiss, "Animal patent debate heats up", *Science News*, vol. 132, no. 5 (August 1987).

[85] Gary Slutsker, "Patenting Mother Nature", *Forbes*, vol. 147, no. 1 (7 January 1991).

[86] Gina Kolata, "Biologist's speedy gene method scares peers but gains backer", *The New York Times* (28 July 1992).

[87] *The Economist* (28 July 1990), pp. 7-58.

[88] Debora MacKenzie, "Europe debates the ownership of life", *New Scientist* (4 January 1992), pp. 9-10.

[89] *African Diversity*, nos. 2 and 3 (June 1990).

[90] Joyce Christopher, "Prospectors for tropical medicines", *New Scientist* (19 October 1991), pp. 36-40.

[91] Celestous Juma, *The Gene Hunters: Biotechnology and the Scramble for Seeds* (Princeton, New Jersey, Princeton University Press, 1989).

[92] Hoffman, op. cit.

[93] M. Yuanliang, *Modern Plant Biotechnology and Rural Society: Today and Tomorrow* (Shanghai Institute of Scientific and Technical Information, 1989).

[94] Vibhuti Patel, *Misuse of Prenatal Diagnostic Techniques in India — A Case Study of Sex Determination Tests Leading to Female Foeticide* (Bombay, SNDT Women's University, 1989).

[95] Marge Berer, "The perfection of offspring", *New Scientist*, vol. 124, no. 1725 (14 July 1990), pp. 58-59.

[96] Jean Bethke Elshtain, "Reproductive ethics", *Utne Reader*, no. 44 (March 1989).

[97] Ibid.

UNIVERSITY OF MAINE AT AUGUSTA

3 2304 00060201

APR. 25 1996

Printed in USA                                        United Nations publication
94-93440—February 1995—5,000                          Sales No. E.94.IV.4
ISBN 92-1-130161-0